Divine Love

Also by Jeff Levin

Faith, Medicine, and Science: A Festschrift in Honor of Dr. David B. Larson
Edited with Harold G. Koenig

Religion in the Lives of African Americans: Social, Psychological, and Health Perspectives
With Robert Joseph Taylor and Linda M. Chatters

God, Faith, and Health: Exploring the Spirituality-Healing Connection

Essentials of Complementary and Alternative Medicine
Edited with Wayne B. Jonas

Religion in Aging and Health: Theoretical Foundations and Methodological Frontiers

Also by Stephen G. Post

Altruism and Health: Perspectives from Empirical Research

Human Nature and the Freedom of Public Religious Expression

Unlimited Love: Altruism, Compassion, and Service

Altruism and Altruistic Love: Science, Philosophy, and Religion in Dialogue
Edited with Lynn G. Underwood, Jeffrey P. Schloss, and William B. Hurlbut

The Moral Challenge of Alzheimer Disease: Ethical Issues from Diagnosis to Dying

More Lasting Unions: Christianity, the Family, and Society

Spheres of Love: Toward a New Ethics of the Family

Divine Love

PERSPECTIVES FROM THE
World's Religious Traditions

WILLIAM C. CHITTICK ▪ VIGEN GUROIAN
RUBEN L. F. HABITO ▪ WILLIAM K. MAHONY
JOHN S. MBITI ▪ JACOB NEUSNER
CLARK H. PINNOCK ▪ DAVID TRACY

Edited by Jeff Levin and Stephen G. Post
Foreword by Seyyed Hossein Nasr

TEMPLETON PRESS

Templeton Press
300 Conshohocken State Road, Suite 550
West Conshohocken, PA 19428
www.templetonpress.org

Designed and typeset by Gopa & Ted2, Inc.

Library of Congress Cataloging-in-Publication Data

Divine love : perspectives from the world's religious traditions / edited by Jeff Levin and Stephen G. Post.
p. cm.
Includes bibliographical references and index.
ISBN-13: 978-1-59947-249-2 (pbk. : alk. paper)
ISBN-10: 1-59947-249-X (pbk. : alk. paper) 1. Love—Religious aspects. 2. God—Love. 3. Religions. I. Levin, Jeffrey S. II. Post, Stephen Garrard, 1951-
BL626.4.D58 2010
212.'7—dc22

2009036976

Printed in the United States of America

10 11 12 13 14 15 10 9 8 7 6 5 4 3 2 1

For Lea, my love (J. L.)

For Sir John Templeton and Samuel H. Miller (S. G. P.)

Contents

Foreword

Seyyed Hossein Nasr

What wondrous harmony and tone does the musician of love possess;
The spirit of whatever song he creates traces a path to an abode of refuge.
May the world be never empty of the lamentation of lovers,
For how melodious and exhilarating a sound it does possess.

Hafiz (trans. by S. H. Nasr)

[M]a già volgeva il mio disio e'l velle,
sì come rota ch'igualmente è mossa,
l'amor che move il sole e l'altre stelle.

(But now was turning my desire and will,
Even as a wheel that equally is moved,
The Love which moves the sun and the other stars.)

Dante, *Paradiso*, Canto xxxiii (trans. by H. W. Longfellow)

All human beings in no matter what time or clime they live or have lived have experienced love either given or received or most likely both. Therefore, one can assert with certitude that love exists and all that exists must have its origin in the Source of all existence. That Source, which is none other than the Divine, is the origin of all love, ultimately love of whatever it might be that one loves, for whatever we love is in its inner reality the love of the Divine, even if this love be experienced through the myriad of cosmic veils that hide the Divine Face from many a human being. Nor is this love confined to the human state; rather, it flows through the veins of all of cosmic existence. It manifests itself in the love of animals for their offspring, of plants for light, and even in the so-called material world in the attraction of atoms and particles to each other. It is what draws *yin* and *yang* together on all planes of reality. According to a famous sacred dictum of the Prophet of Islam, quoted so often in Sufi texts, God, speaking in the first person, says, "I was a hidden treasure. I *loved* to be known; therefore I created the world so that I would be known." If then the goal of creation is knowledge of God, its cause is Divine Love.

Love is not just a sentiment, although that precious sentiment is also a form of love. But love as such is an ontological reality, as much an ontological reality as the reality of existence itself. It is, therefore, impossible to experience existence, to experience life without experiencing some form of love, the form, extent, and degree depending on the mode of existence of the subject who or that loves. For the human being, who is given the privilege of living on different levels of existence and of having different modes of consciousness, the more he or she *is*, the more intense his or her state of being, and the more pure his or her state of consciousness, the greater the experience by that person of love leading finally to the stage of Divine Love.

Religions are messages from the Divine whose aim is to return us to the Divine; *religat*, from which comes the word "religion," means to bind. Religion is what reestablishes for fallen humanity that binding to the Source. And so Divine Love, which of course includes binding and attraction, cannot but be central to all authentic religions no matter how different their external form might be. There are religions such as Christianity that define the Divine Itself as Love. Others such as Islam envisage the Divine primarily as the One in essence beyond all attributes and yet possessing many attributes of which an essential one is Love or rather what one could call Merciful Love. And then there are other religions such as Buddhism that are nontheistic and yet there appears within them the blinding reality of love in the form of compassion. There is, in fact, no religious universe to which we can turn without finding therein the presence of Divine Love in one form or another.

Now, Divine Love can have two meanings: our love for the Divine and the Love of the Divine for us, us here meaning not only ourselves and our co-religionists, not even only the whole of humanity, but the whole of creation. These two meanings are, metaphysically speaking, bound to each other and have a causal relationship. It is the Love of the Divine for Itself and for Its creation that allows creatures to have love for the Divine. As human beings, we are the only creatures given the possibility of being aware of this reciprocity and endowed with the freedom even to reject this Love. From the spiritual point of view it can be said that God wants us to love him on the basis of the freedom he has given us, the choice to love or not love him and/or his creation. He does not want us to love him on the basis of coercion and so he has made us all aware of the truth that love based on coercion is not love at all. Furthermore, there is a mysterious reciprocity hidden in this relationship between the human lover and the Divine Beloved. From the human point of view, it appears that we can decide to love or not to love the Divine; but from the inner point of view, no one can love God unless God loves him or her not in the ontological sense of the love of God for his creation which is always there, otherwise the created order would cease to exist, but in a personal and individual sense.

Many traditional accounts of anthropogenesis speak of our preexistence in the Divine Order before our appearance here on earth. To use the language of Sufism, we were in intimacy with the Divine and in the loving embrace of the Beloved before being cast here below. All the love we experience here below is a faint reflection of that primordial Love. And in all human climes there have been those who have sought to go beyond those dim reflections to that original Divine Love whose recovery brings with it also the sense of love for and compassion toward all beings.

The presence of teachings concerning this universal love and compassion in all of our religions has caused many who seek accord between religions today to base themselves solely on a sentimental understanding of love. On that basis they have come to claim that we should simply love each other putting aside all the different sacred forms and doctrines of various religions—which as a matter of fact alone make the realization of Divine Love possible—in order to reach a superficial and sentimental humanism that lacks efficacy and certainly has not succeeded in bringing followers of different religions closer together. What has been needed, therefore, is the exposition in a serious and in-depth manner of the reality of Divine Love within different religions while remaining faithful to the authentic teachings of each tradition and not basing oneself merely on a sentimental and superficial consideration of human nature. The present book is valuable precisely because it seeks to accomplish such a task. We are presented here with authoritative voices from different religions presenting the reality of Divine Love according to the language, symbols, and doctrines of each religion, voices brought together in harmony and with authenticity in this important collection of essays. We must be grateful to the editors, Jeff Levin and Stephen Post, as well as to the authors of the individual essays for having made the appearance of such a work possible.

Ours is a world in which awareness of the universality of the doctrine of Divine Love and its reality in religious worlds other than our own is a dire necessity. Of course, love is not only to be discussed in conceptual terms and only written about; it is to be experienced. In fact, as that supreme troubadour of love, Jalāl al-Dīn Rūmī, has sung,

> Whatever description or explanation I give of love,
> When I reach Love I am ashamed of my exposition.
> Although commentary by the tongue clarifies,
> Love that is tongueless is of greater clarity.
> As the pen was hastening to write,
> When it came to Love it split upon itself.
> In expounding Love, reason becomes mired like an ass in mud,
> It is Love alone that Love and being in love has explained.
>
> *Mathnawī*, Book I (trans. by S. H. Nasr)

But even writing about Divine Love authentically can only be done through love, and the present work is certainly itself the fruit of a labor of love. Let us hope that it will help to lead its readers to the experience of Divine Love itself, to a clear recollection of the experience by us all, in "preeternity" and existing still deeply within our being here and now, of the love and embrace of the Beloved. Let us hope that it will help us to attain a state of being wherein we could look at the heavens and experience like Dante "the Love which moves the sun and the other stars."

Bethesda, Maryland
September 2009

Acknowledgments

THE EDITORS WOULD LIKE to thank all of the chapter authors for the wonderful and groundbreaking works of scholarship that they contributed to this project. We know that for some of these chapters the task was equivalent to constructing an edifice out of bricks that themselves had to be fabricated from scratch. There are rewards, but also great challenges, in pursuing scholarship on a topic that has heretofore been relatively deemphasized in academic theological writing within many religious traditions. This book might even have been a couple of chapters lengthier, but for a few of the potential authors whom we approached, the prospect of composing an essay on this subject from the perspective of their respective faith tradition was simply too daunting; there were almost no sources on which to draw. We are thus deeply grateful to our contributors for not having begged off when we first extended our invitation to them. We are hopeful that the end result is not simply a thoughtful and provocative book on the topic of divine love but also the starting point for future scholarship by other theologians and religious scholars within these and other traditions of faith.

We would also like to express our deepest gratitude to all of the wonderful folks at Templeton Press who have contributed to this project. Our editor, Natalie Lyons Silver, has been a delight to work with and is an author's dream: friendly, knowledgeable, hardworking, detail-oriented, understanding, accessible. Many others at Templeton have been so helpful to us throughout the writing, editing, and publishing processes, and we thank them all.

Besides the Press, the John Templeton Foundation (JTF) itself merits so much of our appreciation for having the foresight to promote scholarly research and writing on the subjects of altruism and an unlimited love that, for the late Sir John Templeton, described the essence of divinity underlying the best elements of the great world religions. His exalted vision was instrumental in the founding of several academic centers of excellence pertaining to what variously have been termed classical sources of human strength or essential capacities or prosocial behaviors. These faith-grounded virtues are typically said to include forgiveness, spirituality, gratitude, humility, self-control, wisdom, hope, and love.

Among the centers that JTF has helped to establish is the Institute for Research on Unlimited Love (IRUL), as named by Sir John, located first in Cleveland's University Circle and currently in Stony Brook, New York. One of IRUL's key ongoing projects is the Flame of Love, which applies the methods of the social sciences to the study of self-reported experiences of godly love, and to which this book contributes directly at the conceptual level. The two editors of this book play lead roles in IRUL: Stephen Post as president and Jeff Levin as research advisory consultant for public health. The work of this book's contributing authors was also underwritten by IRUL, and thus, ultimately, by JTF. We are therefore doubly blessed by the Templeton family: the Foundation has supported our work and the Press is publishing our results.

Finally, we would like to thank our own families for their support and encouragement as we worked on this project: Lea Steele Levin and Mitsuko, Emma, and Andrew Post. Our prayer is that this book both honors their faith in us and also does justice to all those innumerable saints whose lives have been paragons of selflessness, compassion, and divine love.

Divine Love

Introduction

Divine Love in the World's Religious Traditions

JEFF LEVIN

IN THE MIDRASH, A telling anecdote from the life of Asshur illuminates a troubling facet of human nature, as much a source of crisis for our day as for the ancient days of the biblical patriarchs. The book of Genesis states that Asshur, a son of Shem and forerunner of the Assyrian people, lived in Nimrod's wicked land of Bavel until "out of that land [he] went forth."[1] According to the Rabbis, Asshur had heard about idolatrous plans to build a great tower to heaven and "from that scheme Asshur dissociated himself."[2] To his credit, the Midrash notes, "When he saw them come to wage war against the Holy One, blessed be He, he quitted his country."[3]

Asshur went on to make a name for himself in the world. He was an accomplished builder of many cities, Nineveh his crown jewel—an "exceeding great city"[4] with wide avenues and considered a center of civilization. But this worldly success and renown had predictable results. The Rabbis explain: "Yet he [Asshur] did not remain constant [in his righteousness], and when he came and joined them in destroying the Temple God said to him: 'Yesterday a chicken and to-day an egg! Yesterday thou didst soar aloft with religious actions and noble deeds, whilst now thou art shut up like [a chicken in] an egg.' . . ."[5]

Here then is a universal dilemma: while the stated ideals of religious traditions may ennoble us and steer us to acts of courage and benevolence, sometimes this incentive is just not enough. For various reasons, imperfect humans fail to live up to these ideals and fall into sin and decrepitude, either backsliding from an earlier attempt to match their actions to these ideals, like Asshur, or never managing such an effort at all.

To construct and live a life in accord with the highest of religious principles is a challenge. The pull of the world is a fierce counterweight, for us as much as for ancients such as Asshur. The approbation of opinion leaders, the material rewards of conformity, the safe feelings of fellowship with like-minded others—against this force, religious ideals sometimes fail.

But another force works against living by the highest principles of religion. Our faith traditions themselves may betray us. Alongside lofty ideals, expounded upon repeatedly within sacred texts, is the testimony of history. The manifest reality of religious history is often quite divergent from the whitewashed stories of selfless saints motivated only by truth and goodness that are held up as models for the religious life. Ugly perversions of the noblest religious impulses—into obsessions of hatred, injustice, cruelty, and greed—drive many souls into the intellectual and spiritual prison of fundamentalism, the parched desert of secularism and materialism, or the swamp of ersatz religions derived from misreadings of older wisdom traditions imported from elsewhere.

The challenge to the world's religions is to match the highest principles of their respective sacred writings to the messages that they communicate and to the actions that they sponsor, undertake, and hold up as representative of their traditions. This collective and global challenge is mirrored by a more individual and personal one, shared by every religious believer. Over a century ago, Rabbi Moses Mielziner, a great Talmudic scholar, elucidated this challenge: "The ultimate aim of religion is to ennoble man's inner and outer life, so that he may love and do that only which is right and good. This is a biblical teaching that is emphatically repeated in almost every book of Sacred Scripture."[6]

Religion, ideally, serves to inspire, to elevate, and, most of all, to synchronize human behavior with the most exalted principles revealed by respective world teachers and sacred texts. Only by fulfilling the ubiquitous golden rule in our actions toward others can it be said that we have fully taken such guidance to heart. The noblest and holiest words spoken by the great wisdom traditions must incline our hearts and, in turn, our deeds to holiness. The inner and the outer must become one.

The intrepid reader can find this same teaching, in one form or another, articulated throughout the writings of other sacred traditions: in the Hadith literature and Sufi tales, in the collective writings of the Zen masters, in the hagiographies of the Roman Catholic saints, in Chasidic legends and *bubbe meises*, in the epic stories of the *Mahabarata* and in the *sutras* of the *Upanishads*, in the words of moral guidance found in the *Dhammapada* and in the narratives of the lives of the Jain *tīrthankaras*, and in the folk legends of Asian shamans and their counterparts in African and Native American cultures.

The world's religious traditions constitute an enormous font of moral instruction. Unfortunately, as happens all too often, the message may get lost in the translation from sacred text to human action. It must remain a conundrum, a frustration, and an outrage to the Creator and Source of being that magnificent and inspired words endorsing justice, kindness, and mercy pass through filters of human construction and produce acts in service of quite the opposite.

Striving to understand why and how this terrible state of affairs comes to pass is the ever-present challenge and life's work of theologians, clergy, religious teachers and scholars, pastoral counselors, and apologists in every tradition. These efforts would be overwhelming, and in vain, were it not for a great truth that sustains those laboring in this task. Somewhere outside of the destructive impulse to kill or oppress for God, as in fundamentalist distortions of religion; the lure to deny or reject God, as urged by postmodern secular materialists; and the temptation to supplant or become God, as in the New Age mythology; there lies a fourth way, truest to the sacred texts of the major religions: to love God and all of God's creation.

The Core Meaning of Love

To love and be loved by God—to live in connection with the Divine, in union with the Beloved, reconciled with the Ultimate—this describes the holy grail for religious believers throughout the world's faith traditions. Externalizing this soteriological quest, in turn—recapitulating it in our relations with all sentient beings—this represents the redemptive charge set before each believer seeking to translate the moral wisdom of respective religions into ethical actions that elevate the holiness of God's creation.

Languaged differently across faiths, although conceptually more alike than distinct, a common and central aim of religions is to draw down the *ain sof or*, the limitless light, from the macrocosm of divine relations to the microcosm of human relations. "As above, so below," the mystics teach, no less a statement of metaphysical fact than of earthly mission. To that end, *homo religiosus* is tasked with ensuring that the limiting strictures of manifest reality—the man-made things and concepts that constitute our shared psychic grid—do not obscure or befoul or destroy what is essentially unlimited. Redeemed, they may become vessels of the light and radices of further redemption.

In this book, eight of the preeminent religious scholars in the world share their perspectives on the what, how, and why of divine love, as well as on the whither of divine love—the who, when, and where of what might be termed divine love, lost and found. These topics are explored within the context of Judaism, Christianity, Islam, Hinduism, Buddhism, and the sacred traditions of Africa. Naturally, the calculus related to unpacking these questions and the associated core concepts drawn on by authors vary considerably across religions. Further, certain issues are more meaningful and more resonant within some traditions than others. Still, while the authors have been given carte blanche in organizing their material, several common points of focus and reflection have seeded these discussions.

In approaching the topic of divine love, four general questions are posed:

1. *What is divine love?* This question addresses the definition and conceptual boundaries of divine love. What about divine love is distinct—different from other types of love and different from other ways of relating to or responding to the sacred? Are there subtypes or categories of divine love? Have these concepts evolved over time in response to changing historical circumstances? What do sacred texts and holy people have to say?

2. *How do we access and manifest divine love?* This question addresses the expression and experience of divine love. What does it mean to be in relationship with or reconciled to God or the Divine? Is divine love experienced unconditionally, or is there an expectation of something from us in return? Are our love of God and our love of our fellow beings associated in some way? Are they inseparable (one joined to the other), conditional (one upon the other), hierarchical (one trumps the other), or nested (one defined in terms of the other)? Are norms of fellowship, connectedness, and mutual obligation expressed through commandments or other scriptural prescriptions or proscriptions?

3. *Why is divine love important?* This question addresses the instrumentality and salience of divine love. Does divine love matter? To what end does divine love influence the lives of individual human beings, the communion of believers, and the state of the world? Does divine love figure

into discussions of personal or collective redemption or of eschatology? What are the forces arrayed against the apostles of divine love, and what are the challenges to be overcome? What are the prospects of success? Are there global consequences should we fail?

4. *Whither divine love: how is it lost and how is it found?* This question addresses the distortions of divine love that arise within religions and how they can be countered. What are the major ways in which divine love has been distorted? When and where have distortions occurred in the past? Are they present and visible today? How can such distortions be avoided or corrected? Who are the great historic exemplars of divine love? How did they confront apostasy and distortions of divine love? Were they ultimately successful in their work of restoration? In what ways did they fail? Are the resources that they drew upon, internal to their faith tradition, available to believers in the present day?

In answering these and other provocative questions, important common themes emerge across religions. Each of these faith traditions offers guidance on how we may grow toward identifying with the One rather than the fragment, and on how each of us may come to see ourselves in the other. Each tradition seeks to shape a normative religious experience that guides its adherents toward recognition of a common humanity, of kinship and fellowship with believers on different spiritual paths. Finally, each tradition affirms that engaging the divine is the best and only way to redress the problems that religion has caused and to resolve the moral crises that plague our world.

Defining and describing this ultimate expression of love is no easy task. Its characteristics and functions, its antecedents and consequences, in some ways may seem to defy our best efforts to represent them in words. How does one use a delimited tool such as human language to depict and interpret a phenomenon that exists principally in the realm of subjective experience? Moreover, unlike other subjective experiences involving features of our inner psychological life—our cognitions, affects, conations—the kind of love of which we speak also comprises a transcendental quality that resists the prodding of empirical validation. For good reason, love has been famously described as "a subject whose boundaries recede with each attempt to characterize them."[7] How much more difficult to characterize divine love, in its many facets and manifestations?

To begin, it would serve to identify what one of the editors of this book has termed the "core meaning of love."[8] Among love's many constituent elements and functions are celebration, compassion, forgiveness, care, companionship, and correction.[9] These dimensions and expressions of love are notable for their voluntary, unselfish, and other-regarding characteristics. Compassion, especially, a higher octave of empathy, is empowering, both to the one who loves and the one who is loved. Compassion may also be liberating and transformative, both in the sense of self-actualization and as an antecedent and marker of spiritual rebirth. Moreover, by motivating courageous acts in the pursuit of justice and mercy, the experience of love is self-replicating, extending its reach out into the world.

Divine love in its fullest expression, then, is about far more than the experience of these elements and functions in a purely vertical context, to borrow the language of theologians like Paul Tillich.[10] Divine love is not simply reducible to God's love for us or our love of God, but rather implies each of us actively participating in the love that God has for us all. How is this possible? To most authentically engage the divine, in love and in the fullness of relationship, we must overlay our love of God upon the maze of human social relations in which each of us is entangled. Accordingly, the vertical becomes horizontal: by recognizing the indwelling Presence of God in our fellow beings, we can "love thy neighbor as thyself."[11] In service to this end, religious piety and obedience engage the believer in a covenantal web of reciprocities and obligations. Love of God is not fully manifest unless and until translated into love of others.

This theme, ably captured by the term "unlimited love,"[12] is present in the sacred writings and the ideals of the world's great religions. Why then does it seem so distant from the realities of religion as experienced in the daily lives of those who profess allegiance to these traditions? It is not difficult to identify the culprits: the lure of the world, assimilation, moral neutrality, and compromise with the pack mentality that thirsts for the lowest common denominator of ethics, all fueled by pop-culture icons and marketers and flaks, more often than not given over to the grossest materialism and profane values.

The historic religious traditions thus have found themselves on the verge of surrender to the basest default values of the postmodern liberal ethos, the decomposing corpse of an earlier, more optimistic ideology that promised to replace so-called religious superstition with a utopian secular age of progress and peace. That many of the great intellects tacitly cited as apostles of this new, secular humanism in fact never endorsed anything like the antipathy to religion expressed by contemporary partisans is no matter. The philosopher John Dewey, for one, while skeptical of the truth claims of specific religions, was warmly sympathetic to the religious impulse and recognized faith in God as an essential force motivating benevolent actions.[13] Nevertheless, by acquiescing to the dominant culture's misreading of their mission and motives, contemporary religions have allowed a core part of themselves to die on the vine, abrogating their calling and their responsibilities to (literally) godless institutions incapable of accessing the human heart and soul and thus unable to fully marshal the forces of good.

Regrettably, this irresolute surrender has cleared the field for the spread of more sinister forms of religion. The current crisis is thus owed in no small part to the cowardice and timidity of traditional religions, who have been cowed into silence and have enabled their own co-optation by destructive influences. The spiritual void left behind has found potent faux spiritualities anxious to fill the lacuna: New Age–isms of one sort or another, heterodox syncretisms of irreconcilable spiritual paths, oversimplifications of profound Eastern or mystical teachings transplanted into postmodern Western contexts, a newly militant scientism masquerading as an arbiter of ontological truth, and a rising tide of fundamentalism within all of the major religions.

The Crisis of Our Age

The dissolution and moral failure of the great religions have not occurred overnight, nor have they developed in a social or historical vacuum. Famed Russian sociologist Pitirim Sorokin, writing at the onset of World War II, provided one of the most concise and eloquent discussions along these lines. Sorokin observed, with great alarm and pity, that militant atheism and sensate materialism had begun to overwhelm religion from within. He termed this moment "the crisis of our age."[14]

According to Sorokin, civilization and humanity cycle through centuries-long epochs of idealistic, ideational, and sensate value systems that inform and dominate all of the institutions of culture. These include philosophy, law, ethics, the arts, politics, and science. At the vanguard of a new sensate era, religion, he observed, was relinquishing its prophetic role as a voice of "superrational, supersensory, superempirical, absolute truth and reality—namely, God,"[15] and instead racing to add its name to the list of social institutions that the new ethos had co-opted. Sorokin lamented the resulting faith as "pseudo-religion" and a mere husk of its former glory, "the charismatic gift of mystic experience" replaced by worship of science, rationality, and empirically verifiable truth.[16] His critique of this type of go-along-to-get-along religion concluded with a scathing prediction:

> The sensate society, with its sensate ethics, has prepared its own surrender to the rudest coercion. "Liberating" itself from God, from all absolutes and categoric moral imperatives, it has become the victim of undisguised physical coercion and fraud. Society has reached the nadir of moral degradation and is now paying the tragic price of its own folly. Its vaunted utilitarianism, practicality, and realistic expediency have turned into the most impractical and unrealistic dis-utilitarian catastrophe. Nemesis has at last overtaken it![17]

The prescience of these terrifying words, written on the eve of Hitler's final solution, the West's failed political appeasement, and the Christian church's concomitant silence,[18] needs no explanation.

Who can deny that the institution of religion has been a willing servant of the forces precipitating this crisis and thus a major contributor to the world's present tenuous state? As traditional religious values have receded into the background of moral discourse, distortions of religion have filled the resulting vacuum. That a love-infused bond connects God and God's creation in a covenant of mutual obligations is a statement that would meet strident objection from religious fundamentalists and religious appeasers of the rational-utilitarian humanism spoken of by Sorokin. "Divine love," as an ideal and a foundation for the construction of the kingdom of God on earth, is under assault from both sides: the fundamentalists objecting to "love," the rational humanists objecting to "divine."

The decline of the historic faith traditions as arbiters of moral values has left a vacuum ably filled by the ascendancy of dangerous spiritual forces anxious to adjudicate in matters of personal and social ethics. Each of these distortions of religion threatens the rediscovery of a divine love that issues in profound compassion for all creatures. The fundamentalist distortion, fueled by an arrogant absolutism sanctioned by a favored group status, demonizes and dehumanizes outsiders, redefining them as unworthy of God's love and grace. The New Age distortion, found in individual seekers enraptured by a self-focused ecstatic mysticism, forgets the other, rather than seeking his or her redemption. The secular or humanist distortion, in reaction to both of these currents, presumes that one can love the neighbor without the mediating experience of divine love; compassion is reduced to social engineering.

In *Divine Love*, we seek a solution to this crisis of our age. We identify a way out of the present situation, orthogonal to perversions of religion found in the haughty triumphalism of both dogmatic fundamentalism and creeping atheism and in the smug self-obsession of those New Age religions that masquerade as esoteric insight into the nature of the divine. The hijacking of religion by any of these forces represents a calamity for humankind. Each of these distortions of religion, history attests, can fuel divisiveness, separation, judgment, indifference, antagonism, oppression, and cruelty. Each debases the core values that underlie and nourish the great faith traditions. Each leaves the world woefully unprepared to deal with the moral challenges that confront it, abrogating a role that religion and its revealed wisdom traditionally filled.

A Poisoned Spring

The malign influence of fundamentalism has received considerable attention, including scrutiny in recent comprehensive works of scholarship.[19] Its associated evils, albeit often overstated by haters of all forms of religion, are well detailed and commented upon and by now are a feature of the lingua franca of contemporary cultural discourse. But typically unobserved is an egregious concomitant of the rise, spread, and increasing hegemony of fundamentalism within the religions of the world. French religious philosopher Jean Borella paraphrased traditionalist-school esotericist Frithjof Schuon in articulating this tragedy: "The only remedy for our present suffering is found in religion, but the entire modern world diverts us from our return. We die of thirst beside a spring because we are persuaded that it has been poisoned."[20]

In other words, by avoiding one unacceptable expression of religion, we risk ending up driven into the arms of another. The distortions of religion symbiotically complement each other, each responsible in part for the growth of its counterparts. Fundamentalism sends many religious seekers, repelled by its values, into the void of vacant spiritualities. At the same time, the spiritlessness of dead and dying mainline creeds and congregations sends its fallen away to empty promises of "that old-time religion." Still others abandon their faith entirely, or wind up ensnared by the cheesy counterfeits populating the fringes of the spiritual terrain.

Huston Smith, revered dean of religious scholars, astutely dissected this trend in his identification of the "two dogmatic fundamentalisms in America today," one of which he termed "dogmatic secular modernity."[21] The mainline denominations, he lamented, "are digging their own graves, for without a robust, emphatically theistic worldview to work within, they have nothing to offer their members,"[22] and thus have waved a white flag at the secular onslaught. This, in turn, has further fueled the rise of fundamentalism within Western faiths.

No wonder so many of us are ambivalent about religion. Due to an emphasis on tribalistic elements in religion, over and above moral and ethical imperatives, norms of religious devotion may be observed to elicit harmful tendencies. Thoughtful people recognize this effect and are thus driven further from the deepest well available to quench the destructive fires of atheism and materialism. Religion, debased by fundamentalism, sanctions glorification of a favored identity (e.g., election, salvation), its adherents glorifying in this status, vulnerable to reifying the otherness of outsiders. This approach distorts the messages of love, unity, justice, compassion, kindness, and mercy that lie at the core of the great religions, that serve to instill humility in religious believers, and that denote the essence of divine love.

To be fair, there is tribalism and then there is tribalism. A faith tradition as keenly cognizant of, and defined by, notions of peoplehood or nationhood as Judaism, for example, recognizes these distortions as a derogation of an implicit moral responsibility to those who are "strangers."[23] Laying at the feet of a generic tribalism indirect blame for the crisis of our age is not helpful. Common sense calls us to delineate the morally functional and dysfunctional, the good and the bad, in cultically bounded and supernaturally sanctioned communities.

As Emile Durkheim observed, the members of tribal clans live in relationship with each other not primarily on account of shared kinship but due to mutual affiliation with totemic entities, including beliefs, that defines the associative relations as sacred.[24] For example, Jewish tribalism is covenantal—grounded in special obligations and burdens voluntarily contracted to with God on account of being "a holy people unto the Lord thy God."[25] Hindu and Shinto tribalism, likewise based on national origin, encompass responsibilities regarding the maintenance of ceremonial ritual, order, and purity. These tribalisms are functional, morally speaking; they serve to reaffirm and elevate the holiness of a people and thus ideally inspire and enable greater and more successful acts of communal and worldly service to exemplify that holiness.

By contrast, the tribalism of fundamentalists is prone to moral dysfunction. In extremis, the tribal instinct as manifested within contemporary religious fundamentalists is not so much about affirming or elevating one's own holiness or sacred status for instrumental purposes as about judging, disfellowshipping, and distancing oneself from otherness. The separatism of ultra-fundamentalists is less in service to marking off a private space or sanctuary for the important business of making holiness—for purposes, for example, of preparing the tribe for going out into the world in order to serve as agents of redemption. Rather, it is about leaving a perceived evil and wicked world dominated by others to stew in its own juices and suffer its presumably deserved fate. Rats jumping from a sinking ship may be the most apt metaphor here. The other is stigmatized, condemned, and avoided like the plague—and left to its reward in hell. This begs the question whether such a worldview does not leave an even worse hell, on earth, in its stead.

This discussion of "good" and "bad" expressions of tribalism is, of course, a simplification. Fundamentalism has reared its head in Jewish, Hindu, and Shinto communities throughout history, to be sure, but these episodes are debasements of the ideal found within normative beliefs. The same can be said of flare-ups of Christian, Muslim, and Sikh fundamentalism in recent decades. The ideals of a body of Christ committed to neighborliness and *agape* love or of a holy people in submission to Allah and devoted to pursuit of *adl*, or justice, for example, are faithful reflections of the earlier Mosaic covenant enshrined within the scriptures of these successor faith communities.

In the contemporary world, fundamentalists have used systems of political economy in attempts to marginalize and even criminalize the other, which runs counter to the founding principles of the aforementioned tribal religions. It is also quite contrary even to the earlier history of fundamentalism in the monotheistic West, which was decisively separatist, stridently nonactivist—that is, diffident to or disinterested in taking action against (or in) the outside world—and certainly not expansive. That is, while at times moderately evangelical in temperament, Christian fundamentalism in North America, for one, at least until the mid- to late twentieth century, was self-interpreted as a utopian soteriological vision and not as a template for sociopolitical redemption through direct action.[26]

But, sadly, the history of cultures coming into contact with each other has long had deleterious consequences, especially for new or tenuous nation-states, usually as a result of competition and conflict among religions.[27] As the real and psychic distances among members of the global community continue to shrink, and cherished traditions are discarded in favor of profane and life-denying idolatries, a uniquely reactive and crusading fundamentalism has appeared on the world scene. This sacrilegious trend is not a figment of the fundamentalist imagination, to be fair, so their concerns cannot be callously ignored or dismissed. There is a healthier way, however, to respond to the challenge of the crisis of our age.

Instead of engendering withdrawal or, alternatively, militant reaction within our tribal borders, our contacts with the other can present challenges of learning and growth. We can come to see in our brothers and sisters distinct reflections of our mutual oneness that perhaps we cannot see through our own cultural lenses. Engaging the divine in our fellow beings thus presents opportunities to better recognize our own divine nature. The coming together, the interfacing of religions, rather than presenting a clash of titans and reifying our age's great crisis of separation and hatred, can serve as a springboard to what Mircea Eliade termed "a new humanism."[28] Grounded in humble recognition of the great religions' shared phenomenology across unique historical contexts, through the human encounter with religion we can all come to recognize our own highest aspect in the life of the other.

How to elicit the best of religion, and to extinguish the worst, has great currency and urgency in the present day. Tribalism is not the enemy. That would instead be the exploitation of tribalistic impulses dormant in respective religious traditions in order to marginalize, condemn, and attack other tribes. Like the twelve tribes of Israel, we may see ourselves as delineated communities, each with a special mission, but, viewed through an alternative lens, we also are akin to the twelve sons of Jacob, children of a single father. Together, all human beings, regardless of tribe or clan or religion of birth, constitute one meta-tribe united in kinship through a common Creator.

Bridging the Abyss

In *Divine Love*, we seek to identify the universal in the particularities of respective faith traditions. This effort is guided by the maxim that what unites us is greater than what separates us. Throughout the chapters of this book, several meta-themes emerge from respective discussions of the nature, experience, instrumentality, and distortion of divine love within specific religions. Regardless of the chapter authors' innate perspectives—theological, ideological, theoretical—three themes are consistently developed:

1. *Divine love is critically important for humankind.* If we are to survive as a species, perhaps even as a living planet, then an ethic of mutual respect and love must guide our actions and those of our leaders and institutions. This respect and love must extend to all humans—to all sentient beings, some would say—and must replace the predominant ethic that defines social relations, local and global, in terms of concepts such as power, control, competition, possession, and dominance. Souls infused with divine love see life as a journey into greater service, not as a game in which some of us must win and others must lose.

In Sorokin's famous taxonomy of the multiple aspects and dimensions of love, most germane to this discussion is what he termed the "extensity" of love.[29] This he conceived of as a continuum, with "love of all mankind, all living creatures, and the whole universe," and, ultimately, of God, at one end.[30] At the other end, the "zero point of love extensity," was not hatred, but, tellingly, "a love of oneself only."[31] Selfishness and self-obsession represent our greatest sins and lead to all other destructive forms and expressions of interpersonal behavior. Directing our regard outward, just as, Christians affirm, did the God Who "so loved the world that He gave His only begotten son,"[32] is the beginning of our salvation.

2. *Divine love is irreducible to a mere feeling located within the psyche of the lone individual.* Recent scientific studies inform us of significant psychological and even physiological correlates and sequelae of certain spiritual states of consciousness and spiritually or altruistically motivated actions. This fascinating and provocative research is detailed in respective works by the two editors of this book.[33] If true, this is a wonderful blessing, a grace that we can all welcome. But these salutary personal outcomes ought not be construed as the most objective markers of divine love nor as its most certain validation. If we are not careful in our interpretation, we risk reducing divine love to a passive emotional or psychophysiological gift,

"received" in some way in consequence of creedal orthodoxy or acceptable thoughts. This smacks of what the German martyr Dietrich Bonhoeffer famously termed "cheap grace," a kind of self-centered actualization sought without cost or sacrifice or discipleship.[34]

We all seek to feel good. There is nothing intrinsically immoral in wanting to experience warm, comforting feelings, such as being held in the loving embrace of a divine being. But we are challenged to keep in mind that maximizing pleasant emotions or our physical status does nothing, by itself, to serve the common good or to help bring a solution to the core problems of the world. Where religious messages have been constructed and construed to serve such ends, promising all manner of holy and unholy benefits and gains to the individual believer, religion tragically separates itself from its historic function as prophetic voice and acquiesces to an identity as mere self-help philosophy, a barker of what Sydney Ahlstrom aptly termed "the superficialities of mere . . . peace-of-mindism."[35] This is not just a reference to some New Age groups and recent Eastern imports, by the way—"seed faith," "abundant Christian living," the "prosperity gospel," and the like retain great bewitching power in the present milieu.

If the message of divine love is reduced to just another desirable personal outcome of the practice of religion, then it risks corruption by what the great social historian Christopher Lasch perceptively called a "therapeutic sensibility."[36] This product of the hedonistic and sensate-materialist years of the 1970s, Lasch described, denominated a world of privileged Western opinion leaders and yuppies increasingly obsessed with themselves—their inner growth, their lifestyles, their pursuit of happiness, their fitness, their longevity. All nice things, to be sure, but not so savory if our existing social, economic, and political systems are rebooted with the maximizing of these outcomes as their foundational principle. The transformation of religion from a system of transcendental moral teachings and values guiding groups of believers to build and maintain a just or otherwise ideal social order to a narcissistic program of personal growth with individually defined endpoints, as in the neologistic rebranding of the term "spirituality," has further divorced religion from its communal and moral contexts and contributed to the fracturing of human unity.

This historic moral function, according to British Chief Rabbi Jonathan Sacks, is contained within a "covenantal morality"—an affirmation of mutual obligations on the part of God and humankind.[37] Rabbi Sacks explains that this is the truest representation of the social contract as sanctioned by the Western monotheistic traditions in sacred writings dating to the earliest lessons of the Hebrew Bible. Then, as now, divine love, in the form of God's mercy for human beings, is made manifest in the world through the agency of humans themselves acting collectively to show mercy by effecting justice.

3. *Divine love demands collective action to relieve suffering and to promote the common good.* The inseparability of mercy and justice, and the drawing down of God's mercy and justice principally through and consequent to our own exercise of these great divine traits, are common themes of the world's religions. We find these ideas present in Judaism and Islam, as in the former's *chesed* and *tzedek* and the latter's *hanan* and *adl*—mercy (or compassion) and justice—the most valued attainments of character to be cultivated among believers. Another shared inseparability of these great faiths is of contemplation and action.[38] Jews and Muslims value learning, of course, but most of all as a means to informed action. Similar is the Roman Catholic imperative, as articulated most recently by Pope Benedict XVI, that humans reproduce God's love by way of effecting acts of justice and mercy.[39]

Likewise, among religions of the East, this same theme is developed. In Hinduism's yogic tradition, the *jñana* and *bhakti* paths, of learning and devotion, respectively, are in service to the *karma* path, the way of action. In Buddhism, *dharma* and right conduct are emphasized above all. In Jainism, the most treasured and memorable stories in the lives of the *tīrthankaras* highlight their remarkably devout avoidance of even the tiniest acts of cruelty and harm. Foremost within these traditions is a shared emphasis on compassion, as in the Buddhist *karunā*, the Jain *daya*, and the Hindu *ahimsā*.

These three religions each lay claim to concepts akin to *dharma* as central to their cosmogonies, such as related to the evolution of consciousness and the workings of the laws of *karma*, or to understandings of the moral order of creation, inasmuch as guiding principles can be deduced for defining ethical human behavior.[40] Moreover, these traditions converge in recognizing the divinity that resides in all things, all sentient beings, and all manifestation. Our duty to be diligent in refraining from unkindness, in cultivating compassion, and in loving others is thus an obligation to love God. This is our only valid response to the inscrutability of theodicy, as it is required of us in order to sustain the universe.

If indeed we are all interconnected and one, then to the extent to which the exoteric faith traditions ignore this truth, they contribute to the dire straits in which our world finds itself. The grace of divine love demands more than just passive receipt; it testifies to a communal imperative. Its experience points to a Source of infinite blessing Who calls us to pass along our grace and to build reciprocities of love with our fellow beings. We are called to action, to externalize this love to our brothers and sisters, both co-religionists and people of other faiths.

This is not to suggest that imitation of any of God's traits, such as translation of God's justice into ethical acts, is ever easy. It is fraught with danger, in fact, in two ways. First, we can fail. We are not God, after all, no matter that we may experience God's Presence. This speaks to the danger of our refusing to acknowledge anything but our smallness and weakness in relation to God. Yet God believes in us, so we ought to believe in God's good judgment. Second, by contrast, we can become so swelled with self-pride over our incremental gains in worldly knowledge that we delude ourselves into believing that we can and have usurped God's sovereignty. Such is the danger of falling victim to the delusion of our grandeur, as among prideful evangelists of the scientistic faith. These dangers are ever present, as respected rabbinic scholar Ephraim E. Urbach alludes to:

> Recognizing the enormous interval between the transcendental God—a consciousness that exists in every religion that has passed the mythical stage—and himself, the believer also yearns to attain to the realization of his nearness, without reverting to dangerous identification. A great part of the history of religions, including the religion of Israel, consists of the quest for the solution of the problem of bridging the abyss that cannot be closed.[41]

To heed the call of an untouchable transcendent Source of being to become co-creators of God's sovereignty upon the earth is a mighty task, a quest indeed. But it is within our grasp. Through exhibiting in our actions the same quality of loving-kindness that God exhibits in elevating justice and mercy above all else in God's dealings with us, we can become agents of divine love and thus, ideally, rescue the world from the clutches and consequences of a demonic ethic that glorifies separation, divisiveness, dominance, and cruelty. This great call lies at the doctrinal core of each of the world's major faith groups, regardless of the public messages of its leaders or proponents, at this or any other time, which might seem to argue quite the opposite.

It behooves us to ever remember that invoking the Divine Name is the province of saints and sinners. The great psychologist Gordon Allport described as "paradoxical" the role of religion in human affairs: "It makes prejudice and it unmakes prejudice."[42] Presuming to act in God's stead, or in God's manner, can serve to separate and divide as well as to bring together and unify. It is up to us to sanctify God's name by acting out of love.

The Light Invisible

This book represents the collective response of the editors and chapter authors to the crisis of our age. Divine love, we assert, is at the core of the world's great religious traditions. The spring is not poisoned after all, although it is fast becoming muddy and polluted, and the well is caving in. Only by our reconciliation with the Ultimate can we hope to recover the redemptive moral wisdom that we seek. But the abyss is not so easily bridged. If it were, would the world find itself in its present state?

Good intentions may not be enough. Whatever our spiritual inclinations, distractions as well as too-easy solutions steer us astray. Sometimes the contemplative, for example, may become so wrapped up in ecstasy that the sentient world is forgotten. Thus is the tendency to identify divine love with the noetic experience of union through a simple-minded moralism. God is everything, everything is God, we are all each other, all is one, all is well. The mainline believer, by comparison, may settle on an ethic that concludes that the commandment to love God can be set aside in favor of just getting on with one's neighbor. God *is* the orphan, God *is* the widow, God *is* the oppressed. In the first instance, God is solely transcendent, and we can experience divine love without engaging the world. In the second instance, God is solely immanent, or a vague pantheistic force, and we can only experience divine love by conjuring schemes to fix the world. In both instances, the vertical context gets lost as a fundamental experience of a higher source for animating the human or horizontal expression of love.

The greatest contribution of *Divine Love*, we pray, will be to describe individuals throughout the great spiritual traditions who have experienced the divine and then returned to the world with wisdom and devotion to a purer benevolence for all people without exception. Each of these great traditions is replete with canonical writings that unreservedly endorse this ideal, and each faith contains exemplars of divine love whose actions in furtherance of this ideal are fulfillments of explicitly normative religious teachings. The perversions of religion described in this introduction are and always have been distortions of the impulse to respond in kind to God's unlimited love that lies at the core of every major religious tradition. Our choice to respond to God's love for us with an equal outpouring of love for others is the truest, most authentic expression of religion.

In his poem "The Great Light," T. S. Eliot uses a metaphor based on water and light to idealize our humility before the unseen Divinity that created us and merits our praise:

> Our gaze is submarine, our eyes look upward
> And see the light that fractures through unquiet water.
> We see the light but see not whence it comes.
> O Light Invisible, we glorify Thee![43]

One may imagine oneself a fish that jumps up toward this great light at the surface of the water, experiences it in its full glory though never seeing it with one's eyes, and then dives back down into the water to do good and lead others to the surface. So many of us, though, caught up in the glamour of having managed a glimpse of something above the surface, never dive back in. Others of us, by contrast, mistakenly presume that there is nothing above worth experiencing, so this world of unquiet water goes unredeemed. But there is indeed something above the surface, it is well worth experiencing, and the Light Invisible desperately needs us to dive back in and alert the other fish. This act of unlimited faith and compassion is the very paragon of divine love that we seek to elucidate in this book.

Notes

1. Genesis 10:11.
2. Genesis *Rabbah* 37:4.
3. Ibid.
4. Jonah 3:3.
5. Genesis *Rabbah* 37:4.
6. Moses Mielziner, *Introduction to the Talmud* (1894; repr. New York: Bloch Publishing, 1968), 267.
7. Robert Brown, *Analyzing Love* (Cambridge: Cambridge University Press, 1987), vii.
8. Stephen G. Post, *Unlimited Love: Altruism, Compassion, and Service* (Philadelphia: Templeton Foundation Press, 2003), 41–53.

9. Ibid., 1–7.
10. Paul Tillich, *The Protestant Era*, trans. James Luther Adams (Chicago: University of Chicago Press, 1948), 185–91.
11. Leviticus 19:18.
12. John Templeton, *Pure Unlimited Love: An Eternal Creative Force and Blessing Taught by All Religions* (Philadelphia: Templeton Foundation Press, 2000).
13. John Dewey, *A Common Faith* (1934; repr. New Haven, CT: Yale University Press, 1962).
14. Pitirim A. Sorokin, *The Crisis of Our Age: The Social and Cultural Outlook* (New York: E. P. Dutton, 1941).
15. Ibid., 111.
16. Ibid.
17. Ibid., 163–64.
18. Stuart E. Rosenberg, *The Christian Problem: A Jewish View* (New York: Hippocrene Books, 1986), 183–205.
19. Martin E. Marty and R. Scott Appleby, eds., *Fundamentalisms Observed*, vol. 1 of *The Fundamentalism Project* (Chicago: University of Chicago Press, 1991); and Bruce B. Lawrence, *Defenders of God: The Fundamentalist Revolt against the Modern Age* (San Francisco: Harper & Row, 1989).
20. Jean Borella, "René Guénon and the Traditionalist School," in *Modern Esoteric Spirituality*, ed. Antoine Faivre and Jacob Needleman (New York: SCM Press, 1992), 330–58; quotation on 351.
21. Huston Smith, *The Soul of Christianity: Restoring the Great Tradition* (New York: HarperSanFrancisco, 2005), xx.
22. Ibid.
23. Exodus 22:20.
24. Emile Durkheim, *The Elementary Forms of Religious Life*, trans. Joseph Ward Swain (1912; repr. New York: The Free Press, 1915).
25. Deuteronomy 7:6.
26. Karen Armstrong, *The Battle for God* (New York: Ballantine Books, 2000), 167–316.
27. Joachim Wach, *Sociology of Religion* (Chicago: University of Chicago Press, 1944), 287–330.
28. Mircea Eliade, *The Quest: History and Meaning in Religion* (Chicago: University of Chicago Press, 1969), 1–11.
29. Pitirim A. Sorokin, *The Ways and Power of Love: Types, Factors, and Techniques of Moral Transformation* (Boston: Beacon Press, 1954), 15–35; Sorokin, "Love: Its Aspects, Production, Transformation, and Accumulation," in *Explorations in Altruistic Love and Behavior*, ed. Pitirim A. Sorokin (Boston: Beacon Press, 1950), 3–73.
30. Sorokin, *Ways and Power of Love*, 16.
31. Ibid.
32. John 3:16.
33. Jeff Levin, *God, Faith, and Health: Exploring the Spirituality-Healing Connection* (New York: John Wiley and Sons, 2001); Stephen Post and Jill Neimark, *Why Good Things Happen to Good People: The Exciting New Research That Proves the Link Between Doing Good and Living a Longer, Healthier, Happier Life* (New York: Random House, 2007).
34. Dietrich Bonhoeffer, *The Cost of Discipleship* (1937; repr. New York: Macmillan, 1959), 35–47.

35. Sydney Ahlstrom, *A Religious History of the American People*, 2nd ed. (New Haven, CT: Yale University Press, 2004), 984.
36. Christopher Lasch, *The Culture of Narcissism: American Life in an Age of Diminishing Expectations* (New York: W. W. Norton, 1979), 7–13.
37. Jonathan Sacks, *A Letter in the Scroll: Understanding Our Jewish Identity and Exploring the Legacy of the World's Oldest Religion* (New York: Free Press, 2000), 77–90.
38. Leo Schaya, "Contemplation and Action in Judaism and Islam," in *Contemplation and Action in World Religions: Selected Papers from the Rothko Chapel Colloquium "Traditional Modes of Contemplation and Action,"* ed. Yusuf Ibish and Ileana Marculescu (Seattle: University of Washington Press, 1978), 151–94; Seyyed Hossein Nasr, "The Complementarity of Contemplative and Active Lives in Islam," in Ibish and Marculescu, *Contemplation and Action in World Religions*, 195–204.
39. Pope Benedict XVI, *God Is Love: Deus Caritas Est* (San Francisco: Ignatius Press, 2006), 51–93.
40. Heinrich Zimmer, *Philosophies of India*, ed. Joseph Campbell (Princeton, NJ: Princeton University Press, 1951), 40–41, 152–53, 163, 271, 513–15.
41. Ephraim E. Urbach, *The Sages: Their Concepts and Beliefs*, trans. Israel Abrams (Cambridge, MA: Harvard University Press, 1979), 39.
42. Gordon W. Allport, *The Nature of Prejudice*, 25th anniversary ed., unabridged (New York: Basic Books, 1979), 444.
43. T. S. Eliot, "Choruses from 'The Rock,'" *The Complete Poems and Plays, 1909–1950* (New York: Harcourt Brace & World, 1952), 113.

1 "If God Did Not Love Me, God Would Not Have Made Me!"

Exploring Divine Love in African Religion

John S. Mbiti

In the largely oral traditions of African peoples, there are obviously no written views about divine love or other topics. I have also found no extended discussions of this theme by individuals, communities, or academic institutions, other than references to the love of God in Christian circles.

Nevertheless, in their traditional life, people are aware of the divine love, and do say something about it, without necessarily using this terminology. The notion belongs to the wide spectrum of ethical concepts that includes God's love, mercy, kindness, providence, generosity, creative activity, and saving acts (salvation). We find such views in the vast areas of proverbs, beliefs, ethics, myths, stories, and symbols that every community cherishes. People speak about life in ways that point to their love-based relationship with God. In this oral context, such opinions are community opinions since they cannot be tied to an individual by virtue of his or her writing them down.

In each of Africa's roughly two thousand languages (plus many more dialects), there are obviously words for love and related concepts, with various usages. Similarly, in every one of these languages and among the peoples who speak them, there is at least one word for God and many ideas about God. Thus, "love" and "God" are common concepts in African life and religiosity. This chapter examines three areas in which the concept of divine love would be concealed in traditional life: proverbs, prayers, and names of God. As a point of entrance, we consider first the concept of God's relationship to human beings (persons).

A strong feature of traditional African life is its religiosity (or religiousness), which is today commonly called "African religion." It defines the landscape of people's lives at the deep level of their awareness of existence, worldviews, and participation in life. We find religion in various forms in every ethnic community or people (not to use the discarded word "tribe"). Yet, over the vast continent, there exists an assortment of commonalities and similarities of belief, praxis, worldviews, and values, to make it possible to speak of African religion in the singular, allowing for variations in location and time.

God and the Creation of Persons

One of these strong commonalities of African religion is people's acknowledgment of God. We find this religious component in every people and language, constituting a monotheistic view of and belief in God. Everywhere, people confess or acknowledge God to be the Creator and Sustainer of all things. While they have no physical representations of God, people use symbolic language and anthropomorphisms to speak about God. Through such uncomplicated affirmations or anthropomorphic symbols, communities disseminate and perpetuate knowledge about God, which they articulate especially in proverbs, sayings, prayers, and names of God. Proverbs are short and easily memorable. Everybody can use proverbs spontaneously at any occasion as he or she may see fit, but family and ritual elders generally say the prayers for their families and communities.

Besides speaking of the many activities (works) of God, people reflect also about the nature and being of God. In many cases, they use symbols and anthropomorphisms to fathom the mysteries of God. They have also many concepts that describe the ethical nature of God. In this range of concepts we unearth how people speak of God as being kind, loving, good, and just. In relation to people, they perceive and describe God as Parent, Mother, Father, Ruler, Judge, Friend, Savior, Protector, Giver of Children and Rain, Healer, and Preserver. They pray and perform rituals, calling upon God in whom they trust.

All these references to God indicate and illustrate how the belief in God is the anchor of African religiosity. It is a communal value, an integral part of people's heritage and identity. It plays an essential role in explaining the world, in putting ethical values into action, and in relating to the day-to-day situations and experiences of life. People refer to God in all situations, in connection with life experiences and puzzles. This strong belief in God colors traditional views about the world and human persons, starting with the creation of the world.

We spotlight the creation of humans, in which innumerable myths feature God as the ultimate Creator. In some myths, God created persons from clay; in some, God created the first persons and pulled them out from a hole, or from marshes, or from a tree (of life). In other myths, people tell that God made the first persons in heaven and brought them to earth. Still other myths present the creation of persons in a process over a period of days, to equip them fully to live on the earth. Many variations of these mythical accounts of creation exist, and some of them incorporate spiritual (or ancient human) figures in the work of creation, whom God assigned particular roles in the creation process.

Creation stories commonly tell that the original state of persons was one of happiness. God granted them immortality, or rejuvenation upon getting old, or the ability to rise again after dying. God provided for their necessities of life. That is already a demonstration of divine love at the initial creation. But persons lost this original state of bliss. In some cases that happened through their own fault, in others through an animal (like the chameleon, the hare, or the hyena), or by accident. Calamitous consequences followed when that happened. Among them, there came the separation of God from persons, the disconnection between heaven and earth, and the loss of resurrection and rejuvenation. Death, diseases, misfortunes, and the termination of free provisions also resulted.

For example, the Shilluk people in the Sudan narrate that God made the first persons (male and female) out of clay. Then God gave them legs with which to walk and run, hands with which to plant grain, eyes with which to see that grain, and a mouth with which to eat it. Afterward God gave them the tongue, with which to sing and talk; and finally ears, so that they may enjoy the sound of music, dance, and the speech of great men and women. Then God sent them out, as complete persons, encased with full dignity, or, one would say, "divine dignity."

In various ways, people express this notion of the completed, perfected, and dignified nature of the first humans. Some depict them as "children of God," living with God as a family; some depict them as existing in harmony with God and the rest of creation; and some assign to them privileged duties, positions, or oversight toward other creatures. But that was not an assignment of dominion over other creatures.

Creation as Basis for Divine Love

African ideas revolving around creation, especially the creation of human beings, point to this as the most explicit expression of divine love. The simple saying that many people would be heard to utter is an obvious statement, but it amounts to a profound confession of faith: "If God did not love me, God would not have made me!" The traditional adherents of African religion often talk like that in response to other persons (Christians) trying to convert them, by telling them that God loves them. Converts to Christianity would also talk like that, through sermons and teaching about the love of God in the Christian tradition. In both cases, the people are saying in effect that being alive is witness enough to the fact that God loves them. Divine love is for them an ontological fact of life—an obvious reality by which they live. It is an integral part of their identity, for without it they would not exist. Itself, life is an expression of divine love. That love is personalized in the creation of the individual person. Any message based on that fact makes sense; it is welcome. It fits into their religious worldviews. People thus confess their conviction, positive rephrasing of which would read as follows:

> God made me, because God loves me.
> God loves me, since God made me.
> God "must" love me, for God to have made me.
> Because God made me, God loves me.
> Since God made me, God really loves me.
> I am the living evidence that God loves me.

This conviction is expressed in proverbs such as, "God conceals himself from the mind of man, but reveals himself to his heart." A person may not (cannot) comprehend or feel God with the head. But a person feels God's love through the heart. The mental picture of God is fleeting, but the love of God in the heart is continuing. The head aspires to grasp the greatness and the being of God, an exercise that can be neutral or detached. Head knowledge may not reach the heart. The heart, on the other hand, is open to emotions, one of which is love. To say that God "reveals God's self" to a person's heart is to say that God penetrates into the seat of emotions. A contrast emerges here: with regard to the human mind, God "conceals" God's self; with regard to the human heart, God "reveals" God's self. People cannot "research" God through the mind. But people can get in touch with God through the heart, and love can best achieve that. God loves persons and therefore reveals God's self to them through the receptacle of love. God "pours" God's self out toward people, and that happens in the heart. The heart is the receptacle of not only love but also other emotions, which are attributed to and derive from God. These include God's compassion, mercy, kindness, care, and goodness.

There are many dangers and threats to life, such as famines, wars, diseases, accidents, disasters, catastrophes, and human injustices. People experience and appreciate the kindness and compassion of God in the face of these hardships and threats. For example, out of God's kindness, God supplies the family with what it needs; as an Oromo (Ethiopia) proverb says, "By the kindness of God the house (family) is satisfied." Even individuals are aware of God's kindness for their lives and they trust God to meet their needs, in spite of what other people may do to them. We consider later other proverbs that take up this idea.

Names of God That Explicitly or Implicitly Point to Divine Love

Name Giving in African Society

One of the widespread African customs is the giving of personal names that describe the outstanding features or activities of the person, or that anticipate such meanings. Traditionally the giving of additional names can take place at any age, after the initial naming of the child. The name may even be a strengthening of the current name. People assign names to fit some features such as the seasons, diseases, places, animals, human and natural events, physical features, general characteristics like the beautiful (poetical) sound of the name, and names of historical or mythical figures. A person may be named "Locust" if he or she was born at a time when there was a locust invasion in the land. A person may be named "Morning" if born in the morning. A person may be named "Runner" if in the course of growing up he or she develops superior running skills. A person may be named "Happy One" if, as a child, he or she was notably cheerful and happy. Another may get the name of a departed member of the family, such as a parent, grandparent, or sibling who died before. This is a way of remembering the departed (living dead), and saying that the departed has now symbolically returned through the birth of the new baby.

There are also names that outwardly seem unpleasant, but they serve to stress the contrary, such as "The Ugly One," "The Bad One," "The Hated One," and so on. Such names evoke or indicate feelings of love but without verbalizing them and without praising the person, lest something bad befalls her or him. "The Ugly One" tells how the parents consider the child to be so beautiful that they dare not call him or her "The Beautiful One," in order to avoid a misfortune striking the child. Some names, on the other hand, specifically give titles, honor, respect, praise, and flattery, particularly those that are self-given by or accorded to public figures, such as "Defender of the Land," "Father (never Mother?) of the Nation," "Great Hero," and so on. Names may also describe the wicked doings of political figures like "Slaughterer," "Disappear" (because he takes away other people who are never seen again alive), or "Sharp Knife." Some such names are not necessarily used openly for fear of the consequences.

Most African names have a lot of compact meaning in them. They may summarize the character of the person, the circumstances of the person's birth or life experiences, the historical happenings at the time of birth or even later, the activities of the family members, or weather conditions, prevailing diseases, wishful thinking, etc. Names also have power in them; in many cases they are the identity of the persons who bear them.

When we transpose this custom or system of using names to point to real (or imaginary) identities of persons onto the names given to God, we are faced with very solid concepts about God. The names have evolved in the course of generations. Since they are common property of the ethnic group or community concerned, they come out of community wisdom and views about God. They are the theological expressions of the people. Most likely they evolve through an informal process of careful formulation, and the names become theological pointers about God. I have collected about two thousand such names of God, personal and attributive names, from all over Africa. From this list, I give examples of names that point to people's recognition or affirmation of divine love.

Human Confidence and Trust in God as Friend

Akan (Ghana): *Nyaamanekose* (He in whom you confide troubles which come upon you)
Banyarwanda (Rwanda): *Ndagijimana* (in God I entrust my property)
Banyoro (Uganda): *W'omukago* (the Friend)

This set of descriptive names of God reveals people's attitudes toward God. They have complete confidence and trust in God, which arises from the unspoken certainty that God loves them and loves the created world. To name God "friend" is to elevate people's confidence in God to great heights, acknowledging that God loves them like a real friend in human relations. They feel safe and secure before God. People sense that God accepts and recognizes them, that their identity before God is valuable. The concept puts the people in a reciprocal status as friends of the Creator Friend. People are free to respond to that friendship. Other concepts derive from this name, some of which we consider below.

God as Consoler, Comforter, Savior

Akan (Ghana): *Abommubuwafre* (Consoler or Comforter who gives salvation)
Banyoro (Uganda): *Mujuni* (the Author of safety and security, the Savior)
Ganda (Uganda): *Ssewaunaku* (He who has pity on the poor and the suffering)
Ila (Zambia): *Luvhunabaumba* (Deliverer of those in trouble)

These names point to people's feelings toward God, feelings of being safe and secure in the sight of God. Only where there is love do people feel secure. Not only that, but God saves them and delivers them when trouble or danger arises. Only through definite love would God do that freely, and the people do not have to pay God for such delivering and saving acts. There can be no deliverance or salvation without divine love. People experience and take note of such deliverance and salvation from dangers and threats to life, of which there are many. These include sickness, accidents, death, famines, threats from animals and natural catastrophe, threats from human beings, and weather conditions such as storms and droughts; dangers may befall people in journeys, in the night, in hunting or fishing expeditions, and even in disputes and fights with fellow human persons. Expressed negatively, if God did not love them, God would not deliver or save them from such dangers.

God as Giver

Abaluyia (Kenya): Giver of all things
Akan (Ghana): *Amosu* (Giver of rain), *Amaomee* (Giver of sufficiency), *Totorobonsu* (causes rain to fall copiously); Giver of the Sun and Light, Giver of Sunshine
Banyoro (Uganda): *Mugabi* (He who distributes things), *Muliisa* (He who feeds), *W'emigisa* (He who has and gives blessings)
Bemba (Zambia): *Kaleka-Misuma* (He who gives complete [whole] gifts), *Kapekape* (He gives to each and every creature all their needs), *Nalusandulula* (Multiplier, He who makes all things multiply)
Ewe (Benin, Ghana, Togo): *Mawu* (Sky, Rain, All-wise Creator and Giver of all good things)
Shilluk (Sudan): Giver Who looks after the country
Shona (Zimbabwe): Gracious One

With these names and attributes of God, people are expressing God's constant provision toward them and the world. One major item in the background is the supply of rain (water), on which people depend for their lives. Rain is life for the community, for the land. And when the Akan of Ghana speak of God as "*Totorobonsu*" (causes rain to fall copiously), they are symbolically saying, in effect, that divine love is as plentiful as the rain, that it is for all people, for the whole land, for the whole earth. Divine love is the water of life, and God gives it freely and generously.

People acknowledge also that God gives them not only rain, but in reality all things. That includes, besides rain, big items like the sun and light, what nourishes, good things that sustain life and make it meaningful. On the human level, it is God that gives children to parents. In their name for God, "*Mawu*," the Ewe (in Benin, Ghana, and Togo) make this an essential aspect of God's creative activity that goes on all the time. The

Shilluk in the Sudan have a comprehensive view that God is the "Giver Who looks after the country." God's love is not just toward human persons alone but is inclusive, embracing the whole country. In effect it is directed toward the whole world, the whole of creation. This is explicitly expressed in the Bemba (Zambia) name for God, "*Kapekape*" (He gives to each and every creature all their needs). Similar views are contained in the Banyoro (Uganda) name, "*W'emigisa*" (He who has and gives blessings).

African traditional society highly values blessings, which are given or pronounced in the context of love between the giver and the recipient. It is assumed that blessings ultimately come from God and that it is God who fulfills them. Human beings are simply God's agents in dispensing God's blessings at the personal, family, community, or national levels. One of the attributive names of God among the Banyoro (in Uganda) is "*W'emigisa*" (He who has and gives blessings). The Bemba (of Zambia) emphasize this concept of God through three names: "*Kaleka-Misuma*" (He who gives complete [whole] gifts), "*Kapekape*" (He gives to each and every creature all their needs), and "*Nalusandulula*" (Multiplier, He who makes all things to multiply).

Whether these blessings are in terms of whole gifts, needs, all things, or other unspecified items, God provides them out of divine love. They are concrete expressions of God's love, even without talking about love as such. There is no ending to God's love. Everyone acknowledges it by using the names of God that refer to love. Whenever people dispense or receive blessings, they are in effect invoking the love of God. These blessings are abundant and God is disposed to give them out generously.

God Is Kind and Merciful

Banyoro (Uganda): *Mbabazi* (He who is kindness)
Barundi (Burundi): *Rufashaboro* (He is merciful)
Bemba (Zambia): *Nafukatila* (He who is "as kind as the hen to her chicks")

Here God is depicted as being kind and merciful. There are many occasions in life situations when people feel or acknowledge the kindness of God. For the Banyoro (Uganda), this aspect is so strong that they see God as being truly "*Mbabazi*" (He who is kindness). That kindness springs from divine love. By implication, God is that love.

God as Helper with Loving Care

Banyoro (Uganda): *Atalemwa* (He who never fails), *Atugonza* (He who loves us), *Asumurra* (He who unties all difficulties)
Bulu (Cameroon): *Mebee/Membe'e* (the One who bears the world)
Chewa (Malawi): *Mlezi* (Caretaker of Children), *Wolera* (same as *Mlezi*)
Shilluk (Sudan): Giver Who looks after the country
Sidama (Ethiopia): *Halalancho* (the True One), addressed as Father, loving and caring for His children
Sukuma-Nyamwezi (Tanzania): *Kube-Nyangasa* (the One who furnishes us with what we need)

With these names, people highlight the loving and providential care that they experience from God. They are so convinced of such care that the Banyoro see God as "*Atalemwa*" (He who never fails). God's faithfulness in caring for them never fails. There are those who specifically connect this aspect of God with children, and who like the Chewa (of Malawi) designate God as "*Mlezi*" and "*Wolera*" (Caretaker of Children). In human life, children need the most care, and God is here the supreme One who provides it. Just as God cares for the little ones, so God also provides that care for everyone. People are satisfied with such care, and so the Sukuma-Nyamwezi (Tanzania) call God "*Kube-Nyangasa*" (the One who furnishes us with what we need). The Banyoro (Uganda) refer to God with the names "*Atugonza*" (He who loves us) and "*Asumurra*" (He who unties all difficulties). This is a highly significant and rare expression in African societies, to speak of God directly as loving us. That God takes care of children is enough to say that God loves them. There is no care of children without love, even on the human level.

The Sidama in Ethiopia refer to God by the name "*Halalancho*" (the True One), and address God as "Father, loving and caring for His children." The Shilluk in the Sudan elevate the concept further to refer to the whole country and call God the "Giver Who looks after the country." God's loving care is not confined to human society. It extends over the entire physical country. That idea is universal among the Bulu (in Cameroon), who describe God as "*Mebee/Membe'e*" (the One who bears the world). The "world" here would certainly mean the whole of creation, the whole cosmos. That is a fitting attribute of God, seeing that God has created everything; God thus cares for everything in creation, God "bears" the world, God is the nursing Caretaker of the universe. That image derives from the way that parents and other family members may carry (bear) children especially on their back or front. It implies safety, security, care, provision of food and shelter, protection from danger, and sustaining life in all its ramifications. For human parents it implies constant contact with the children. For God it also implies constant contact with the world, with creation.

God as Maker, Father, Mother, Parent, and Origin

Akamba (Kenya): *Asa, Mumbi* (Father, Mother, Parent, Creator)
Akan (Ghana): *Nana Nyankopon* (Grandfather who alone is the Great One), Artist-in-Chief, *Borebore* (Excavator, Hewer, Creator, Originator, Inventor, Carver, Architect)
Alur (Uganda): *Jok Odudu* (God of birth)
Banyarwanda (Rwanda): *Habyarimana* (God only brings forth children), *Ruremabibondo* (Maker of children), *Naluntuntwe* (Father/Mother, the Progenitor, "Parent" of every creature), *Nafukatila* (He/She who is as kind as the hen to her chicks)
Banyoro (Uganda): *Muzaire* (the Parent)
Duala (Cameroon): *Ebasi* (Omnipotent Father)
Ewe (Dahomey, Ghana, Togo): Mother of People
Fiote (Congo), Fjort: *Nzambi Mpungu, Nzambici* (the Father God who dwells in the sky)
Fon (Benin): *Genitor* (Father)
Hottentot (South Africa): Father of our fathers and mothers
Luo (Kenya): *Were* (Father of grace), *Tham, Wuonwa* (Our Father), *Wuon kwere* (Father of the "ancestors"), *Wuon ji* (Father of all), *Uworo* (Father)
Maasai (Kenya, Tanzania): my Feathered One, Nursing Mother
Namaqua (Namibia): Grandfather
Nuba (Sudan): Great Mother
Pygmy (Democratic Republic of the Congo): Father of our ethnic group

Sidama (Ethiopia): *Halalancho* (the True One), addressed as Father, loving and caring for His children
Sukuma (Tanzania): Creator of all people (Father/Mother)

Here we have a whole range of names of God pointing to a number of insights or designations. They describe God in intensive family and anthropomorphic language: Mother, Nursing Mother, Great Mother, Mother of people, Father, Our Father, Father of our ethnic group, Father of all, Father of grace, Omnipotent Father, Father of the ancestors, Grandfather, Parent, Parent of every creature, Progenitor, Genitor, Maker of children, Giver of children, God of birth, Creator of all people. The Akan word "*Borebore*" describing God summarizes many of these concepts in its comprehensive and dynamic images: "Excavator, Hewer, Creator, Originator, Inventor, Carver, Architect."

These family attributes place people in the position of children—God's children. They convey images within which love is supreme. It is divine love that links God to the children, to the family, to the world, to creation. It is divine love that links past generations (living dead, ancestors) to the present and those yet to be born. Divine love is cosmic, creative, sustaining, nursing. It is intimate vis-à-vis creation, as it embraces all within its outreach. Divine love is family oriented, and God is literally the Father-Mother of all, who originates all creation and cares for it. Within the sphere of these relations, people express most intensely what for them amounts to divine love. They are terms of intimacy, where communion and communication between them and God is best possible. The Banyarwanda have a beautiful image in one of their names of God: "*Nafukatila*," meaning "He/She who is as kind as the hen to her chicks." Divine love is parental love; it translates into family love.

These terms, however, do not necessarily overlook the agonies of life, the destructive dimensions of life for humans and the world at large. But they go beyond these destructive elements and, in a sense, overcome them. Severe destructive elements may appear to eclipse divine love, but they cannot conquer it and cannot root it out. To the contrary, divine love conquers them. It is what upholds human life, the world, and the cosmos at large. Divine love is distributed everywhere in creation. The world (cosmos) is the theater of divine love, and everything is involved in that love, including paradoxically those seemingly destructive elements.

God as the Source of Protection and Security

Banyoro (Uganda): *Mujuni* (the Author of safety and security, the Savior)
Barundi (Burundi): *Rutunga* (Protector), *Rutangaboro* (Protector of the poor), *Ntirandekuva* (He has not let me drop yet)
Chewa (Malawi, Zambia): Great Rainbow
Ganda (Uganda): *Ddunda* (Pastor, Shepherd), *Ssewaunaku* (He who has pity on the poor and the suffering)

People experience the love of God in the area of their security; God provides ultimate security for their lives. This feature comes out through saving them for which, for example, the Banyoro call God "*Mujuni*," which means "the Author of safety and security, the Savior." The name comes out through God protecting them against threats to life. People recognize the protective love of God particularly in connection with the poor.

God is also considered to be the Pastor and Shepherd, as the Ganda name "*Ddunda*" indicates. God feeds, God guides, and God gives direction. God provides what sustains people, what keeps them healthy, and what makes them prosper. Divine love is healing, nourishing, protective, and responsive to people's sufferings. It is sensitive to their life situations and responds to their needs. Every individual lives on God's love, so the Barundi call God by the name "*Ntirandekuva*," which means, "He has not let me drop yet." It is a sustaining, uplifting, and assuring love. Divine love confers dignity to individuals. As such they matter infinitely, whether they are healthy or sick, whether they prosper or suffer, and whether they are rich or poor. Divine love has no discrimination whatsoever. It is not limited to a particular time or place.

This conviction about divine love encourages and enables people to carry on and face the difficulties, hardships, hurdles, and tragedies of life. They know that God is on their side as the ultimate Protector. In struggling to overcome the difficulties or contradictions of life, they do not feel abandoned, even if they may wonder why God allows difficulties to come upon them. In their conversations and in their prayers, they maintain that God is their Protector, their Savior, their Helper, their Guard, their Shepherd, and their caring Parent. We have seen other names that fall into this category, all pointing to people's awareness of divine love. One set of sayings among the Igbo in Nigeria clearly articulates this attitude of the people: "God! I am in your hands! What you say will happen! Nothing baffles you!"

Prayers as a Source of Declaring and Claiming Divine Love

African Religion Is Rich in Prayers

African prayers exist in oral form; only a few of them have been recorded in writing. From a study of some three hundred such prayers, about 90 percent are addressed directly to God. The remaining 10 percent make mention of other "spiritual" beings, like mythical heroes, some spirits, (so-called) ancestors, the departed (living dead), and personifications of natural phenomena and objects. But even these 10 percent assume that God is in the background and is the ultimate recipient of the prayers concerned. The idea that God is in the background comes out clearly where the petitioner asks one or more of the living dead (or ancestors) to plead with God on his or her behalf.

"Officials" and older persons normally say the prayers on behalf of their families, communities or (ethnic) people, the whole country, and the world at large. Praying is community oriented, and even when an individual says a private or personal prayer, it is generally applicable for others in the family or community. This is intimately linked to the reality that belief in God is first and foremost a community belief, a community value, and the ultimate point of reference for the community's spirituality. Some of the prayers require the response of the community. In this case, the leader intones a prayer while the assembled group responds by repeating certain words, in a song or in a dance. Individual needs may be passed on to the prayer leader or the elders, who would normally also know such needs in the family and community.

Largely in and through these prayers, the people use different personal and attributive names of God. As the prayers address God directly or indirectly, they portray a certain picture of God that people have. The people address God as Father, Mother, Creator, Maker, Parent, Elder, Grandfather, Source of life, Protector, Savior, Healer, Giver of children and rain, Shepherd of the people, and Protector of people and land. In many cases, a personal pronoun is attached to the name of God: "my" or "our" (Protector, Healer, Giver of children, etc.). In praying, the people refer to themselves as God's ("Your") children. Whether they offer prayers of blessings, protection, healing, or petition for children and rain, they clearly address God in a personal way, convinced that God listens to people addressing God. People's impression of God is that God loves them, cares for them, gives to them generously to meet their various needs, and accepts their praise and thanksgiving.

The prayers clearly bear witness to people's awareness of divine love. They facilitate channels of communication that are only possible where love, God's love, is at work. Thus, when people petition God to give them offspring, they do so believing that God loves them. When they praise and thank God for protecting them, they do so believing that God loves them. When they pray at a funeral ceremony that God would look after the departed member of the family, they do so because they believe (know) that God loves both the dead and the living. When they pray for the welfare of their cattle or land, they do so believing that God loves their animals and land and cares for their welfare. When they pray and address God as the Eternal, the One "who knows no death," they do so convinced that God's love is also eternal and endures without end.

Indeed, the names of God used in prayers are born out of the understanding, the belief, the conviction, the feeling, and the awareness that God loves people, land, and creation. Divine love is the common assumption that enables people to give different attributes to God, and to make them address God directly or in some cases through the chain process of asking the departed to convey the requests to God. These names that people give to God, the invocations or prayers that they say using those names, and the picture of God that emerges from them portray God as personal, approachable, kind, a giver and preserver of life, and above all loving toward people and creation.

Concepts of divine love also emerge in the depiction of the persons praying before God. Through the prayers, the persons come out as the prime objects of divine love. This is a liturgical picture and paints persons at prayer, communicating with God (and other alleged spiritual realities). Some prayers portray persons in a state of humility, before God the Almighty. So one prayer goes, "Today we, your creatures, prostrate ourselves before you in supplication. We have no strength." Persons consider themselves to be in a child-parent relationship with God, depending entirely on God, and pray from that standpoint. Thus, another prayer calls upon God as the Parent: "O God of our forefathers and mothers, all our lives depend on you and without you we are nothing. . . . Without you we can't live because we shall have no food or water to drink. You are the source of life." God's love sustains the people.

The life of persons on earth is fleeting, accompanied by many forms of suffering and faced with inevitable death. Yet persons address God as Father, Creator, Protector, and Giver of life. With that posture toward God, they are confident that God listens and responds. In one example of prayers, people respond by shouting in unison in a chorus, "He [God] will grant it!" In another prayer, they regard God as the One "upon whom men [*sic*] lean and do not fall." Even where persons struggle in the face of suffering, they hold fast that God does not abandon them, and that God will respond to their requests. Good examples of such prayers are the ones prompted by drought, which makes people desperate for water and rain: "We make this sacrifice in order to have rain"; "God, have-we-prayed-to-Thee, Give us rain"; or, "We come to ask for water, we who are dying from thirst." In another prayer, the people regard God as the Water of life: "Come to us with a continued rain, O *Lesa* [God], fall!"

Blessings are an intensive area of prayers. They depict persons as dependent on God, since it is God who ultimately grants the realization of blessings. They are the symbols of God's love, divine love. Persons of a "higher" status pronounce blessings upon those of a "lower" status, in terms of age (parents, grandparents, aunts, uncles, etc.), social position (community and ritual elders), religious position (priests, diviners, healers), and political position (chief, king, queen, ruler). Blessings are given for personal and community needs, such as protection, good fortune, success, childbearing, longevity, peace, good harvest, happiness, rain, and victory. Blessings are the channels through which persons may experience God's love in tangible ways. This love is, however, for all people and for all lands. It knows no boundaries, and God grants it without discrimination. One proverb from Cameroon bears this out clearly: "Rain does not fall on one roof alone."

The prayers contain elements that can be grouped, for example, into the following categories:

- Blessings, curses, justice, peace, good health for people, animals, and land.
- Celebrations in connection with the rites of passage—namely birth, naming, initiation, menstruation, betrothal, marriage, death, funerals, and contact with the departed.

- Communal/community welfare, harmony, peace, cooperation, resolving frictions, sharing resources.
- Formal festivals, rituals, music, dances, making of sacrifices and offerings.
- Health, increase, and prosperity of human life; healing; prosperity of land and animals; relationships with the living dead (departed), ancestors, and spirits (benevolent and unwanted); passing the day and night.
- Personal welfare and harmony in the family, life together of husband-wife-children, passing of examinations, finding jobs, promotions, successful election, finding life partner, love affairs, and family welfare.
- Praise, thanksgiving, "wrestling with God," theodicy, dealing with broken taboos, failure to keep formal promises or covenants, ritual uncleanness, moral breaches.
- Protection; removal of evil and threats to life, such as war, epidemics, locusts, witchcraft, troublesome spirits, and sickness.
- Provision of children, food, rain, and success in undertakings and travels.
- Seasonal conditions and activities like rain, planting, harvesting, hunting, or fishing.

God, Save Us. God, Hide Us.

A prayer from the Samburu people in Kenya:[1]

> When we sleep, God do not sleep.
> If we sleep, God do not get drowsy.
> Tie us around your arm, God,
> Like a bracelet.
> Guard us now, my God, guard us and save us.
> God, guard for us our little ones
> Both people and beasts,
> Whether awake or asleep.
> God, look on us with a countenance that is happy.
> Hit us with the black cloud of rain like the long rains.
> God, give us your waters.
> God, give us what we ardently desire in regards to children,
> and to cattle.

God, do not make our land barren.
God, give us places where there is life.
God, divide us fairly into dead and alive.
And God said, "All right."

This is a prayer for the family and community. God exercises care, love, watchfulness, and protection over the people. They are convinced that God will not cease to do so, whether they sleep or stay awake. God's love does not cease, or "get drowsy," no matter in what conditions people may find themselves. People feel that this love binds them firmly to the protective arm of God. Before God they are precious and beautiful, like a bracelet.

The love of God guards and saves people, with particular attention to "our little ones" who are not strong and need to be safeguarded. That love extends to people, animals, and land, the items they value most. Domestic animals (cattle, sheep, goats, donkeys, dogs, etc.) are the livelihood of the Samburu people. As they live in barren and semi-barren parts of the country (Kenya), water has great value. In dry seasons people and animals may walk far and wide (up to ten kilometers) in search of water. The land becomes literally barren. This prayer thus puts a lot of emphasis on rain and water in its pleading with God:

Look on us with a countenance that is happy.
Hit us with the black cloud of rain like the long rains.
God, give us your waters.
God, give us what we ardently desire in regards to children,
and to cattle.

So then, for the people, God's love is manifest most intensely in matters of rain and water. That is what they consider to be "places where there is life." God's love restores and affirms life.

This prayer is a comprehensive plea for God's love toward the people, their animals, and their land. The people feel confident in asking for it, being convinced that God loves them and will grant them their request, whether they are alive or dead. They are so sure of God's love in this respect that they have to declare at the conclusion of the prayer, "And God said, 'All right.'" In that case, God is almost obliged to grant the material essence of this prayer, indicative of their conviction about divine love.

A Prayer of a Hungry Man

From the Barolong (Mafikeng) in South Africa:[2]

> God of our ancestors, I lie down without food,
> I lie down hungry,
> Although others have eaten and lie down full.
> Even if it be but a polecat or a little rock-rabbit.
> Give me and I shall be grateful.
> I cry to God,
> Father of my ancestors.

This is one of the fairly few individual or personal prayers on written record, but it captures the experience of many persons, from time to time. Otherwise most of the prayers are voiced on behalf of the community. The praying person, who is evidently a hunter, is preoccupied with a deeply personal need. He is very hungry and needs food. Perhaps he spent the day and all his hopes in the task of hunting, but killed nothing. He is desperate. Now, his only hope is God, the ultimate point of reference for his life. He turns to God in a childlike voice and calls out of the depths of his heart, "God of our ancestors." Through blood, he is linked to his ancestors. But in faith he is also linked to God, whom he calls at the end of the prayer, "Father of my ancestors." He is praying to the very Father of all peoples, the Parent of all parents. He views and addresses God from a supremely parent-and-child position. As Father/Mother, God loves him as much as God loved his physical ancestors. That divine love has not diminished along the line of generations. God's love is faithful love. At the start of the prayer, the hunter speaks to "God of *our* ancestors," thus including all people. At the end, he claims the personal dimension of God's love and speaks of "Father of *my* ancestors." There is the communal dimension to divine love, and there is the personal individual dimension to the same love. He is aware of both dimensions.

The hunter (petitioner) claims this love of God on a personal level: "I lie down hungry, / Although others have eaten and lie down full." He compares himself to other people who have eaten enough. The tone tells God that they have had a full share of God's love, and it is now his turn to get a portion of the same. That love is inexhaustible. He is not complaining, or is he? The man will be completely satisfied with even the least portion of God's love, be it in the form of "a polecat or a little rock-rabbit" that he can kill and eat. Even the smallest portion of God's love satisfies, for God does not give it according to any measure. The hunter is fully aware of that. When he receives this portion of love, he will be grateful. The divine parent has shown immense love for him. He cries to God to have pity on him. God shows love in acts of pity. God loves him the same way that God loved his (their) ancestors. God's pity, hence God's love, does not get rusty and does not grow old. The hunter hopes that, as God had pity upon the ancestors, so God will have pity on him. He will eat, be satisfied, be thankful, and spend the night with a full stomach.

The prayer does not tell whether the hunter got food that night. At least he did not die of hunger; otherwise his prayer would not have become known.

We Do Not Tire in Giving Thanks to You

Prayer of the Maasai of Kenya and Tanzania:[3]

> Creator God, we announce your goodness because it is clearly visible in the heavens where there is the light of the sun, the heat of the sun, and the light of night. There are rain clouds. The land itself shows your goodness, because it can be seen in the trees and their shade. It is clearly seen in water and grass, in the milking cows and in the cows that give us meat.
>
> Your love is visible all the time: morning and daytime, evening and night. Your love is great. It has filled the land; it has filled people. We say: "Thank you. Our God," because you have given us everything we have. You have given us our fathers and mothers, our brothers and sisters, our children and friends. You have given us cows, grass and water. We have nothing except what you have given us.
>
> You are our shield; you protect us. You are our guard; you take care of us. You are our safety, all days. You stay with us forever and ever. You are our Father and Mother. Therefore we say: "Thank you." We worship you with our mouths. We worship you with our bodies. We worship you with everything we have, because only you have given us everything. We say: "Thank

you," today. And tomorrow. And all days. We do not tire in giving thanks to you.

This prayer is longer than average. It is based on God's creation. It is not a petition. It is a kind of confession of faith, a form of adoration, based on what the community believes about God. The phrase "your goodness" is central to the prayer. God's goodness fills the whole creation. It translates into love. This is one of the very few traditional African prayers I have seen that directly speaks about the love of God in an intensive language—visible love, enduring love, ever-present love, great love, the love that fills land and people:

Your love is visible all the time:
Morning and daytime, evening and night.
Your love is great.
It has filled the land;
It has filled people.

The people see God's goodness (read: love) as an expression of divine love. They see it, feel it, and experience it through what God has created and given to them. God's goodness (love) is visible through the light and heat of the sun. God's goodness (love) is seen through the rain, which enables trees and grass to grow. People experience God's goodness (love) in their cattle that give them food—milk and meat—the traditional staple food of the Maasai people. When it is available, God has blessed them with plenty.

The people see the goodness (love) of God in "everything we have." "Everything" embraces family members, including "our fathers and mothers, our brothers and sisters, our children and friends." The family is God-given, an expression of God's goodness (love). "Everything" also includes animals, rain, grass, water, sun, air, and land. Furthermore, God is their "shield," providing protection, guarding them, taking care of them, granting them their security, and remaining with them forever. In their traditional life, the Maasai men carry spears and shields and use them for hunting, defending against wild animal and human attacks. The shield is a very powerful and practical symbol to use for God.

Such is the goodness (love) of God, as the people feel it, experience it, rejoice in it. It binds them with God. Through it they are almost "mystically lost in God." Inevitably they pour out their spirit, to plead, profess, and venerate:

> You stay with us forever and ever.
> You are our Father and Mother.
> Therefore we say: "Thank you."
> We worship you with our mouths.
> We worship you with our bodies.
> We worship you with everything we have,
> Because only you have given us everything.
> We say: "Thank you," today.
> And tomorrow. And all days.
> We do not tire in giving thanks to you.

These are expressions of a profound awareness of God's goodness (love), derived from the visible creation. It is God's goodness (love) in geography, so to speak. It is tangible and spread out in space and time. And everyone is a partaker of this divine love. It evokes thanksgiving to God and worship with mouth, body and everything, without tiring, as the prayer asserts. The people sense God's goodness (love) so intensively that it binds them intimately with God. They tell God, "You are our Father and Mother. Therefore we say, 'Thank you.'" That statement reaches a great height of spiritual awareness. People experience divine love not as an abstract thought, but in concrete forms that they reciprocate in enduring thanksgiving. Divine love here is active on two dimensions: the goodness that people receive from God, and the worship that they render to God in turn.

Kwambaza: A Cry for Help

Prayer from Rwanda-Burundi:[4]

> O *Imana* [God] of Urundi/Ruanda, if only you would help me!
> O *Imana* of pity, *Imana* of my father's home [country], if only
> you would help me!
> O *Imana* of the country of the Hutu and the Tutsi,
> If only you would help me just this once!
> O *Imana*, if only you would give me a homestead [*rugo*]
> and children!

> I prostrate myself before you, *Imana* of Urundi/Ruanda.
> I cry to you: Give me offspring, give me as you give to others!
> *Imana*, what shall I do, where shall I go?
> I am in distress: where is there room for me?
> O Merciful, O *Imana* of mercy, help this once!

The woman who says this prayer is in great social, emotional, and spiritual agony. It is a prayer that is echoed in every society, all over the world. In a traditional African community, for someone, particularly a married woman, to be childless is a deep social and emotional burden that in turn generates spiritual ripples. Traditional African society does not know how to tolerate childless marriages. Without children there is no family and there is no social peace. Society seeks various ways to neutralize or cope with such situations.

This prayer thus responds to personal, emotional, social (communal), and spiritual dimensions of life. The petitioner is very open about her problem and her relationship with God. She appeals to God ("*Imana*"), the God of all peoples. There is "no" exclusively individual God. Belief in God is a communal value in African society, and an individual relates to God in that context. So, here, the woman addresses "*Imana* [God] of Urundi/Ruanda . . . of my father's home [country]."

The prayer is an appeal to God who exists for all times and all places. Without hesitation, the woman claims personal access to God. She has confidence in God's love for all people, including her. The love she claims from God is in terms of pity and mercy. She feels and believes that God is merciful and shows pity. Therefore, she is confident to address her prayer to the "*Imana* [God] of pity." It is as if God is so full of pity, she could say, "God is pity." For her, God's pity is God's love. Because God is pitying, God can help her. In a litany for help, she calls four times on God to help:

> "If only you would help me!" (line 1)
> "If only you would help me!" (line 2)
> "If only you would help me just this once!" (line 4)
> "O *Imana* of mercy, help this once!" (line 10)

The prayer begins with this earnest appeal for help; it repeats it ("this once") and concludes with it. It is a very vivid prayer. We can hear the cry of the woman. We can hear her knocking on God's door of pity. It is a universal cry, and it is not confined to the women, since (married) men are also affected by the state of being childless.

In the prayer, "help" means, concretely, homestead and children. In traditional life, the homestead and children belong together. They are the family, the physical space and the human substance. That is the ideal setting of life, according to traditional values. Without them, life is incomplete. To have no homestead, no children, and no offspring amounts to being essentially nonexistent and nonhuman. Hence, in this cul-de-sac situation, she makes her desperate appeal:

> *Imana*, what shall I do, where shall I go?
> I am in distress: where is there room for me?

No human person can answer these questions. Only God can rescue and save from that brink of nonexistence, that brink of being nobody, the brink of (social) death. Inwardly in her own eyes and outwardly in the sight of society, without a child she is nobody, no person as persons should be.

So the petitioner cries for help that, at this point, can only come from God. She looks upon God as "*Imana* of pity" and "*Imana* of mercy." These are strong attributes of God through which to address the love of God. Love is pity and mercy, which are personified in the form of help that provides children, offspring, and family (homestead). Only such help can remove the physical, social, and spiritual distress in which the woman finds herself.

She does not question God. She does not blame God. But perhaps rightly feeling jealous, she tells God about other persons (women) whom God has given children. So she pleads, "If only you would help me just this once!" She prostrates herself before God and pleads for God's love to take concrete form in her—mercy, pity, and tangible help. That would give her all the room—physical, social, and spiritual—that she needs to live the true life. She has no doubt about it, that she will get from God the answers regarding her quest for and meaning of life:

> *Imana*, what shall I do, where shall I go? . . .
> Where is there room for me?

These are profound questions of life. Different people receive different answers from God. We do not know what answers the woman may have received. God's love manifests itself in different forms. On her part, she believed that only God's love (through pity, mercy, and help) could provide ultimate answers to her search, the fulfillment of her life.

Divine Love in Proverbs

Proverbs Abound in African Communities

It is estimated that Africa has about 8 million proverbs in its roughly two thousand languages plus thousands of dialects. Most of them are not recorded in written form and circulate orally. But since about 1970, more and more collections are being published, with numbers ranging from a few dozen to several thousand proverbs from different ethnic-language regions. Many African proverbs are also being made available on the Internet. Universities and other institutions of higher learning are taking up academic studies of proverbs, and scholars are collecting them directly from the indigenous speakers.

Among other things, proverbs play an important pedagogical role in traditional society. One great advantage of proverbs is that each can be used again and again to deal with different occasions or purposes. They address every possible item about people's lives and the world. Some communicate, others teach and educate; some warn, others give moral and ethical directions; some entertain, others make commentaries on society; some tell extra-short stories or relate historical and mythical events. Many proverbs are rich in religious, philosophical, and literary values. As a whole, proverbs contain a concentration of traditional wisdom and knowledge. Being in the form of short statements, people easily take note of them, learn and apply them, and reflect on them when someone quotes them. Proverbs fit extremely well into the oral culture, and they serve as spices in that oral tradition.

Proverbs are thus well incorporated into conversations, speeches, discussions, formal teachings, counseling, giving advice, settling disputes, and the upbringing of children and young people. Using proverbs never becomes a dull exercise. Sometimes people also employ them as a hidden language (or weapon) in communicating concealed messages or information. Teachers utilize them in schools for teaching, and preachers in churches for preaching and catechumen for instruction. Today, some proverbs are provided on the Internet as sayings of the day, week, or month; some are printed in calendars or as quotations in various publications; and others are provided for particular occasions and themes. In eastern Africa, proverbs are printed on clothes known as *kanga* and *kitenge*, which women wear or that are used as tablecloths and curtains. When so used, the proverbs convey a message about relationships like love, marriage, friendship, jealousy, respect, patience, complaint, justice, warnings, and good wishes. They become an important platform for women's voices, where otherwise women may not have much freedom to speak their minds openly.

Through the use of proverbs, people articulate their views on everything about the world. These are communal views, even if individuals employ proverbs to make personal points. They are generally wrapped up in cultural contexts, but some have a global or universal applicability. Proverbs are generated by society, with certain individuals having greater ability than others in formulating and using proverbs. They are without known authors, but occasionally some are attributed to a given person. The process of formulating proverbs goes on all the time. Some proverbs die out through their not being relevant any more for use. New proverbs emerge all the time, some of which address the current situation of society. However, as the African populace moves more and more to become a literary society, the origination and use of proverbs in oral communication seem to decrease.

We look at some proverbs here that point to divine love. These proverbs talk about God being merciful, kind, and compassionate; caring, providing, and saving. Those are the points of reference in which people experience or observe (and interpret it to be) the intervention of God in their lives and in the world, or when they call upon God to intervene for particular purposes. A proverb can be used to speak to different purposes and occasions, and for that reason we quote some of them here more than once.

God Is Compassionate and Kind

Many proverbs speak about God being kind and compassionate. The Oromo (Ethiopia) state that, "By the kindness of God the house is satisfied." They are convinced that satisfaction for the family (house) comes ultimately from the kindness of God, who provides, as we shall see further below.

An Akan proverb from Ghana states, "If God gives you a calabash full of [palm] wine and a living man kicks it over, God fills it up again." This is to encourage people to know that if someone tries to do harm to them, God's love is bountiful enough to continue to bless them, to fill their calabash again and again with wine. God's compassion cannot be extinguished by the wickedness of people. This thought is also affirmed from the Oromo (Ethiopia) proverb, "God does not abandon a person." People are assured that God's love toward them is so strong that they do not or should not feel left on their own, even in times of great difficulties. God is ever present to save, to comfort, to support, and to encourage them.

In the light of God's compassion, no one has an unfair advantage over another. God's compassion and care are upon those who are underprivileged as well as those who are strong and healthy. Two proverbs provide examples. Looking at one end of human conditions, a Swahili proverb from eastern Africa states, "What God preserves for the poor does not rot." God also cares for people at the other end, as stated by an Oromo proverb in Ethiopia: "The mother of a brave man is God." In these two proverbs, God is depicted as the caring, loving, compassionate Mother of all, of both the weak and the strong. Such is God's compassion, God's love toward all. The Ovambo in Namibia verbalize the same idea, in a proverb that calls God "Spirit of the homeless, God of the poor and the rich." At the same time, God exercises protective care as indicated in an Oromo proverb, "That which [the Lord] put aside for the blind person, the one who sees will not take." God is with the blind to protect their welfare and sustain them.

People experience God's care and compassion especially in times of sickness. The Akan in Ghana are ready to face such times, prepared with the proverb, "If God gives you sickness, God gives you its cure." Likewise the Ga people of Ghana put it this way: "When God gives you a load, God also gives you a soft pad to carry it." God's compassion, mercy, and consolation are present in all conditions of life. They never end, and the Ga have another proverb to drive this point home: "The salty taste never ceases in a salt-pot." God is the source of mercy, compassion, and grace that never cease. Of such love among people, another proverb says, "Love knows neither shame nor fatigue." If that can be said of people, it must apply even much more to God's love.

About God's mercy the Akan say, "Even for the handicapped, God provides help and sustenance," and "It is God Who pounds *fufuu* for the one-armed person." *Fufuu* is the Akan traditional staple food prepared from plantain, cassava, or yams. After boiling these food items, a person puts them in a mortar and pounds them with a pestle, holding the pestle with both hands. The proverb assures a one-handed person that God will help him or her pound the *fufuu*, so that the person can eat and not die of hunger. The person will not go hungry because of being handicapped. God stays near to help. God's kindness and compassion do not run out; another Oromo proverb affirms, "The home of a person runs out of kindness. In the home of God it never ends."

God's caring love extends to the whole creation. The Akan of Ghana thus quote the proverb, "If you cheat the crab, God sees your buttocks." In catching a crab, one has to bend down and thereby expose the buttocks. God sees what you are doing and will deal with you, in matters of justice to the crab, for God cares for the crabs. For that reason, the Akan also say, "God is not asleep." God is keeping watch over the whole creation. The Ovambo in Namibia agree when they say, "God speaks a foreign tongue." By this proverb, they warn against tormenting God's creatures, as that would evoke punishment. God is compassionate toward creation.

God Is Good

The following proverbs illustrate the belief that God is good by nature, and therefore is good toward people and creation. Goodness is an element of God's love. God loves and therefore God is good; this would be the line of reflection when people talk about God's goodness. So, the Akan (Ghana) say categorically, "God does not like evil."

Considering how much people hate robbers and would severely deal with them by beating, stoning, or setting them on fire to die, people imagine that also God feels the same way. This is stated by the Maasai (Kenya and Tanzania): "God never listens to the robber," which could mean that God's goodness is subject to ethical application and justice.

People experience the goodness of God through the good things that God gives to them, without failing and without ceasing. The Oromo (Ethiopia) state, "That which the Lord filled will not fail." Such unfailing goodness can only be an expression of God's love. In two other proverbs, people actually "eat" the goodness of God. Trusting God to supply food, the proverb says, "The appetite that is open, God is able to close." But God does not let food fall into the mouth from the clouds above. God supplies the means through which people get food. They point this out through the proverb, "The mouth eats because of God and the clouds." The rain is (potentially) food for the people, but God forms the clouds that bring rain. Nevertheless, people must play their part, by growing the food, leaving it up to God to create rain and make the crops grow. There is also the food supply through wild fruits, fishing, and hunting, for which God is the Giver, the Supplier, directly through rain.

There is another human dimension in respect to God's goodness. The Oromo (Ethiopia) are conscious that the goodness of God has to be distributed and shared, so they remind one another, "To the person who gives, God will give." God's goodness is not to be monopolized. It is destined for all, because God loves all. Giving something out of God's goodness means receiving even more of it from God. The recipient of God's love cannot exhaust it.

People ought to be aware of God's goodness and respond not only toward others but first and foremost toward the Giver. So, the Ovambo (Namibia) urge firmly, "What is given by God [Kalunga], receive it with both hands." To do that is an expression of profound gratitude. In this case, "both hands" symbolizes and represents the whole person: the head is there, the heart is there, the mind is there, the feelings are there, the mouth is there, the stomach is there, and other parts of the whole person—all embracing the gift of God, the goodness of God, and the love of God. The whole person should embrace the love of God with both hands, with deep appreciation and gratitude.

When people go through hardships and suffering, such experiences do not eclipse the goodness of God. Even if some people may consider that to be a form of punishment, an Akan (Ghana) proverb would urge them to take courage and remember, "When God picks up God's stone, God does not throw it at once." God is compassionate and good, and God does not hasten to mete out punishment, even if God acts with justice. The idea of God punishing individual persons is hardly found in African religious thought. Otherwise, it is the community—such as parents, local community, the chief, queen or king, and maybe the living dead or some spirits—that punishes at different levels. It is thought or assumed that God is "too good" to mete out punishment upon individuals, the community, or ethnic groups. However, some events that affect the wider community, such as drought, epidemics, catastrophe, locust invasion, and wars, may be interpreted as punishment from God. In that case, the community takes measures to appease God, such as making animal (or formerly even human) sacrifices and performing rituals to plead with God.

God Is Providential

Providence is a common concept, and people give God attributive names like Provider, Helper, Keeper, and Shepherd. They trust God to meet their needs, as one Oromo (Ethiopia) proverb states, "I who made this hole in my ear lobe will fill it with an earring. Let Him [the Lord] who made this hole [my mouth] fill it." They are saying that God loves them and will feed them—will provide rain, work, and other means of producing food to fill up their mouths. They trust, but at the same time, they work to get food, with God enabling them to do so.

Many proverbs point to God's providential dealings with people. Indeed all what God does toward people and creation can be interpreted as God's providence. For that reason, an Akan (Ghana) proverb calls for awareness, discernment, and patience, while waiting for God's work upon individuals to bear fruit: "If God is weaving for you a rich silk fabric, be patient and do not interrupt God's plans, else your fabric may turn into an inferior jute material." Even though the weaving is done by persons, God is working through them. If the person becomes impatient waiting for a new silk fabric to be completed, and asks the weaver to hurry up and finish the piece, the result would not be as good as normal.

The Oromo (Ethiopia and Kenya) speak also about the need to wait patiently for the providential goodness of God to take effect. They declare, "That which the Lord filled will not fail." God will not fail to provide again and again. So in another proverb they remind one another, "The mouth is God's gourd; He knows what to fill into [it]." In yet another proverb they point out the same understanding: "The mouth eats because of God and the clouds." God provides rain, so that people can grow (or gather) their food. According to another proverb, the result is that "the people of God gather pumpkins." God cares and provides food for people, and they should not worry or fear. The Ovambo (Namibia) proverb can be quoted here again: "What is given by God [Kalunga], receive it with both hands." God provides so much that people need both hands to be able to receive enough of it.

God Is Helpful

As a whole, people offer prayers because they believe that God will help them. Indeed, they are aware of God's help even when they do not ask for it. In the Democratic Republic of the Congo people say, "A blind man can pick up a bird." The help of God enables even a blind man or woman to find food. Similarly, the Akan (Ghana) hold, "It is God who drives away the flies from a tailless animal." God's help comes to the rescue of people when they reach the end of their own strength, or when they are handicapped, as the case may be. A Maasai woman praying to get a child would say in a proverb, "Oh God, give me shade and not that of the tree." It is said that people use this proverb today, even for anything they need.

But people also recognize that they have to play a certain part in receiving God's help. This is demonstrated in a Gikuyu (Kenya) proverb (with parallels elsewhere) that says, "Help yourself so that I may help you." The idea of self-help is a widespread motivation for people to do something in response to their own life situations. The Maasai (Kenya and Tanzania) are sure that, in the end, God's help will arrive: "There is nothing which can delay help (permanently)." This proverb is particularly supportive when people work to realize particular goals for their lives. They will in due course achieve their goals, which is due to God's help.

People recognize and experience boundaries to God's help. The parents of a sick child may pray and call upon God's help, but the child dies. The community may perform ritual and pray for rain during a severe drought, but the drought may continue longer. Yet people do not seem to lose hope or to grumble against God. Their trust in God's goodness is unbeatable. This comes out in a number of proverbs. An Oromo (Ethiopia) proverb recognizes this limit and states, "The Lord shepherds a person all days, then one day He pulls the man down." This proverb is used to indicate that "God is dependable until the end." The Barundi (Burundi) stress the point in three of their names for God that have proverbial meanings: "*Imana, Ntakimunanira*" (God does no evil), "*Rufashaboro*" (He is merciful), and "*Ntirandekuva*" (He has not let me drop yet). They are conscious of God's goodness (love) that sustains them up to the end.

Concluding Observations

From the many examples of traditional names of God in African religiosity, from the prayers and proverbs that are integrated into people's lives, it is evident that African religion recognizes clear pointers to divine love. God loves people as their Father, Friend, Giver (especially of children and rain), Healer, Helper, Keeper, Maker, Mother, Parent, Protector, Provider, and

Savior. People not only use these terms to speak of God, but they also pray to God out of that relationship, and spice their conversations with proverbs on almost every subject. These expressions indicate God's loving relationship toward people and creation at large. Generally the proverbs hold that the people are children of God, that God cares for them, that God supplies their needs, and that God saves them from danger and death.

At the same time, people indicate a paradoxical dimension to God's love, which comes out also in some of the names, prayers, and proverbs they use.

The Banyoro (Uganda) call God, among many other names, "*Kagingo*," meaning "the Creator of death." Two of the Ila (Zambia) names of God are "*Ipaokubozha*," which means "He who gives and causes to rot," and "*Chaba-wakaaba-ochitadiwa*," which means "the Giver who gives also what cannot be eaten." The Meru (Kenya) describe God, among other ways, as "the All-giver, Master of life and death." Likewise, the Yoruba (Nigeria) explain God as "the One who kills and saves." But even if death must come to all, the Sukuma (Tanzania) see God as "Victor over death."

In their proverbs, the Oromo (Ethiopia) say, "To make the poor full, God kills a rich man's cow that gives milk." The Banyarwanda (Rwanda) assert, "God [*Imana*] who sends famine also provides a place to buy food." The Akan hold fast what other people also experience: "If God gives you sickness, God gives you its cure."

Thus, there is a paradoxical dimension to God's love. Divine love provides human life with children, rain, health, food, protection, and security. That is the creative, saving, and sustaining manifestation of God's love. At the same time, life is under pressure from many forms of suffering, pain, sickness, accidents, tragedies, and ultimately death and destruction. People hold the view that also these forms of suffering come from that same Source. That is a paradox. God kills the cow of the rich person to feed the poor. God sends a famine, but also shows where to buy food. God allows sickness, but also the cure for it. It is the love of God that "gives and causes to rot." It is a paradox of divine love that makes people call God "*Chaba-wakaaba-ochitadiwa*," which means "The Giver who gives also what cannot be eaten." People acknowledge this, but also thank and praise God for giving it.

African religion does not seem to be bothered by this paradox, nor does it attempt to resolve it. The people live with it in a working balance, turning it into a kind of practical theodicy. Persons lost the initial bliss after creation, as the myths tell. However, divine love did not vanish with the bliss, but remained, so people put more weight on their living experiences of divine love in its different manifestations. In reality, they go on with life, with a smile and not a complaining heart. With right they claim and leave it at that: "If God did not love me, God would not have made me!" In other words, collectively, "God made us, because God loves us!" For that reason, "We do not tire in giving thanks to you, God."

Notes

1. Anthony Gittins, comp., *Heart of Prayer: African, Jewish and Biblical Prayers* (London: Collins, 1985), 157.
2. John S. Mbiti, *The Prayers of African Religion* (Maryknoll, NY: Orbis Books, 1976), 84ff.
3. Gittins, *Heart of Prayer*, 15.
4. Mbiti, *Prayers of African Religion*, 86.

2 "In the Beginning, Love Entered That One"

Divine Love from a Perspective Informed by Vedic Hindu Thought

William K. Mahony

Among the first thoughts that rose in my mind when the editors asked me to contribute a chapter to this book was that, yes, I would like to do so, for the topic of divine love is certainly, for me, an interesting and even compelling one and I would be happy to offer comments on it informed by my studies of Hinduism. I would also want to say before beginning that it is hard to imagine a wider range of ideas and practices than those associated with what has come to be known as Hinduism, for Hindu religious sensibilities encompass many traditions, practices, and schools of thought.

Among my subsequent thoughts, therefore, was that I probably should focus my comments on a particular thread within Hinduism. Accordingly, I have decided to weave my reflections in this chapter on ideas and practices represented specifically by texts expressing Vedic religious sensibilities. The English adjective "Vedic" is formed from the Sanskrit word *veda*, which means "sacred knowledge." The word connotes a knowledge gained through seeing: it is originally a visionary knowledge of the holy, and thus insight into the nature and meaning of existence and the way to life in effective harmony with it. Grounded in this sense, the Veda also refers to an extensive religious system based on this sacred knowledge and on a particular complex of songs, rituals, sacred narratives, contemplative investigations, philosophical musings, and normative ethics that express that knowledge. When used in the plural, the term "the Vedas" refers to the set of sacred literatures and practices that present and hold that knowledge.[1]

I have chosen this strand because Vedic ideas, practices, and intuitions have found expression in India for four thousand years or more and, it could be said, have served as a foundation of sorts for various Hindu perspectives throughout the many centuries since then.[2]

Scholarship is not unanimous in dating the rise of the Veda as an identifiable system of religious thought and expression. General agreement holds that the earlier phases of such sensibilities can be dated to 2000–1100 BCE, with the first singing of sacred songs and hymns in praise of the Vedic deities. A somewhat later period from about 1100 BCE to roughly 800 BCE brought the telling of mythic narratives and delineation of instructions associated with the performance of sacred rituals. A third period from roughly 800 BCE to about 500 BCE offered the presentation of teachings based on the contemplative, mystical apprehension of a divine presence within all beings and on philosophical reflections into the nature of that presence, and a fourth period from 500 BCE onward through the centuries consisted of the systematizing of these various components as a whole.[3]

I realize that my decision to concentrate on the Veda may surprise some people. I suspect that, when asked to think about the theme of divine love in Hinduism, those familiar with the field would tend to think more immediately of the devotional thread of Hinduism—that is to say, *bhakti*—represented by such texts as the *Bhagavad Gītā* and the *Bhāgavata Purāṇa*[4] and by numerous theological and philosophical texts stemming from them, as well as the sentiments expressed by worshippers, poet-saints, pilgrims, and devotees aligned with various sectarian *bhakti* traditions.[5]

When there are discussions specifically of Vedic sensibilities, they usually and appropriately turn on such important themes as the description of the many gods and goddesses in the Vedic world, the nature and function of sacrifice, the performance and interpretation of the meaning of sacred public and domestic rituals, and the value and effective function of contemplative meditation.[6] Relative to these important themes, Vedic thought gives less explicit attention to the nature and expression of love. Yet, as we will see, Vedic visionaries, liturgists, and contemplative sages did indeed recognize the power, presence, and importance of what could be called divine love.

"Ponder This, Wise People: On What Did the Maker of All Things Stand When He Made All Things?"

We can begin our consideration of Vedic thought by saying that, to those Vedic seers who possessed what was regarded as visionary insight, the world and all things in it were in some way to have been brought into being, sustained, and enlivened by otherwise hidden forces they identified as various deities. Vedic poets and singers of sacred songs responded to and invoked those deities with verses of praise, calls for protection, and prayers for forgiveness and grace. An operative word for "deity" here would be the Sanskrit *deva*, which linguists know to be related to the English "divinity" and thus "divine." There was the god Agni, for example, who brought forth and dwelled within the many forms of fire: the sun, the flame in the domestic hearth, the sacred fire burning on the sacred altar. The mighty Indra protected the world against forces of death. Vedic seers saw the daytime light of the celestial realm as the god Dyaus and addressed the broad earth as the goddess Pṛthivī. Parjanjya fashioned the clouds and lived within the nourishing rain. Vāyu moved as the wind. Puṣān guided cows along their paths. Mitra and Varuṇa looked over the smooth turning of the days, months, and seasons.

At one level, Vedic sensibilities are therefore polytheistic in nature. One Vedic visionary poet sang, for example, of the "thirty and three gods," while another praised 339 deities who served the god Agni alone.[7] On the other hand, Vedic seers themselves wondered: How did the gods and goddesses themselves come into being? Who or what created them?

Such questions may have stood behind the musings of the Vedic sages who sang this song of the god Viśvakarman, whose name means "Maker of All Things":

> Where did he stand when he took his position?
> What supported him?
> How was it made?
> From what did the Maker of All Things,
> beholding all things, fashion the earth
> and shape the splendor of the skies? . . .
> From what lumber and from what tree
> were the heavens and the earth carved?

Ponder this, wise people!
Inquire within your minds:
on what did he stand when he made all things?[8]

Here we see an instance of a type of question that intrigued the Vedic mind: From what do the gods draw their creative and sustaining power? Is there some preexistent principle or force with which they align their artful work in the universe? These sorts of questions imply others that Vedic sages pondered and expressed in various ways: If there is such an underlying or transcendent Ultimate Reality, what is the relationship within it between the gods and the world? What is the relationship between the gods and one's own existence? Is there something that unites one's existence with the existence of all things?

Vedic sacred songs, paeans, prayers, liturgical texts, and contemplative intuitions variously indicate that the answer to such questions is "yes," and that this universal source and continuing foundation of reality itself is in some ways associated with the power of love.

Love as the Divine Yearning-to-Be

In the following song from the *Ṛg Veda* from roughly 1200 BCE we hear the musings of one who has pondered the otherwise incomprehensible fact that existence actually exists. Displaying a sense of wonder and a visionary spirit, the song presents its understanding of this mystery in the form of a creation narrative:

There was neither nonbeing nor being then.
There was no region of air nor sky beyond it.
What moved? Where? Under whose protection?
Was there water, deep and unfathomable?
There was neither death nor immortality then.
There was no distinction between night and day.
By its own inner power that One breathed, windless.
Beyond it, there was nothing whatsoever. . . .
Love-yearning entered that One, in the beginning:
That was the first seed of thought.
Searching within their hearts with wisdom,
Sages found the bond of being within nonbeing. . . .

Who really knows? Who will proclaim it?
Where was this creation born? Where did it come from?
The gods were born after the creation of the universe:
Who, then, can know from where it comes?
No one knows whence this creation has come into being.
Perhaps it formed itself. Perhaps not.
Only he who looks down from the highest heaven truly knows.
Or perhaps he does not know.[9]

The seer here asks a question that has drawn the attention of people throughout the millennia: How is it that existence came into existence? What transforms nonbeing into being? The seer has his listeners try to imagine a state of infinite potential. Such a state, if we can speak of it in this manner, would necessarily be beyond duality of any sort, for any kind of distinction implies the existence of that which is being distinguished. So, this state is beyond day and night. It is beyond death, and yet also beyond immortality. It is beyond even the distinction separating nonbeing and being.

As the source of existence, that state, or principle, or power, would exist independently of existence, and yet would also be inseparable from existence, for it would embrace both existence and nonexistence. In some ways, it is impossible to conceptualize such a state, because any concept of it necessarily limits it. Accordingly, "No one knows whence this creation came into being." Only the god who "looks down from the highest heaven truly knows"—and, yet, "Perhaps he does not know." As existent forces in the realm of being, even "the gods were born after the creation of the universe."

Our seer speaks here of an otherwise incomprehensible potentiality-and-actuality, a transcendental yet immanent unity beyond all duality that gives rise to everything in the universe, including the gods. He seems unwilling and perhaps logically unable to name it, referring to it simply as "that One" (*tad ekaṁ*). This One who is real even before the emergence of being is infused with a powerful force that draws existence out of fathomless nonexistence: "By its own power" it breathed—that is to say, it brought forth the life force—though there is yet no wind for it to breathe.

What is this mysterious power that draws forth existence "in the beginning"? The song calls it *kāma*. The word can and has been translated as "desire."[10] In subsequent Indian thought, *kāma* usually refers to desire for sensual pleasure, and from this sense the word has come also to carry a negative connotation of a spiritually harmful desire of any sort that seeks narrowly self-centered, temporary, conditional fulfillment.[11]

In the setting described much earlier by this vision from the *Ṛg Veda*, though, *kāma* cannot logically refer to such a desire for gratification, for there was nothing in existence yet that could satisfy it. Here, the word carries the sense of a desire-to-come-into-reality, a powerful longing-to-be, and thus a profound affirmation of being. I have translated it here as "Love-yearning," for we see reference to a divine desire, a generative, unconditional, nonobjective, gracious impulse that seeks expression and manifestation from within the depths of nonbeing. Raimondo Panikkar translates *kāma* in this hymn as "Love,"[12] a rendering that I will also follow in reference to this power.

This Love releases the latent life force that was covered in emptiness; it pulls the One out of its formless insularity. This creative stirring, this yearning-to-be, expresses a divine intention; it is a loving "first seed of thought." This intention, this generative divine thought of existence, is itself formed and impelled by the power of Love. Without Love there is nothing—nothing whatsoever.[13]

Love as a Bond between Human and Divine Hearts

Vedic songs variously describe the relationship between the deities who have come into existence as a result of Love and those who worship them. To be sure, most often the seers' words express the sentiments of awe, frequently tinged with a sense of fear in front of those powerful and mysterious divine forces. Yet some of those verses express the seers' own longing for a close and familiar intimacy with the gods. In various verses the relevant deity invoked is addressed or described as a most kindly friend, a brother, a mother, a father, or as a father and mother at the same time.[14] Elsewhere the gods are invoked in a manner similar to the way one calls on one's beloved: "I call Indra near, like a groom thinking of his consort."[15] The love the seer directs toward deity is steady, focused, and strong: "My mind, directed toward you, never wavers from you, O Indra; in you I have placed my love-yearning [*kāma*]."[16] Such a Vedic visionary is described in several places in the *Ṛg Veda* as *deva-kāma*, that is, as "loving the gods."[17]

How is it that visionaries came to "see" the otherwise hidden gods and goddesses? Describing visionary sages, the *Ṛg Veda* says that "by the perceptions of the heart they penetrate into the mystery,"[18] the heart, in part, being a component of the human spirit that could see what the eye could not.[19] The heart was also said to be the place of intuition, trust, affection, and spontaneity, and thus the source of realizations and expressions based on these functions.[20] Thus, it is the heart in which Vedic visionaries were understood to see, know, honor, and make contact with the gods, and the heart is where they fashioned their sacred songs to the gods. Referring to Agni, for example, one poet prays, "May our most recent song of praise, born in the heart, reach him whose voice is as sweet as honey," while another sings, "to him we will send forth from the heart the well-fashioned song."[21]

So, too, the gods are understood to receive and enjoy those sentiments in their own hearts and to be moved by them. For example, we hear this from a song to Agni:

> I sing this newest well-crafted song to him,
> the ancient one who loves it.
> May he hear our voice.
> May it come near his heart and stir it with love.[22]

As we will see in a subsequent section, if the heart is the place of contact between divinity and human being, it also refers in the Veda to the core of one's existence, the very center of one's being. So, too, the heart is said to be in some way the home of divinity itself. It is therefore to the heart that one turns to know and become immersed in divine Love. I will return to this idea shortly.

The Divine Commitment to a Sacred World Turning On a Universal Harmony

Looking out over the world, Vedic visionaries saw a powerful and compelling display of existence brought forth by divine forces and intentions and embodied for these seers as the gods and goddesses themselves. Here are some verses from a song to the dawn, seen here to be the form of the goddess Uṣas:

> Dawn arrives, shining—like a lady of light—
> stirring all creatures to life. . . .

Uṣas's light breaks the shadows.
Her face turned to all things across this wide world,
she rises in splendor, enwrapped in bright clothes.
Shining in golden colors, dressed with rays of light,
she guides forth the day like a cow leads her calves.[23]

We might say that, for such visionaries who looked at it in such a way, the world was a *lovely* world, by which I mean both that it is beautiful[24] and that it reflects or expresses a divine love. One seer described the rising sun emerging from the mist and bringing its light to the world as the god Vena, "the loving one," who, following a holy, dynamic universal principle ascends into the daytime sky:

Vena draws forth a wave from the ocean.
Born of the clouds, the loved one's back has appeared.
He shines brightly at the crest of universal order.[25]

When all was in place, when it ran smoothly, the world was for these visionaries one of expansive light and life. To them such a world was *sat*: existence, being, reality; and, to them, the world as *sat* was known to be *satya*: true, the truth. As *satya*, the world was seen to be good. Vedic visionaries saw the various patterns and movements in the world—the emerging light of the dawn, the movement of the sun across the skies, the shifting of the seasons, the falling of rain and flowing of rivers toward the sea—to reflect or express a transcendent principle of universal harmony in which all things fit together properly and effectively.

They called this dynamic and integrating principle *ṛta*, a word literally meaning "that which has moved" in a smooth manner and thus implying "that which has always been." To them, the integrating principle of *ṛta* gave dynamic, harmonious order to the world they saw to be sacred.[26] (The phrase "universal order" in the verse to Vena just quoted translates *ṛta*.) That the concepts of *satya* and *ṛta* are closely related is suggested by what is regarded to be their respective opposites. That which went against *sat* was *asatya*, untrue, unreal, false; and that which is *asatya* is regarded as *anṛta*: "without *ṛta*" or "against *ṛta*" and thus unholy "chaos." The principle of *ṛta* precedes even the birth of the gods, who are known to be "true to *ṛta*, born of *ṛta*, strengtheners of *ṛta*, fearful haters of *anṛta*."[27]

Vedic visionaries knew the world to be a fragile place. They saw what they understood to be forces they identified as demons that continually threaten to destroy the balance, vitality, and beauty of a universe aligned with the patterns of *ṛta*. While they saw the gods supporting *ṛta*, they saw the demons debilitating and endangering it. Their leader was Vṛtra, the "Encloser," depicted as a demon-serpent whose coils entrapped and imprisoned the nourishing and powerful living forces that brought energy and growth to the world. If the gods were forces of expansiveness, light, and life, the demons were forces of constriction, darkness, and death. The demons were therefore, for Vedic seers, forces that lead to *anṛta* and *asatya*.

Vedic thinkers saw the deities as supporting, protecting, and maintaining *ṛta* and *satya* against the constant threat of nonbeing. They did so in part by bringing light, nourishment, and vitality into a world made sacred by the divine affirmation of existence. Doing so, they were in their various ways "true to *ṛta*, strengtheners of *ṛta*." Each deity had its particular *vrata*, which is to say that each had its own unique obligation, its own solemn vow, to the world.[28] A verse to the celestial gods Varuṇa and Mitra, for example, declares that these deities make sure that the sun rises in the morning, impelling creatures into wakefulness and dispersing the night: "true to their *vrata*, the rulers of secure realms raise the sun into the heavens. With unceasing consistency they impel the Impeller to drive away the darkness."[29]

Divine Love as Benevolent and Merciful Grace

We might take a moment here to step back and note that both the impulse of divine Love and the dynamic structure *ṛta* precede the emergence of the gods. It could be said, therefore, that, in aligning themselves with *ṛta*, the gods support the affirming dynamics of Love and are, thereby, worthy of people's adoration. In a hymn from the *Atharva Veda* we again see the idea that Love—addressed in this instance by the proper noun Kāma—is a divine power that preexists and is superior even to the gods:

> Neither the gods, nor the fathers, nor mortals
> are as lofty as he.
> You, Kāma, are superior to all, ever-great.
> To you, I offer reverence.
> However broad the expanse
> of heaven and earth, or rivers, or fire,

You, O Love, are superior to all, ever-great.
To you, I offer reverence.[30]

A few verses later in that song to divine Love we hear this declaration and prayer:

You have many excellent and favorable bodies
through which, O Love, you choose to become manifest.
With them, enter fully into our hearts
and banish all harmful thoughts![31]

According to this verse, Love is embodied, as it were—it is manifest, revealed, made real—in the heart. We also have a suggestion here that it does so through an act of a benevolent divine will. Divine love "choose[s] to become manifest." Furthermore, the prayerful request that Love "enter into our hearts and banish all harmful thoughts" expresses the ideas that a person may be infused with this same divine Love and that a person's own will and intention can be purified and transformed by its power.[32]

Our verse does not say just what these "bodies" are in which Love chooses to become manifest. Given the reference in a subsequent line to "harmful thoughts," though, perhaps we could say that such manifestations of Love take the form of one's own benevolent thoughts, one's own best hopes, one's own loving care and concern.

Vedic texts recognize the fact that there are, of course, such things as harmful thoughts, and as these lines just quoted suggest, the texts acknowledge the need for the gracious power of Love to clear the human heart of them. Elsewhere, we hear a plea for divine purification expressed in this prayer to Agni; the image here is that of the divine Fire burning and carrying away one's impurities:

If we have committed offense, whether awake or asleep,
knowingly or unknowingly, through harmful curse,
then may Agni bear to distant places
all our hateful acts and destructive deeds.[33]

These lines express the sense that people at times feel uncertain about whether they are thinking and acting in alignment with divine forces. Accordingly, at times we see in Vedic texts pleas for divine forgiveness, as in this prayer to Varuṇa, which expresses the seer's fear that he may "pass into the house of clay"—that he may die—before he has the chance to realign himself and to become strong in fulfilling his responsibilities to the sacred universe:

> Let me not yet pass into
> the house of clay. O majestic Varuṇa.
> Forgive me, mighty Lord. Have mercy. . . .
> If because of weakness
> I have in some way erred or strayed,
> forgive me, mighty Lord. Have mercy. . . .
> Whatever law of yours in thoughtlessness we transgress:
> punish us not for that misdeed.[34]

In their various ways, these passages stress the quality and importance of one's mindfulness. One's mind can slip from its awareness of and appreciation for the world as sacred. When there is this thoughtlessness and forgetfulness, though, there is the possibility that one can realign oneself with a divine intention. Love can return to one's heart and again become manifest.

The Vedic Call for Sanctifying Activity within a Sacred Universe

The idea that there are ways of being in the world that are consonant with and supportive of a divine foundation of life finds suggestion in a set of Vedic creation stories—there are several such narratives in Vedic literatures—that can be interpreted to express the idea that life as a whole is to be lived as a sacred offering that sanctifies and heals a broken world.

One such mythic narrative tells of a single god, Prajāpati, the universal "Lord of Creatures." In this version, like that in the account of the One we noted previously, we hear it said that, in the beginning, before there was either any universe or anything in it, Prajāpati existed all by himself. He wished no longer to be alone, so he created the universe and the gods who lived in it. (We again note the presence of a divine yearning for a world of existence.) He did so by stoking a fervent creative heat, *tapas*, within his body through ascetic discipline and, bursting with that blazing inward energy, exploded outward, just as a well-stoked fire produces innumerable sparks that rise into the darkness. He emitted his life force outward, and his dispersed body became the many components of the world:

> Prajāpati wished, "May I be propagated, may I be multiplied." He practiced ascetic fervor. Having practiced *tapas* he emitted these worlds: the earth, the atmosphere, and heaven. He warmed up these worlds, and when he did so, the bright ones [that is, the luminous deities] were born. Agni was born of the earth, Vāyu from the atmosphere, Āditya from the heavens.[35]

Similar Vedic narratives hold that Prajāpati's emanational, sacrificial act of creating the world breaks his once-unified body and drains him of his own life force. As one instance of the sacred story tells it:

> Prajāpati produced the creatures. Having produced the creatures . . . he became broken. When broken, his vital breath left from within; when broken, his living energy left from within: they having left him, he collapsed. . . . Truly, there was no firm foundation whatever for anything here.[36]

His body broken and drained of life force, Prajāpati yearned to be made whole again:

> Having created the creatures . . . he fell to pieces. Having fallen to pieces, the vital air went out of him. When it had gone out of him the gods left him. He said to Agni: "Put me back together again!"[37]

The gods gathered together food, the sun and the wind, and other components of the dismembered form and offered them to a sacred fire, the transforming power of which refashioned Prajāpati's enervated body, making it whole again:

> Thus heated, the fire rose around him. That same vital breath which had left him from within returned, and they put it back into him. They put back into him the living energy that had

> left him. They put back into him the food that had flowed out from him. Having constructed him entirely and completely, they stood him upright; thus, because they stood him upright, he is these worlds.[38]

This line of thought acknowledges that the world we live in is a fragile one. Accordingly, it also holds that human beings share with the gods the need to reintegrate what in some ways has become a disintegrated world. It holds that Prajāpati's body can indeed be renewed, reinvigorated, and made whole.

From the Vedic perspective, this is done through acts of sacrifice.[39] The English word "sacrifice" (literally, an action that sanctifies)[40] is a customary translation of the Sanskrit term *yajña*, a word formed on a linguistic root meaning to "consecrate, hallow, honor, offer." One of the verbs most frequently associated with the *yajña* is *karoti*, "one makes." The verb *karoti* is related to the Vedic noun *karman*, and thus to the word *karma*: "action, activity" that brings results. In the Vedic worldview, sacrifice is beneficial action par excellence; by means of sacrifice one participates in the consecration of being itself, helping as one does so to make a better world.

The importance of sacrifice as *yajña* stands as the ideological basis for the performance of various solemn rituals in which the sacred world is symbolically renewed.[41] Some of these rites are to take place on an episodic basis, as at the installation of a new king; some are performed on periodic basis, as, for example, at the rising sun and at the new and full moon. These sacred rituals are intricate, complicated, and highly structured events that can require the participation of up to sixteen highly trained and specialized priests and some of which last as long as a year to perform. The performance of some of them depends on so many resources that they require sponsorship by wealthy patrons, including at times the king.

Yet Vedic sensibilities also include the notion that the protective, integrating, beneficial purposes of these large public *yajñas* could also be performed in the family home at such times as a child's entry into adulthood, at marriage, and after a person's death, and symbolically be expressed in one's own personal daily life.

Indeed, all of one's life, from childhood through old age, is to be considered a sacred offering. For example, noting what it sees to be a homology between the stages of one's life and the components of sacred ceremonies performed over the length of a day, the *Chāndogya Upaniṣad* says that, "A person is himself the *yajña*. His first twenty-four years correspond to the morning offerings. . . . His next forty-four years correspond to the noontime offerings. . . . His next forty-four years correspond to the third offering."[42]

Tradition based on the Veda also came to include the practice of what are known as the five great offerings (*pañca-mahāyajñas*) to be performed by householders every day in a spirit of benevolence and gratitude. These are symbolic expressions of the desire for the welfare of all beings throughout the universe and across the generations.[43] The practice of the personal offering to the gods, *devayajña*, consists of symbolically offering small amounts of nourishing food to a small flame while chanting the names of the gods or of one god in particular. The symbolic sacrifice to the ancestors, *pitṛyajña*, typically takes the form of the daily dedication of small amounts of grain, rice, water, milk, fruit, and so on, in loving memory of those deceased family members. In performing the symbolic offering to living creatures, *bhūtayajña*, one places food on clean ground so that animals may eat it, even animals that are normally shunned. The offering to one's fellow human beings, *manuṣyayajña*, turns on the kind treatment to others, the typical attitude being based on the notion that people are to be treated as guests in one's home and that guests are to be treated as gods. The offering of one's study of sacred words, *brahmayajña*, consists of the daily study and contemplation of sacred texts.

These personal offerings are to be performed throughout one's lifetime.[44] Though in some ways quite simple, one can see how they could arise from and inspire larger and encompassing feelings of gratitude, appreciation, compassion, tolerance, and kindness toward all beings in the world.

When generalized and universalized, the larger and foundational sentiments expressed in these symbolic offerings of care and concern recollect the divine body that has become all things. In Vedic terms, they revitalize the body of the Lord of all Creatures and, in so doing, renew the life and heal the fractures of a sacred world that otherwise has become enervated and broken.

With this in mind, we can turn our attention for a moment to the Vedic notion of *dharman* and thereby to the general Hindu notion of *dharma*. Based on a linguistic root meaning "support, uphold," the word *dharma* refers to a stabilizing state of correctness, responsibility, and duty. Understood in a descriptive sense, *dharma* is a steadfast principle or rule, guided by which one's activity supports the world as a whole. In this sense, it is related to the Vedic concept of *ṛta* mentioned earlier. So, too, the commitment to following this rule of integration and harmony is reminiscent of the Vedic notion of *vrata*. We see expression of the idea that the gods follow *dharma* in overseeing the manner in which all beings are to live their lives in effective support of the world: "O Mitra and Varuṇa, full of wisdom, by means of *dharman* you watch over the *vrata* [of all beings] and rule the whole world by means of *ṛta*."[45]

Based in part on these Vedic ideas, the larger Hindu notion of *dharma* as the set of actions, responsibilities, and obligations by which one serves the integrity of the world can be understood in both a descriptive and normative sense. Each person is understood to have his or her *svadharma*; in other words, each has a particular set of responsibilities, and each person is to live one's life in alignment with those obligations. For example, a young student's responsibility to learn about the sacred world is different in some ways than the responsibilities of a householder who is raising and supporting a family, and a merchant's responsibilities in producing and distributing goods is different than a soldier's in protecting the community from martial danger.

Yet, all people are also said to share responsibilities or modes of behavior that apply to everybody. Such universal obligations are said in classical Hinduism to express *sādhāraṇa-dharma* or *sāmānya-dharma*, that is to say, *dharma* that is shared by all and common to all, respectively. The *Arthaśāstra* notes, for example, that everyone is to refrain from wishing injury on others and is to tell the truth, live purely, practice goodwill, be forgiving, and exercise patience at all times.[46] Similarly, the *Bṛhadāraṇyaka Upaniṣad* tells of Prajāpati as a teacher who, when asked by his students for instruction, repeats the syllable *da* three times to refer to three imperatives they should follow: *dāmyata*, *datta*, *dayadhvam*—"Control yourself. Give. Be compassionate. One should observe this same triad: self restraint, generosity, compassion."[47]

To live in this way is to bring oneself to the world in a way that holds it together against forces that would otherwise pull it apart; it is to live one's life as a responsible and responsive offering to a world consecrated by the divine presence. Said differently, from the perspective of our current concern, to live according to *dharma* is to live in alignment with the integrative power of divine love.

The Heart as the Abode of Divinity

We have seen that Vedic visionaries, philosophers, and sages sensed and variously spoke of the presence of a single divine power, principle, or state in which all things have their existence. Over time, they increasingly referred to this universal ground of being as Brahman, a word meaning "possessed of the nature of expansive pervasiveness, great." Vedic philosophers and contemplatives came to teach that all the deities are images or personifications of the one Brahman. We see such an understanding expressed in a set of questions a student addresses to his teacher, presented here in abbreviated form:

> "How many gods are there, Yājñavalkya?"
> "Three hundred and thirty-three."
> "Yes, but how many gods are there really?"
> "Thirty-three."
> "Yes, but how many gods are there really?"
> "Three."
> "Yes, but how many gods are there really?"
> "One."
> "What is that one god?"
> "It is Brahman. It is what they call 'That.'"[48]

A song from the *Atharva Veda* praises Brahman as a single foundation in which all things have their being:

> Homage to that supreme Brahman. . . .
> In it dwell everything that lives and breathes,
> all that opens and closes the eye. . . .
> It is that which, though multiform,
> is concentrated into a single whole.
> It sustains the world.[49]

As one of the Upaniṣads succinctly proclaims: "Truly, this whole world is Brahman."[50]

So, too, the Upaniṣads and works based on them speak of Ātman, the universal Self, the single essence of which variously dwells within all of the manifold forms of the world. As one text says, "There is one power that lies hidden within all creatures. All pervasive, it is the Self [*ātman*] of all beings."[51] Another declares, "Truly, this Ātman is Brahman."[52]

Vedic contemplative sages thus came to the insight that all of the gods praised by the sacred songs and honored by all the sacred rites were actually images of Brahman/Ātman, and that this single divine presence dwelled at the core of all beings. Accordingly, they saw that its light shines deep within their own being, too. As one text proclaims, "All the gods are within me,"[53] an understanding that is similarly expressed in these lines:

> In the heart reside all the gods;
> in it are established the vital breaths.
> In the heart are life and light. . . .
> [All this] stands within the heart.[54]

The Vedic vision of a divine world-soul that sanctifies the immense expansiveness of Creation yet also dwells deep within the human spirit has reverberated throughout Hindu thought for nearly three thousand years. As the *Chāndogya Upaniṣad* says,

> This is the Self [*ātman*] within my heart: smaller than a grain of rice, or a corn of barley, or a mustard seed, or a grain of millet, or the kernel of a grain of millet. This is the Self within my heart: more vast than the earth, more vast that the atmosphere, more vast than the heavens, more vast than all the worlds. . . . This is the Self within my heart. This is Brahman.[55]

Vedic sages and teachers saw the importance and value of entering the heart on a regular basis:

> As far as the space of this [universe] extends, that far extends the space within the heart. Within it are held both heaven and earth, both fire and air, both sun and moon, lightning and the stars. . . . Truly, the [divine] Self abides in the heart. Knowing this, [the wise person] enters daily into the heavenly world.[56]

A later Upaniṣad influenced by such ideas similarly notes that a way to do this is through the practice of meditation:

The highest meditation should be on
the Self of the universe,
which is seated in the heart:
the size of an atom, peaceful, quiet
both manifold and subtle, as well as neither of these.
That alone should be the meditation of sages
as well as of ordinary people.[57]

In the Vedic worldview, moral action, compassionate behavior, and meditation support, inform, and nourish each other. All are based on the recognition that the divine Self lives within all beings. All three are based finally in that divine foundation, which is itself of the nature of love.

Whither Divine Love?

According to Vedic sensibilities, one can therefore align oneself with the divine power and presence that pervades and supports the world by treating others with true compassion and generosity, and one can gain access to that power and presence by looking deep within one's own heart.

Informed by this perspective, we could therefore say that the recognition of the power of love within one's heart and immersion into that love thereby joins one's being with the divine Love in and through which the whole world itself has come to exist and by which it is sustained. One's own experience of love itself derives ultimately from that same divine Love. In a song from the *Atharva Veda* we hear:

Through Love, love has come to me;
from Heart, to heart.
The thought of distant others:
may that thought come to me, here.[58]

From a Vedic perspective, the problem is that people don't always cultivate an understanding of the world illumined by wisdom. They tend toward narrow self-centered lives, seeking to gratify desires that come and go, driven by motivations that do not necessarily support the well-being of the larger world. Forgetting Prajāpati's body, as it were, they live in a dismembered world. From this point of view, there is need therefore to re-member the Lord of Creatures, and one participates in remembering the divine body, in part, by living one's life in a responsible way that supports the integrity of the world as sacred. We recall Prajāpati's call to the gods—"Put me back together again!"—as perhaps a call to human beings, too. And, as the gods are then said to have put back into Prajāpati the living energy that had left him, so, too, perhaps human beings could return their attention and appreciation to that divine body, remembering it, and thereby again seeing that "he is these worlds."[59]

The *Kaṭha Upaniṣad* distinguishes between those values based on ignorance of the divine Self, on the one hand, and values based on appreciation of that Self, on the other hand. It sees the former, which it describes as the "pleasant," to be driven by one's temporal, narrowly selfish conditional desires. It regards the latter, which it calls the "good," to be oriented toward immersion into the eternal unconditional nature of the true Self:

> The pleasant is one thing; the good is quite another.
> Both, of different aim, bind a person.
> Of these two, it is well for one who takes hold of the good,
> for one who chooses the pleasant is never fulfilled.[60]

The call here is thus to turn away from focusing one's attention solely on one's own narrowly selfish demands on the world and on others. Such a motivation keeps one stuck in a cycle of disappointment leading, finally, to death. Rather, one is to turn toward awareness of and appreciation for the Self that dwells in its completion and perfection mysteriously within all things and, as the divine source and fulfillment of all that exists, does not die. Vedic texts therefore note that when one sees, knows, and experiences the universal Self, one attains what they call "immortality." As the Upaniṣad just quoted says,

> It has no beginning and no end.
> It does not decay. It is eternal.
> Discerning it, firmly established and beyond the immense,
> one is freed from the jaws of death.[61]

Conclusion: "Seeing Oneself within All Beings and All Beings as Oneself, One Never Turns from the Lord"

As we have seen, Vedic texts in various ways speak of a single divine presence that in mysterious yet vital ways gives rise to all things, dwells within all things, and is the true fulfillment of all things. Referring to the divine presence as the Lord of Creatures, a later Upaniṣad influenced by Vedic thought says,

> The subtlest of the subtle, the greatest of the great, it abides as the Self dwelling in the heart of this creation. . . . From him arise the seas and mountains; from him run the rivers of all sorts; from it arise all plants and saps. . . . He arose as the [universal] indwelling Self. . . . He has entered into all the worlds. The Lord of Creatures becomes one with all beings.[62]

Vedic thought holds that one aligns oneself with the divine Self when one enters into the pure heart, a heart in which there is reflection of the divine Love that has given rise to and supports the whole of creation. That Love is eternal: it never dies, and it has never been born, for it exists unbounded by the constraints of time. As one enters into one's own true heart, one can also see and know the divine presence within others. Such a person lives in a constant revelation of the divine Self, no longer disjoined from the rest of the universe: "The Unborn One ever lives in the cave [of the heart]. . . . Having known oneself as an embodiment of Ātman . . . one should see Ātman as pervading all things and as existing by itself. . . . This whole universe is Ātman; there is nothing but Ātman."[63]

The *Śvetaśvatāra Upaniṣad* identifies the universal Self as God, whom it describes as benevolent and worthy of adoration. A person who lovingly knows that One in whom "this whole universe comes together" experiences inner peace and expansive liberation of spirit:

> The One who rules each and every source,
> in whom this whole universe comes together and dissolves,
> the Lord, the Bestower of blessings, God, the Adorable one:
> by discerning him, one goes forever to unending peace. . . .
> By knowing him as the Benevolent,

he who is hidden in all things,
like the exceedingly fine film that rises from clarified butter,
who alone encompasses the universe:
by knowing God, one is released from all fetters.
That God, the Maker of All Things, the great Self
is ever-seated in the heart of creatures.
With the heart, with insight, with mind,
has he been contemplated.[64]

Vedic thought holds that the divine Self that is of the nature of divine Love is ever-present and ever-accessible to those who cultivate, refine, and strengthen their awareness of its presence within all beings and who deepen their reverence for it, for such a person sees and honors the light of divinity within all things. Referring to that universal Self as the Lord, the *Īśā Upaniṣad* says,

This whole world is to be enfolded into the Lord:
everything that lives in this world. . . .
Seeing oneself within all beings and all beings as oneself,
one never turns from the Lord.[65]

Notes

1. Readers unfamiliar with the Veda and Vedic religion can find concise help by consulting R. N. Dandekar, "Vedas," in *The Encyclopedia of Religion*, 2nd ed., ed. Lindsay Jones (Detroit: Thomson Gale/Macmillan Reference USA, 2005), 14:9549–52, and Jan C. Heesterman, "Vedism and Brahmanism," in Jones, *Encyclopedia of Religion*, 9552–74. For what one reviewer describes as a "gentle tour" through Vedic literatures, ideas, and practices, see William K. Mahony, *The Artful Universe: An Introduction to the Vedic Religious Imagination* (1998; repr. Delhi: Satguru Publications, 2002), which is written in a style that is similar to this current chapter and includes a bibliography for those interested in reading further on the topic at a more specialized level.
2. For an argument on the Veda as the foundation of Hinduism, see Brian K. Smith, *Reflections on Resemblance, Ritual, and Religion* (New York: Oxford University Press, 1989), 3–29. On the influence of the Veda on classical Indian philosophy, see Wilhelm Halbfass, *Tradition and Reflection: Explorations in Indian Thought* (Albany: State University of New York Press, 1991), 23–50.
3. Following Dandekar's view, which is shared by many scholars, literature associated with these general periods would be the Mantra Saṁhitās (ca. 2000–1100 BCE); Āraṇyakas and Brāhmaṇas (ca. 1100–800 BCE); the major Upaniṣads (ca. 800–500 BCE); and

Sūtras, Vedāṅgas and Dharmaśāstras (ca. 500 BCE onward). See Dandekar, "Vedas," 14:9550.

4. For a recent work on divine Love as presented in the *Bhagavad Gītā*, translated and interpreted in a spirit similar to that of this current chapter, see Graham M. Schweig, *Bhagavad Gita: The Beloved Lord's Secret Love Song* (San Francisco: HarperCollins, 2007). On love as presented in the *Bhāgavata Purāṇa*, see Subhash Anand, *The Way of Love: The Bhāgavata Doctrine of Bhakti* (New Delhi: Munshiram Manoharlal, 1996). On Bhāgavata philosophy and religion, see Siddhesvara Bhattacharya, *The Philosophy of Śrīmad Bhāgavata* (Calcutta: Visva Bharata, 1960/1962), and T. S. Rukmani, *A Critical Study of the Bhāgavata Purāṇa* (Varanasi, India: Chowkhamba, 1970). See also Edwin F. Bryant, trans., *Krishna: The Beautiful Legend of God, Śrīmad Bhāgavata Purāṇa, Book X* (London: Penguin Books, 2003), and Graham Schweig, *Dance of Divine Love: The Rāsā Līlā of Krishna from the Bhāgavata Purāṇa* (Princeton, NJ: Princeton University Press, 2005).
5. Readers interested in a brief overview of *bhakti* sensibilities and literatures will find help in John B. Carman, "Bhakti," in Jones, *Encyclopedia of Religion*, 2:856–60, which includes a bibliography. Literature on the experience of *bhakti* is extensive and growing. For examples of translations and studies, see David L. Haberman, *Journey through the Twelve Forests: An Encounter with Krishna* (New York: Oxford University Press, 1994), and John S. Hawley, *Three Bhakti Voices: Mirabai, Surdas, and Kabir in Their Times and Ours* (New York: Oxford University Press, 2005).
6. For a bibliography of such studies on the Veda, mostly from the twentieth century, see Norvin Hein, "Hinduism," in *A Reader's Guide to the Great Religions*, 2nd ed., ed. Charles J. Adams (New York: Free Press, 1977), 106–55; the sections on Vedic religion are on 110–14, and the legacy and influence of Vedic thought on subsequent practices and philosophies are covered on 114–26.
7. *Ṛg Veda* 8.28.1 and *Ṛg Veda* 10.52.6.
8. *Ṛg Veda* 10.81.2–4.
9. *Ṛg Veda* 10.129.1–2, 4, 6–7.
10. See, for example, Ralph T. H. Griffith, *The Hymns of the Ṛgveda*, new rev. ed., ed. J. L. Shastri (Delhi: Motilal Banarsidass, 1973), 633.
11. It is in this latter sense that, for example, the *Nārada Bhakti Sūtra*, a set of teachings on the nature of spiritual devotion composed roughly two thousand years after the time of the Veda, places *kāma* in opposition to supreme love (*paramapreman*) when it says that such love "is not of the nature of *kāma*." See *Nārada Bhakti Sūtra* 7.
12. See Raimondo Panikkar, *The Vedic Experience: Mantramañjarī* (Berkeley: University of California Press, 1977), 58.
13. Panikkar describes Love as "the constitutive act by which existence comes into being" and says, "Without love there is no being." See ibid., 57.
14. For examples, as friend: 1.67.1, 1.94.14, 4.17.17, 4.23.5–6, 10.7.13, 10.112.10; as brother: 4.23.6, 4.25.2; as father: 3.53.2, 6.9.2–3; as father and mother: 8.1.6, 8.98.11. See Mrinal Das Gupta, "Śraddhā and Bhakti in Vedic Literature," *Indian Historical Quarterly* 6, no. 2 (1930): 314–33; references to these particular passages appear on 325.
15. *Ṛg Veda* 4.20.5.
16. *Ṛg Veda* 10.43.2.
17. *Ṛg Veda* 2.3.9, 3.4.9, 4.25.1, 10.42.9, 10.160.3.
18. *Ṛg Veda* 7.33.9.

19. For textual references and discussion, see Jan Gonda, *The Vision of the Vedic Poets* (1963; repr. Delhi: Munshiram Manoharlal, 1984), 278–79.
20. On the "heart" in Vedic thought, see R. N. Dandekar, *Der Vedische Mensch: Studien zu Selbstaffassung des Inders in Ṛg- und Atharvaveda* (Heidelberg: C. Winter, 1938), 48, 62ff.; H. D. Velankar, "Mind and Heart in the Rgveda (Manas and Hrd)," in *Proceedings and Transactions of the All-India Oriental Conference*, 22nd session (Gauhati), ed. Maheswar Neog (Gauhati: All-India Oriental Conference, 1966), 2:1–5; Velankar, *Ṛgveda Maṇḍala VII* (Bombay: Bharatiya Vidya Bhavan, 1963), 4; Mahony, *Artful Universe*, 81–82, and under "heart" in the Index, 314–15.
21. *Ṛg Veda* 1.60.3 and 2.35.2. One of greatest of contemporary Sanskrit scholars, the late Venkatarama Raghavan, said this regarding the hymns of the *Ṛg Veda*: "The wealth of devotional mood and attitude here, as well as their literary expression, far outshines anything in the best examples of later devotional poetry." See *The Indian Heritage: An Anthology of Sanskrit Literature*, selected by and trans. V. Raghavan (Bangalore: Indian Institute of Culture, 1956), xxxi.
22. *Ṛg Veda* 10.91.13.
23. *Ṛg Veda* 7.77.1–2.
24. On the Vedic experience of beauty, see Promod Chandra Ray, *Theory of Oriental Beauty (with Special Reference to Ṛg Veda)* (Sambalpur, India: First Orissa Sanskrit Conference, 1974); P. S. Sastri, "The Rigvedic Theory of Beauty," *Proceedings and Transactions of the All-India Oriental Conference, Twelfth Session, Benares Hindu University, 1943–44*, ed. A. S. Altekar (Benares, India: Benares Hindu University, 1946), 232–39; and Mahony, *Artful Universe*, 35–37.
25. See *Ṛg Veda* 10.123.2.
26. Linguists have traced the etymology of *ṛta* to the Indo-European **ar-*, which, in its transitive forms, means "fit together, unite," and, in its intransitive forms, "be fit, be proper." See Julius Pokorny, *Indogermanisches etymologisches Wörterbuch* (Bern, Switzerland: A. Francke, 1959), 1:55. It may be of interest to note that the English "art," "harmony," "ordain," "order," and "rite" are also said to derive from this same Indo-European root. See William Morris, ed., *The American Heritage Dictionary of the English Language* (Boston: Houghton Mifflin, 1981), 1506.
27. *Ṛg Veda* 7.66.13.
28. On *vrata* in the *Ṛg Veda*, see Pandurang Vaman Kane, *History of Dharmaśāstra*, 2nd ed. (Poona, India: Bhandarkar Oriental Research Institute, 1974), 5:1–21.
29. *Ṛg Veda* 4.13.2–3.
30. *Atharva Veda* 9.2.19–20.
31. *Atharva Veda* 9.2.25.
32. The verse could be interpreted as a request that Kāma defend people against harmful thoughts directed at them by other people. Whitney translates it as "make evil devices (*dhī*) enter away elsewhere." See William Dwight Whitney, trans., *Atharva-Veda-Saṁhitā* (1905; repr. Delhi: Motilal Banarsidass, 1971), 2:525. Panikkar translates the verse as, "Send elsewhere all malice." See Panikkar, *Vedic Experience*, 244.
33. *Ṛg Veda* 10.164.3.
34. *Ṛg Veda* 7.89.1, 3, 5.
35. *Aitareya Brāhmaṇa* 5.32. For discussion of Prajāpati's act of creation through emanation, see Brian K. Smith, "Sacrifice and Being: Prajāpati's Cosmic Emission and Its Consequences," *Numen* 33 (1986): 65–99.
36. *Śatapatha Brāhmaṇa* 7.1.2.1.

37. *Śatapatha Brāhmaṇa* 6.1.2.12-13.
38. *Śatapatha Brāhmaṇa* 7.1.2.6.
39. See J. C. Heesterman, *The Broken World of Sacrifice: An Essay in Ancient Indian Ritual* (Chicago: University of Chicago Press, 1985).
40. The word "sacrifice" is said to derive from the Latin *sacrificium*: from *sacere*, "sacred," plus *facere*, "to do, to make." See Morris, *American Heritage Dictionary of the English Language*, 1141.
41. I am using the term *yajña* here rather loosely to refer to a large group of Vedic ritual performances, some of which are known by other names. Vedic ritual texts are indeed voluminous, as are scholarly descriptions and interpretations of them. For a summary of such rites and the liturgical texts associated with them, see V. M. Apte, "Vedic Rituals," in *The Cultural History of India*, 2nd ed., reprint ed., revised and enlarged, ed. Sri Ramakrishna Centenary Committee (Calcutta: Ramakrishna Mission Institute, 1982), 1:234–63.
42. *Chāndogya Upaniṣad* 3.16.1–5.
43. On the *pañca-mahāyajñas*, see Kane, *History of Dharmaśāstra*, 2:696–756.
44. See *Śatapatha Brāhmaṇa* 11.5.2.2–3, *Āśvalāyana Gṛhya Sūtra* 3.1.1–4.
45. *Ṛg Veda* 5.63.7.
46. *Arthaśāstra* 1.3.13. For a summary of different types of *dharma*, see Kane, *History of Dharmaśāstra*, 2:1–19.
47. *Bṛhadāraṇyaka Upaniṣad* 5.2.3.
48. *Bṛhadāraṇyaka Upaniṣad* 3.9.1–11.
49. *Atharva Veda* 10.8.1 and 10.8.11.
50. *Chāndogya Upaniṣad* 3.14.1.
51. *Brahma Upaniṣa*d 16.
52. *Bṛhadāraṇyaka Upaniṣad* 4.4.5.
53. *Jaiminīya Upaṇisad Brāhmaṇa* 1.14.2.
54. *Brahma Upaniṣad* 4.
55. *Chāndogya Upaniṣad* 3.14.3.
56. *Chāndogya Upaniṣad* 8.1.2–8.3.4.
57. *Tejobindu Upaniṣad* 1.1.
58. *Atharva Veda* 19.52.4–5. See also Whitney, *Atharva-Veda-Saṁhitā*, 986–87, and Panikkar, *Vedic Experience*, 245.
59. See *Śatapatha Brāhmaṇa* 7.1.2.6, quoted above.
60. *Kaṭha Upaniṣad* 2.1.
61. *Kaṭha Upaniṣad* 3.15.
62. *Mahānārāyaṇa Upaniṣad* 10.1, 10.3, and 10.7. This rendering is based on Paul Deussen, *Sixty Upaniṣads of the Veda*, trans. V. M. Bedekar and B. B. Palsule (Delhi: Motilal Banarsidass, 1980), 254–55.
63. *Adhyātmā Upaniṣad* 65.
64. *Śvetaśvatāra Upaniṣad* 4.11, 16–17.
65. *Īśā Upaniṣad* 1 and 6.

3 Divine Love in Classical Judaism

Jacob Neusner

A religion sets forth a system of the social order comprising a worldview, a way of life, and a theory of the social entity that appeals to that worldview in explaining that way of life. By "Judaism," I mean the religious system that finds in the Torah of Moses its way of life, worldview, and account of itself as the social group that it calls "Israel." That social group regards itself as the embodiment in the here and now of the Israelites of which the Torah speaks. In classical Judaism attested by Scripture and the rabbinic canon of late antiquity, the Torah or Instruction encompasses two components. One part is contained in writing and known as the written Torah, and the other part is formulated and transmitted in memory and called the oral Torah. The written part of the Torah corresponds to the ancient Israelite Scriptures that Christianity calls "the Old Testament." Judaism and Christianity accept this written part as a divine revelation given to Moses at Sinai, although they interpreted the texts differently. Judaism on its part saw the legal sections of the oral part of the Torah as a separate revelation to Moses in explanation of the written laws. The narrative portions of the Torah were examined no less closely to express the Torah's social theory. Discussions of the oral Torah were preserved. The oral part of the Torah is preserved in written form in the documents produced by the ancient rabbis of the first six centuries CE, from the Mishnah, a philosophical law code of 200 CE, through the Talmud of Babylonia, an exposition of the law and narrative of Scripture, and the Mishnah, of 600 CE. When we wish to define God's love in Judaism, we turn to the classical tradition set forth in the Torah, written and oral.

What Is Divine Love?

Classical Judaism depicts God in human terms.[1] The human emotion of love is therefore imputed to God. Classical Judaism sees God and man as consubstantial, sharing in particular the same emotional traits. God has three major character traits: power, love, and justice. Power pertains to God's creation, control of history, and imposition of morality on humankind.[2] Love invokes the imagery of family. Justice means God metes out measure for measure.[3] What happens to human beings responds to the actions of the person who is subject to judgment, and fairness governs. All relationships come to their final resolution in the resurrection of the dead and the judgment of humanity for eternal life or eternal death.

The gift of the Torah is the most important manifestation of God's love for Israel, and the fact that God has informed Israel of his love for them is still greater evidence of that love:

Tractate Abot 3:14

A. R. Aqiba would say, "Precious is the human being, who was created in the image [of God].

B. "It was an act of still greater love that it was made known to him that he was created in the image [of God],

C. "as it is said, 'For in the image of God he made man' (Genesis 9:6).

D. "Precious are Israelites, who are called children to the Omnipresent.

E. "It was an act of still greater love that they were called children to the Omnipresent,

F. "as it is said, 'You are the children of the Lord your God' (Deuteronomy 14:1).

G. "Precious are Israelites, to whom was given the precious thing [the Torah].

H. "It was an act of still greater love that it was made known to them that to them was given that precious thing with which the world was made,

I. "as it is said, 'For I give you a good doctrine. Do not forsake my Torah' (Proverbs 4:2)."

That God has informed Israel of his love is evidence of his love. The commandments, too, are marks of God's love and concern for Israel.

Mishnah Tractate Makkot 3:16

A. R. Hananiah b. Aqashia says, "The Holy One, blessed be he, wanted to give merit to Israel.

B. "Therefore he gave them abundant Torah and numerous commandments,

C. "as it is said, It pleased the Lord for his righteousness sake. Therefore he gave them abundant Torah and numerous commandments."

The Israelite way of life thus conveys God's love for Israel. And just as God loves Israel, so Israel loves God. Acts of loving-kindness are valued by God. These cannot be coerced but only prompted by the actors' generous heart. When the Temple was destroyed, acts of loving-kindness replaced animal sacrifices as the media of atonement. Yohanan ben Zakkai is portrayed in a late Midrash compilation as saying to his disciple, distressed at the loss of Temple sacrifice as a medium of atonement, "We have another mode of atonement, which is like [atonement through sacrifice], and what is that? It is deeds of lovingkindness."[4] Accordingly, in the aftermath of the loss of the sacrificial cult in 70 CE, love formed the principal relationship between Israel and God.

Love in these contexts is commanded, but not coerced. God yearns for Israel's love, as in proclamation of the *Shema*, the creed of Judaism, "Hear, Israel, the Lord our God, the Lord is one," immediately followed by, "You will love the Lord your God with all your heart, with all your soul, and with all your might."[5] But love by definition can only be freely given, and the commandment to love bears the paradox that God can only beseech, not coerce, love. God can command Israel to love him, but cannot force Israel to obey his commandment. Love in the end is an emotion that is freely given or withheld as an act of will. One's attitude determines the weight of an action, and an act can be one of love or one of mere submission, depending on the feeling of the person who performs the action.

The exposition of the commandment to love God in the Talmud of Babylonia stresses the universality of the commandment to love God. It speaks of acts of love that are material and those that are intangible. Martyrdom means voluntarily giving one's life for the love of God and the sanctification of his name. That is done in public and sets an example for Israelites to follow:

Bavli Berakhot 9:5 61b XVIII.1

A. "You shall love the Lord your God" [M. 9:5B]:

B. It has been taught on Tannaite authority:

C. R. Eliezer says, "If it is said, With all your soul, why is it also said, With all your might? And if it is said, With all your might, why is it also said, With all your soul?

D. "But if there is someone who places greater value on his body than on his possessions, for such a one it is said, With all your soul.

E. "And if there is someone who places greater value on his possessions than on his life, for such a one it is said, With all your might."

F. R. Aqiba says, "With all your soul—even if he takes your soul."

Love defines God's relationship with humanity and each person's relationship with others. Love between one person and another forms the model of the great commandment, "You will love your neighbor as yourself."[6] That is regarded as the most important commandment of the Torah. Hence, the definition of love in Judaism requires the exposition of the meaning of self-love, loving one's neighbor as oneself. The exposition involves practical expressions of forbearance and restraint. Here is the way in which the classical exposition of Sifra, a third-century CE commentary to the book of Leviticus, spells out the Great Commandment.

Sifra CC:III

1. A. "You shall not hate your brother in your heart, [but reasoning, you shall reason with your neighbor, lest you bear sin because of him. You shall not take vengeance or bear any grudge against the sons of your own people, but you shall love your neighbor as yourself: I am the Lord]" (Leviticus 19:17–18).

B. Might one suppose that one should not curse him, set him straight, or contradict him?

C. Scripture says, "in your heart."
I spoke only concerning hatred that is in the heart.

At issue is the definition of hatred, the opposite of love. What is at issue is not bearing a grudge, not preserving an attitude of hatred. It is best to articulate the hatred and negotiate its cause.

2. A. And how do we know that if one has rebuked him four or five times, he should still go and rebuke him again?
B. Scripture says, "reasoning, you shall reason with your neighbor."
C. Might one suppose that that is the case even if one rebukes him and his countenance blanches?
D. Scripture says, "lest you bear sin."

One must persist in removing the cause of hatred from one's heart, and it is a sin to bear a grudge. Once more we see that love and its opposite are matters of attitude and emotion.

4. A. "You shall not take vengeance [or bear any grudge]":
B. To what extent is the force of vengeance?
C. If one says to him, "Lend me your sickle," and the other did not do so.
D. On the next day, the other says to him, "Lend me your spade."
E. The one then replies, "I am not going to lend it to you, because you didn't lend me your sickle."
F. In that context, it is said, "You shall not take vengeance."

Vengeance is forbidden, and love requires the opposite: an attitude of generosity and forbearance.

5. A. ". . . or bear any grudge":
B. To what extent is the force of a grudge?
C. If one says to him, "Lend me your spade," but he did not do so.
D. The next day the other one says to him, "Lend me your sickle,"

E. and the other replies, "I am not like you, for you didn't lend me your spade [but here, take the sickle]!"

F. In that context, it is said, "or bear any grudge."

Once more we see the importance of removing from one's heart the attitude of grudge and recrimination. One liberates oneself through the generosity of spirit that is commanded in loving one's neighbor as oneself. If one loves one's neighbor, one benefits oneself as well, and that is the heart of loving one's neighbor as oneself.

How Do We Gain Access to and Make Manifest Divine Love?

Imitating God affords access to divine love. That is how human beings make divine love manifest. What holy Israel learns in the Torah is to meet God in love. This is what the Torah teaches and what in the *Shema* the Israelite proclaims as faith: "You will love the Lord your God with all your heart, with all your soul, and with all your might."[7] God and Israel in both the written and the oral parts of the Torah act like teenage lovers (in the metaphor of the great Catholic sociologist and novelist, Andrew M. Greeley), whose newfound passion knows no limit. In the relationship of love that binds the Israelite to God, God takes the part of the suitor; Israel, the besought: "I will betroth you to me for ever, I will betroth you to me in righteousness and in justice, in steadfast love and in mercy. I will betroth you to me in faithfulness, and you shall know the Lord"[8]—these words, recited every weekday morning in prayer, capture the relationship to which holy Israel aspires to form with God who loves Israel.

Why Is Divine Love Important?

Israel defines its affective life in accord with God's model, and that is why divine love is important. The representation of Israel's relationship to God as one of love presents no surprise. Everyone learns the *Shema*, which proclaims the commandment to love God. But how, in detail, the Torah portrays that relationship deserves some close attention. The first point is the most telling. The relationship of Israel to God is the same as the relationship of a wife to the husband, and this is explicit in the following:

> **Song of Songs Rabbah to Song 7:10: "I am my beloved's, and his desire is for me."**
> "I am my beloved's, and his desire is for me":
> There are three yearnings:
> The yearning of Israel is only for their Father who is in heaven, as it is said, "I am my beloved's, and his desire is for me."
> The yearning of a woman is only for her husband: "And your desire shall be for your husband" (Genesis 3:16).
> The yearning of the Evil Impulse is only for Cain and his ilk: "To you is its desire" (Genesis 4:7).
> R. Joshua in the name of R. Aha: "The yearning of rain is only for the earth: You have remembered the earth and made her desired, greatly enriching her (Psalm 65:10).
> "If you have merit, the rains will enrich it, but if not, they will tithe it [the words for enrich and tithe differ by a single letter], for it will produce for you one part for ten of seed."

Here we find that gender relationships are explicitly characterized, and, with them, the traits associated with the genders as well. To be "Israel" is to accept God's love.

The rabbinic exegesis turns to everyday experience—the love of husband and wife—for a metaphor for God's love for Israel and Israel's love for God. Then, when Solomon's song says, "O that you would kiss me with the kisses of your mouth! For your love is better than wine,"[9] Israel's sages think of how God kissed Israel. Reading the Song of Songs as a metaphor for that real relationship, the Judaic sages as a matter of fact state in a systematic and orderly way their entire structure and system, that Torah that the world calls "Judaism," and, along the way, the sages permit us to identify the traits they associate with feminine Israel and masculine God, respectively.

If God asks for love, then God acknowledges love as a shared emotion and attitude. So here, too, humanity is like God—not only in intellect but also in feeling. It is love that defines the feeling that links the Israelite to God and God to the Israelite. How people feel toward those who are most cherished is how they feel toward God—and how God feels toward them. Since they take up matters of sentiment and emotion, rather than proposition, Israel's sages paint suggestive word pictures. They evoke feelings and speak empathetically, rather than only sympathetically. Song of Songs

Rabbah tells how to think and feel, forming sensibility into the heart at one with God.

To do this, the sages who compiled Song of Songs Rabbah read the Song of Songs as a sequence of statements of urgent love between God and Israel, the holy people. How they convey the intensity of Israel's love of God forms the point of special interest. For it is not in propositions that they choose to speak, but in the medium of symbols. Sages here use language as a repertoire of opaque symbols in the form of words. They set forth sequences of words that connote meanings, elicit emotions, stand for events, and form the verbal equivalent of pictures or music or dance or poetry. Through the repertoire of these verbal symbols and their arrangement and rearrangement, the message the authors wish to convey emerges: not in so many words, but through words nonetheless. Sages chose for their compilation appeal to a highly restricted list of implicit meanings, calling upon some very few events—for instance, Sinai—or persons—for instance, Abraham—repeatedly identifying these as the expressions of God's profound affection for Israel, and Israel's deep love for God. The message of the document comes not so much from stories of what happened or did not happen, assertions of truth or denials of error, but rather from the repetitious rehearsal of sets of symbols.

In reading the love songs of the Song of Songs as the story of the love affair of God and Israel, sages identify implicit meanings that are always few and invariably self-evident; no serious effort goes into demonstrating the fact that God speaks, or Israel speaks; the point of departure is the message and meaning the One or the other means to convey. Here we find the search for the governing pattern in the realm of emotions, attitudes, and inchoate feelings. Not only so, but in the Torah as Israel's sages teach it, what is personal and private corresponds in structure to what is public and communal. Feelings and events, attitudes and happenings—both yield in the end corresponding paradigms. The message of the Torah explains both what happens and how we feel, points to what should happen and how we are supposed to feel, within a single repertoire.

To take one instance of the patterning, which, strikingly, shows the correspondence of patterns of events and patterns of emotions: time and again we shall be told that a certain expression of love in the poetry of the Song of Songs is God's speaking to Israel about (1) the Sea, (2) Sinai, and (3) the world to come; or (1) the first redemption, the one from Egypt; (2) the second redemption, the one from Babylonia; and (3) the third redemption, the one at the end of days. The repertoire of symbols covers Temple and schoolhouse, personal piety and public worship, and other matched pairs and sequences of coherent matters, all of them seen as embedded within the poetry. Here is Scripture's poetry read as metaphor, and the task of the reader is to know that for which each image of the poem stands. So Israel's holy life is metaphorized through the poetry of the lover and the beloved, Lover and Israel.

Long lists of alternative meanings or interpretations end up saying just one thing, but in different ways. The implicit meanings prove very few indeed. When in Song of Songs Rabbah we have a sequence of items alleged to form a pattern—that is, a set of things that share a common trait—of course what we have is a list. The list presents diverse matters that all together share, and therefore also set forth, a single fact or rule or phenomenon. That is why we can list them, in all their distinctive character and specificity, on a common catalogue of "other things" that pertain all together to one thing. The list here corresponds to the paradigm in the realm of history.

Feminine Israel and Masculine God

Here is the clear characterization of God as masculine, Israel as feminine:

> **Song of Songs Rabbah to Song 6:2: "My beloved has gone down to his garden, to the beds of spices, to pasture his flock in the gardens, and to gather lilies."**
> "My beloved has gone down to his garden, to the beds of spices, [to pasture his flock in the gardens, and to gather lilies]":
> Said R. Yosé b. R. Hanina, "As to this verse, the beginning of it is not the same as the end, and the end not the same as the beginning.
> "The verse had only to say, My beloved has gone down to pasture in his garden, but you say, in the gardens!
> "But my beloved is the Holy One, blessed be he;
> "to his garden refers to the world.
> "to the beds of spices refers to Israel.
> "to pasture his flock in the gardens refers to synagogues and school-houses.
> "and to gather lilies speaks of picking [taking away in death] the righteous that are in Israel."

"My beloved" is God; the choice part of the garden, which is the world, is Israel, its synagogues and houses of study. The nations, moreover, concur that God is the lover, and Israel the beloved, and characterize female Israel as an abandoned woman.

> **Song of Songs Rabbah to Song 6:1: "Whither has your beloved gone, 'O fairest among women? Whither has your beloved turned, that we may seek him with you?"**
> "Whither has your beloved gone, O fairest among women":
> The nations of the world [here] speak to Israel, "Whither has your beloved gone? From Egypt to the Sea to Sinai.
> "Whither has your beloved turned?"
> And Israel answers the nations of the world, "How come you're asking about him, when you have no share in him?
> "Once I had cleaved to him, can I depart from him? Once he had cleaved to me, can he depart from me? Wherever he may be, he comes to me."

Now the speaker is the nations, the addressee is Israel, and the issue is Israel's relationship to God. It is one of love and cannot be sundered. Israel is now the faithful beloved, waiting patiently for her lover, always trusting in God's faithfulness.

> **Song of Songs Rabbah to Song 8:6: "Set me as a seal upon your heart, as a seal upon your arm, for love is strong as death, jealousy is cruel as the grave, its flashes are flashes of fire, a most vehement flame."**
> "for love is strong as death":
> As strong as death is the love with which the Holy One, blessed be he, loves Israel: "I have loved you says the Lord" (Malachi 1:2).
> "jealousy is cruel as the grave":
> That is when they make him jealous with their idolatry: "They roused him to jealousy with strange Gods" (Deuteronomy 32:16). . . .
> Another explanation of "for love is strong as death":
> As strong as death is the love with which a man loves his wife: "Enjoy life with the wife whom you love" (Qohelet 9:9).
> "jealousy is cruel as the grave":

> the jealousy that she causes in him and leads him to say to her, "Do not speak with such-and-so."
> If she goes and speaks with that man, forthwith: "The spirit of jealousy comes upon him and he is jealous on account of his wife" (Numbers 5:14).

Israel's feminine character is now well established, and the ways in which the exegesis of the Song is worked out in response to that fact are clear. Then we have to ask ourselves, precisely what kind of relationship does feminine Israel have with the masculine God? The answer is, the relationship of a wife to a husband.

These traits of submission, loyalty, and perfect devotion do not exhaust the feminine virtues. But, from the perspective of this document, they take priority, because they set forth the correct attitude that feminine Israel must take in regard to the masculine nations, not only in relation to the masculine God.

> **Song of Songs Rabbah to Song 2:7: "I adjure you, O daughters of Jerusalem."**
> **Song of Songs Rabbah to Song 3:5: "I adjure you, O daughters of Jerusalem, by the gazelles or the hinds of the field."**
> **Song of Songs Rabbah to Song 5:8: "I adjure you, O daughters of Jerusalem, if you find my beloved, that you tell him I am sick with love."**
> **Song of Songs 8:4: "I adjure you, O daughters of Jerusalem, that you not stir up nor awaken love until it please."**
> R. Yosé b. R. Hanina said, "The two oaths [Song of Songs 2:7: I adjure you, O daughters of Jerusalem; and Song of Songs 3:5: I adjure you, O daughters of Jerusalem, by the gazelles or the hinds of the field] apply, one to Israel, the other to the nations of the world.
> "The oath is imposed upon Israel that they not rebel against the yoke of the kingdoms.
> "And the oath is imposed upon the kingdoms that they not make the yoke too hard for Israel.
> "For if they make the yoke too hard on Israel, they will force the end to come before its appointed time."
> R. Helbo says, "There are four oaths that are mentioned here

> [Song of Songs 2:7: I adjure you, O daughters of Jerusalem; Song of Songs 3:5: I adjure you, O daughters of Jerusalem, by the gazelles or the hinds of the field; Song of Songs 5:8: I adjure you, O daughters of Jerusalem, if you find my beloved, that you tell him I am sick with love; Song of Songs 8:4: I adjure you, O daughters of Jerusalem, that you not stir up nor awaken love until it please], specifically,
> "he imposed an oath on Israel not to rebel against the kingdoms and not to force the end [before its time], not to reveal its mysteries to the nations of the world, and not to go up from the exile [Simon:] by force.
> "For if so [that they go up from the exile by force], then why should the royal messiah come to gather together the exiles of Israel?"

The point is unmistakable and critical. Israel is subject to an oath to wait patiently for God's redemption, not to rebel against the nations on its own; that is the concrete social politics meant to derive from the analogy of Israel's relationship to God to the wife's relationship to the husband: perfect submission, and also perfect trust. Rebellion against the nations stands for arrogance on Israel's part, an act of lack of trust and therefore lack of faithfulness. Implicit in this representation of the right relationship, of course, is the promise that feminine Israel will evoke from the masculine God the response of commitment and intervention: God will intervene to save Israel, when Israel makes herself into the perfect wife of God.

In the following, feminine Israel is ornamented by all of the jewelry contained in the treasure of the Torah: all of the acts of faith are paraded as marks of the beauty of Israel in the explicit setting of Israel's feminine relationship to the masculine God:

> **Song of Songs Rabbah to Song 1:15: "Behold, you are beautiful, my love; behold, you are beautiful; your eyes are doves."**
> "Behold, you are beautiful, my love;
> "Behold you are beautiful; [your eyes are doves]":
> "Behold you are beautiful" in religious deeds,
> "Behold you are beautiful" in acts of grace,
> "Behold you are beautiful" in carrying out religious obligations of commission,

"Behold you are beautiful" in carrying out religious obligations of omission,
"Behold you are beautiful" in carrying out the religious duties of the home, in separating priestly ration and tithes,
"Behold you are beautiful" in carrying out the religious duties of the field, gleanings, forgotten sheaves, the corner of the field, poor person's tithe, and declaring the field ownerless.
"Behold you are beautiful" in observing the taboo against mixed species.
"Behold you are beautiful" in providing a linen cloak with woolen show-fringes.
"Behold you are beautiful" in [keeping the rules governing] planting,
"Behold you are beautiful" in keeping the taboo on uncircumcised produce,
"Behold you are beautiful" in keeping the laws on produce in the fourth year after the planting of an orchard,
"Behold you are beautiful" in circumcision,
"Behold you are beautiful" in trimming the wound,
"Behold you are beautiful" in reciting the Prayer,
"Behold you are beautiful" in reciting the *Shema*,
"Behold you are beautiful" in putting a mezuzah on the doorpost of your house,
"Behold you are beautiful" in wearing phylacteries,
"Behold you are beautiful" in building the tabernacle for the Festival of Tabernacles,
"Behold you are beautiful" in taking the palm branch and etrog on the Festival of Tabernacles,
"Behold you are beautiful" in repentance,
"Behold you are beautiful" in good deeds,
"Behold you are beautiful" in this world,
"Behold you are beautiful" in the world to come.

What we have is a repertoire of fundamentals, dealing with Torah and Torah study, the moral life and atonement, Israel and its holy way of life, and Israel and its coming salvation. Here is a list, not a set of propositions ("if this . . . , then that . . ."). The power of the repertoire is to elicit certain feelings, to shape certain attitudes, to show the beauty of feminine Israel in relationship to God the teenage lover.

Lest we conclude with the impression that the whole is a static tableau, we turn at the end to the daring conception that the marks of God's physical love for feminine Israel are contained in the Torah and the commandments thereof:

> **Song of Songs Rabbah to Song 2:6: "O that his left hand were under my head, and that his right hand embraced me."**
> "O that his left hand were under my head:
> this refers to the first tablets.
> "and that his right hand embraced me":
> this refers to the second tablets.
> Another interpretation of the verse, "O that his left hand were under my head":
> this refers to the show-fringes.
> "and that his right hand embraced me":
> this refers to the phylacteries.
> Another interpretation of the verse, "O that his left hand were under my head":
> this refers to the recitation of the *Shema*.
> "and that his right hand embraced me":
> this refers to the Prayer.
> Another interpretation of the verse, "O that his left hand were under my head":
> this refers to the tabernacle.
> "and that his right hand embraced me":
> this refers to the cloud of the Presence of God in the world to come: "The sun shall no longer be your light by day nor for brightness will the moon give light to you" (Isaiah 60:19). Then what gives light to you? "The Lord shall be your everlasting light" (Isaiah 60:20).

So much for Israel's response to God's caress—in the Torah. How about the equally concrete representation of God's response to Israel's passion? Here the same picture is drawn:

> **Song of Songs Rabbah to Song 4:9: "You have ravished my heart, my sister, my bride, you have ravished my heart with a glance of your eyes, with one jewel of your necklace."**
> "You have ravished my heart, my sister, my bride, you have ravished my heart":

Said the Holy One, blessed be he, "You had one heart in Egypt, but you gave me two hearts."
"you have ravished my heart with a glance of your eyes":
It was through the blood of the Passover offering and the blood of circumcision.
"with one jewel of your necklace":
this is Moses, who was unique, the hero of all your tribes.
Another interpretation of the verse, "You have ravished my heart, my sister, my bride, you have ravished my heart":
Said the Holy One, blessed be he, "You had one heart at the Sea, but you gave me two hearts."
"you have ravished my heart with a glance of your eyes":
"For you stood before me at Mount Sinai and said, All that the Lord has spoken we shall do and we shall obey (Exodus 24:7)."
"with one jewel of your necklace":
this is Moses, who was unique, the hero of all your tribes.
Another interpretation of the verse, "You have ravished my heart, my sister, my bride, you have ravished my heart":
Said the Holy One, blessed be he, "You had one heart in the wilderness, but you gave me two hearts."
"you have ravished my heart with a glance of your eyes":
this is setting up the tabernacle: "And on the day that the tabernacle was set up" (Numbers 9:15).
"with one jewel of your necklace":
this is Moses, who was unique, the hero of all your tribes.
There are those to say, "This refers to the women of the generation of the wilderness, who were virtuous. When that foul deed came around, they went and took counsel among themselves, and did not give a thing of their jewelry to the making of the calf.
"Further, when they heard that, in their menstrual periods, they were prohibited to them, they forthwith went and locked their doors."
Another interpretation of the verse, "You have ravished my heart, my sister, my bride, you have ravished my heart":
Said the Holy One, blessed be he, "You had one heart in the matter of the spies, but you gave me two hearts."
[Supply: "you have ravished my heart with a glance of your eyes":]

> this refers to Joshua and Caleb: "Except for Caleb son of Jephunneh the Kenizzite and Joshua the son of Nun" (Numbers 32:12).
> "with one jewel of your necklace":
> this is Moses, who was unique, the hero of all your tribes.
> Another interpretation of the verse, "You have ravished my heart, my sister, my bride, you have ravished my heart":
> Said the Holy One, blessed be he, "You had one heart at Shittim, but you gave me two hearts."
> "you have ravished my heart with a glance of your eyes":
> this refers to Phineas: "Then arose Phineas and carried out judgment . . . and that was counted to him for righteousness" (Psalm 106:30–31).
> "with one jewel of your necklace":
> this is Moses.

So much for the feminization of the Torah and Israel, and the masculinization of God. The process comes to fulfillment in the representation as feminine of all of the virtues, all of the saints and heroes, all of the acts of sanctification that God has commanded and that submissive Israel carries out. Once Israel is feminized, so too is everything else. Then the feminine virtues—submission, trust, perfect loyalty—are adopted by Israel. But that is only for now.

This brings us to masculine Israel. We should grossly err if we imagined that the whole story is that Israel is feminine, God is masculine. Far from it. The message of Song of Songs Rabbah is that, if Israel is feminine now, she will resume her masculinity in the world to come. That is a much more subtle and profound statement, a judgment on the androgyneity of Israel that makes the union of traits, feminine and masculine, something other than a static portrait of a world at rest. In fact, the metaphor of the feminine Israel and the masculine God is subsumed within the more profound message of redemption and carries a critical element in that message: Israel must be patient, submissive, and deeply trusting in God now, so that, in the world to come, Israel may resume its fulfilled masculinity. In this age, Israel to God is as a wife to a husband. But in the age to come, Israel assumes masculine identity. It follows that Israel is represented as serially feminine and masculine: androgyne, feminine, then masculine:

Song of Songs Rabbah V.III.4

R. Berekhiah in the name of R. Samuel b. R. Nahman said, "The Israelites are compared to a woman.

"Just as an unmarried woman receives a tenth part of the property of her father and takes her leave [for her husband's house when she gets married], so the Israelites inherited the land of the seven peoples, who form a tenth part of the seventy nations of the world.

"And because the Israelites inherited in the status of a woman, they said a song in the feminine form of that word, as in the following: Then sang Moses and the children of Israel this song [given in the feminine form] unto the Lord (Exodus 15:1).

"But in the age to come they are destined to inherit like a man, who inherits all of the property of his father.

"That is in line with this verse of Scripture: From the east side to the west side: Judah, one portion . . . Dan one, Asher one . . . (Ezekiel 48:7), and so throughout.

"Then they will say a song in the masculine form of that word, as in the following: Sing to the Lord a new song (Psalm 96:1).

"The word song is given not in its feminine form but in its masculine form."

R. Berekiah and R. Joshua b. Levi: "Why are the Israelites compared to a woman?

"Just as a woman takes up a burden and puts it down [that is, becomes pregnant and gives birth], takes up a burden and puts it down, then takes up a burden and puts it down and then takes up no further burden,

"so the Israelites are subjugated and then redeemed, subjugated and then redeemed, but in the end are redeemed and will never again be subjugated.

"In this world, since their anguish is like the anguish of a woman in childbirth, they say the song before him using the feminine form of the word for song,

"but in the age to come, because their anguish will no longer be the anguish of a woman in childbirth, they will say their song using the masculine form of the word for song:

"In that day this song [in the masculine form of the word] will be sung (Isaiah 26:1)."

So the real message lies in the femininity of Israel in this world in contrast to its masculinity in the world to come. Israel is feminized only for a time; Israel is fully masculine in the end of time. Israel is serially androgynous: male and female, both. Israel is whole with God, but God and Israel cannot make peace with the nations of the world except on God's terms. The invocation of the dance, with God as the leader, Israel as the partner, at the end underscores the wholly feminine representation of Israel once more: "like women—like the dance of the righteous." Then feminine Israel plays the role of the wife who stands as mediator between her husband and the world at large; the mother who holds the family together, now the family of the nations and the master, who is God.

The kind of love that God holds toward Israel and that Israel holds toward God is clear: women's love is what men are to emulate. The dual Torah, beginning to end, taught that the Israelite was to exhibit the moral virtues of subservience, patience, endurance, and hope. These would translate into the emotional traits of humility and forbearance. And they would yield to social virtues of passivity and conciliation. The hero was one who overcame impulses, and the truly virtuous person, the one who reconciled others by giving way before the opinions of others. All of these acts of self-abnegation and self-denial, accommodation rather than rebellion, required to begin with the right attitudes, sentiments, emotions, and impulses, and the single most dominant motif of the Classical writings, start to finish, is its stress on the right attitudes leading to the right action, the correct intentionality's producing the besought decision, above all, accommodating in one's heart to what could not be changed by one's action. And that meant, the world as it was.

Emotions lay down judgments. They derive from rational cognition. What Judaism teaches the private person to feel links her or his heart to what Judaism states about the condition of Israel in history and of God in the cosmos. All form one reality, in supernatural world and nature, in time and in eternity wholly consubstantial (so to speak). In the innermost chambers of deepest feelings, the Israelite therefore lives out the public history and destiny of the people, Israel. The genius of Judaism, reason for its resilience and endurance, lies in its power to teach Jews in private to feel what in public they also must think about the condition of both self and nation. The world within, the world without, are so bonded that one is never alone. The individual's life always is lived with the people.

This carries us back to tractate Abot, which presents the most systematic account of the meaning of the encounter with God in love that the Torah sets forth. A simple catalogue of permissible feelings comprises humility, generosity, self-abnegation, love, a spirit of conciliation of the other, and eagerness to please. A list of impermissible emotions is made up of envy, ambition, jealousy, arrogance, sticking to one's opinion, self-centeredness, a grudging spirit, vengefulness, and the like. People should aim at eliciting from others acceptance and goodwill and should avoid confrontation, rejection, and humiliation of the other. This they do through conciliation and giving up their own claims and rights. So both catalogues form a harmonious and uniform whole, aiming at the cultivation of the humble and malleable person, one who accepts everything and resents nothing. Here are some representative sentiments:

> **Tractate Abot 3:10**
> He would say, "Make his wishes into your own wishes, so that he will make your wishes into his wishes.
> B. "Put aside your wishes on account of his wishes, so that he will put aside the wishes of other people in favor of your wishes."

> **Tractate Abot 2:4**
> He would say, "Anyone from whom people take pleasure—the Omnipresent takes pleasure.
> B. "And anyone from whom people do not take pleasure, the Omnipresent does not take pleasure."

True, these virtues, in tractate Abot as in the system as a whole, derive from knowledge of what really counts, which is what God wants. But God favors those who please others. Israel is praised in Song of Songs Rabbah because of its power to conciliate and please others. The virtues appreciated by human beings prove identical to the ones to which God responds as well. And what single virtue of the heart encompasses the rest? Restraint, the source of self-abnegation and humility, serves as the anecdote for ambition, vengefulness, and, above all, arrogance. It is restraint of Israel's own interest that enables us to deal generously with others, humility about ourselves that generates a liberal spirit toward others.

So the emotions prescribed in tractate Abot turn out to provide variations of a single feeling, which is the sentiment of the disciplined heart, whatever affective form it may take. And where does the heart learn its lessons, if not in relationship to God? So: "Make his wishes yours, so that he will make your wishes his."[10] Applied to the relationships between human beings, this inner discipline of the emotional life will yield exactly those virtues of conciliation and self-abnegation, humility and generosity of spirit, that the framers of tractate Abot spell out in one example after another. Imputing to heaven exactly those responses felt on earth—for example, "Anyone from whom people take pleasure, God takes pleasure"[11]—makes the point at the most general level.

How are the masculine and feminine reconciled and made one? The answer is simple and now predictable. Through the feminization of Israel in virtue, attitude, and emotion, Israel will attain that *zekhut* to which God will respond by the sending of the Messiah. Keeping the commandments as a mark of submission, loyalty, and humility before God is the Classical system of salvation. So Israel does not "save itself." Israel never controls its own destiny, either on earth or in heaven. The only choice is whether to cast one's fate into the hands of cruel, deceitful men, or to trust in the living God of mercy and love. The stress that Israel's arrogance alienates God—Israel's humility and submission win God's favor—cannot surprise us; this is the very point of the doctrine of emotions that defines Classical Judaism's ethics.

Whither Divine Love; *Zekhut*, the Love beyond Commanding, the Love beyond Losing

If I had to identify, within the range of encounters with God that the Torah makes possible, a single point of meeting, it is at the intersection between God's yearning for Israel's love, and Israel's gift of Israel's love. That human love lies beyond all power to coerce, or even request: the love beyond commanding. Here is that which Israel gives but God cannot expect, that which lies altogether beyond the measure of the law. It is that form of uncoerced love that in the scale of values of Israel's sages transcends even study of the Torah. Let me spell this out.

While people suppose that the Torah forms the symbolic center of Classical Judaism, and study of the Torah the critical action—so that women, excluded from academies, find no place in Classical Judaism at all—in fact when we reach the systemic center, we find that "the study of Torah" does not outweigh all else, not at all. Time and again, knowledge of the Torah forms a way station on a path to a more distant, more central goal: attaining *zekhut,* merit, but here translated more broadly as "the heritage of virtue and its consequent entitlements."[12] Torah study is one means of attaining access to that heritage, of gaining *zekhut*. There are other equally suitable means, and, not only so, but the merit gained by Torah study is no different from the merit gained by any and all other types of acts of supererogatory grace. And still more astonishing, a single remarkable action may produce *zekhut* of the same order as a lifetime of devotion to Torah study, and a simple ass driver through a noteworthy act of selfless behavior may attain the same level of *zekhut* as a learned sage.

Zekhut is gained for a person by an act of renunciation and self-abnegation, such that heaven responds with an act of grace. As works of supererogation, which heaven cannot compel but highly prizes, *zekhut* defines the very opposite of coercion. It is an act that no one could anticipate or demand, but an act of such remarkable selflessness that heaven finds itself constrained to respond. That is why the systemic center is formed by an act, on heaven's part, of responsive grace, meaning grace that one by definition cannot demand or compel, but only provoke. When we make ourselves less, heaven makes us more; but we cannot force Israel's will upon heaven. When we ask about the feminization of Judaism, Israel's attention rests upon this fact: the right relationship between Israel and God is the relationship that is not coerced, not manipulated, not one defined by a dominant party upon a subordinated one. It is a relationship of mutuality and negotiation, a response to what is freely given through what cannot be demanded but only volunteered. The relationship, in other words, is a feminine, not a masculine, one, when measured by the prevailing, conventional stereotypes.

It is where heaven cannot force its will upon humanity that *zekhut* intervenes. It is that exquisite balance between Israel's will and heaven's will that, in the end, brings to its perfect balance and entire fulfillment the exploration of the conflict of God's will and Israel's will that began with Adam and Eve at their last hour in Eden, and Israel's first hour on earth. And, in context, the fact that we may inherit a treasury of *zekhut* from Israel's ancestors logically follows: just as we inherit the human condition of the freedom to practice rebellion against God's word, so we inherit, from former generations, the results of another dimension of the human condition: Israel's power to give willingly what none, even God, can by right or rule compel.

The final step in the path that began with God's profession of love for Israel, the response of the freely given, uncoerced act of love, *zekhut* stands for the empowerment of a supernatural character that derives from the virtue of one's ancestry or from one's own virtuous deeds of a very particular order. No single word in English bears the same meaning, nor is there a synonym for *zekhut* in the canonical writings in the original. The difficulty of translating a word of systemic consequence with a single word in some other language (or in the language of the systems documents themselves) tells us that what we are dealing with is unique and beyond comparison, and therefore contrast and comprehension.

When we come to the way in which *zekhut* is set forth, we find ourselves in a set of narratives of a rather special order. What is special about them is that women play a critical role, appear as heroines, and win the attention and respect of the reader or listener. It is difficult to locate in Classical literature before the Talmud of the Land of Israel—the Mishnah, the Tosefta, and Sifra, for instance—stories in which women figure at all, so to take up a whole series of stories in which women are key players comes as a surprise. But there is more. The storyteller on the surface makes the man the hero; he is the center of the narrative. And yet a second glance at what is coming shows us that the woman precipitates the tale, and her action, not the man's, represents the gift that cannot be compelled but only given; she is the one who freely sacrifices, and she also is represented as the source of wisdom. So Israel's systemic reversal—something above the Torah and the study of the Torah takes priority—is matched by a still-less-predictable shift in narrative quality, with women portrayed as principal actors.

In all three instances that follow and define what the individual must do to gain *zekhut*, the point is that the deeds of the heroes of the story make them worthy of having their prayers answered, which is a mark of the working of *zekhut*. It is supererogatory, uncoerced deeds—those well beyond the strict requirements of the Torah, and even the limits of the law altogether—that transform the hero into a holy man, whose holiness served just like that of a sage marked as such by knowledge of the Torah.

When Torah stories are told, by contrast, the point is that a man attains *zekhut* by study of the Torah, and a woman attains *zekhut* by sending her sons and her husband off to study the Torah and sitting home alone—not exactly commensurate action. Only *zekhut* stories represent the act of the woman as the counterpart and equivalent to the act of the man; and, in fact, even here, the fact that the woman's uncoerced gift is far greater than the man's—her body, merely his ass—should not go unnoticed. Once more, we find ourselves at the systemic center, where everything is reversed:

> **Yerushalmi Tractate Taanit 1:4.1**
> A certain ass driver appeared before the rabbis [the context requires: in a dream] and prayed, and rain came. The rabbis sent and brought him and said to him, "What is your trade?"
> He said to them, "I am an ass driver."
> They said to him, "And how do you conduct your business?"
> He said to them, "One time I rented my ass to a certain woman, and she was weeping on the way, and I said to her, What's with you? and she said to me, The husband of that woman [me] is in prison [for debt], and I wanted to see what I can do to free him. So I sold my ass and I gave her the proceeds, and I said to her, Here is your money, free your husband, but do not sin [by becoming a prostitute to raise the necessary funds]."
> They said to him, "You are worthy of praying and having your prayers answered."

The ass driver clearly has a powerful lien on heaven, so his prayers are answered, even while those of others are not. What did he do to get that entitlement? He did what no law could demand: impoverished himself to save the woman from a "fate worse than death."

> **Yerushalmi Tractate Taanit 1:4.I**
> In a dream of R. Abbahu, Mr. Pentakaka ["Five sins"] appeared, who prayed that rain would come, and it rained. R. Abbahu sent and summoned him. He said to him, "What is your trade?"
> He said to him, "Five sins does that man [I] do every day, [for I am a pimp:] hiring whores, cleaning up the theater, bringing home their garments for washing, dancing, and performing before them."
> He said to him, "And what sort of decent thing have you ever done?"
> He said to him, "One day that man [I] was cleaning the theater, and a woman came and stood behind a pillar and cried. I said to her, What's with you? And she said to me, That woman's [my] husband is in prison, and I wanted to see what I can do to free him, so I sold my bed and cover, and I gave the proceeds to her. I said to her, Here is your money, free your husband, but do not sin."

He said to him, "You are worthy of praying and having your prayers answered."

This story moves us still further, since the named man has done everything sinful that one can do, and, more to the point, he does it every day. So the singularity of the act of *zekhut*, which suffices if done only one time, encompasses its power to outweigh a life of sin—again, an act of *zekhut* as the mirror image and opposite of sin. Here again, the single act of saving a woman from a "fate worse than death" has sufficed.

Yerushalmi Tractate Taanit 1:4.I

A pious man from Kefar appeared [in a dream] to the rabbis. He prayed for rain and it rained. The rabbis went up to him. His householders told them that he was sitting on a hill. They went out to him, saying to him, "Greetings," but he did not answer them.

He was sitting and eating, and he did not say to them, "You break bread too."

When he went back home, he made a bundle of faggots and put his cloak on top of the bundle [instead of on his shoulder].

When he came home, he said to his household [wife], "These rabbis are here [because] they want me to pray for rain. If I pray and it rains, it is a disgrace for them, and if not, it is a profanation of the Name of Heaven. But come, you and I will go up [to the roof] and pray. If it rains, we shall tell them, We are not worthy to pray and have our prayers answered."

They went up and prayed and it rained.

They came down to them [and asked], "Why have the rabbis troubled themselves to come here today?"

They said to him, "We wanted you to pray so that it would rain."

He said to them, "Now do you really need my prayers? Heaven already has done its miracle."

They said to him, "Why, when you were on the hill, did we say hello to you, and you did not reply?"

He said to them, "I was then doing my job. Should I then interrupt my concentration [on my work]?"

They said to him, "And why, when you sat down to eat, did you not say to us You break bread too?"

> He said to them, "Because I had only my small ration of bread. Why would I have invited you to eat by way of mere flattery [when I knew I could not give you anything at all]?"
> They said to him, "And why when you came to go down, did you put your cloak on top of the bundle?"
> He said to them, "Because the cloak was not mine. It was borrowed for use at prayer. I did not want to tear it."
> They said to him, "And why, when you were on the hill, did your wife wear dirty clothes, but when you came down from the mountain, did she put on clean clothes?"
> He said to them, "When I was on the hill, she put on dirty clothes, so that no one would gaze at her. But when I came home from the hill, she put on clean clothes, so that I would not gaze on any other woman."
> They said to him, "It is well that you pray and have your prayers answered."

Here the woman is at least an equal player; her actions, as much as her husband's, prove exemplary and illustrate the ultimate wisdom. The pious man, finally, enjoys the recognition of the sages by reason of his lien upon heaven, able as he is to pray and bring rain. What has so endowed him with *zekhut*? Acts of punctiliousness of a moral order: concentrating on his work, avoiding an act of dissimulation, integrity in the disposition of a borrowed object, his wife's concern not to attract other men, and her equal concern to make herself attractive to her husband.

*Zekhut c*omes about through deeds of a supererogatory character—to which heaven responds by deeds of a supererogatory character: supernatural favor to this one, who through deeds of ingratiation of the other or self-abnegation or restraint exhibits the attitude that in heaven precipitates a counterpart attitude, hence generating *zekhut*, rather than to that one, who does not. The simple fact that rabbis cannot pray and bring rain, but a simple ass driver can, tells the whole story. The relationship measured by *zekhut*—heaven's response by an act of uncoerced favor to a person's uncoerced gift, for example, an act of gentility, restraint, or self-abnegation—contains an element of unpredictability for which appeal to the *zekhut* inherited from ancestors' accounts. So while one cannot coerce heaven, he or she—for women as much as men enjoy full access to *zekhut*, though they do not to the study of the Torah—can through *zekhut* gain acts of favor from heaven, and that is by doing what heaven cannot require of me. Heaven then responds to one's attitude in carrying out his or her duties—and more than those duties. That act of pure disinterest—giving the woman one's means of livelihood—is the one that gains for me heaven's deepest interest.

The God of the Torah breaks the rules of the Torah, accords an entitlement to this one, who has done some one remarkable deed, but not to that one, who has done nothing wrong and everything right. So a life in accord with the rules—even a life spent in the study of the Torah—in heaven's view is outweighed by a single moment, a gesture that violates the norm, extending the outer limits of the rule, for instance, of virtue. And who but a God who, like us, feels, not only thinks, responds to impulse and sentiment, can be portrayed in such a way as this?

> "So I sold my ass and I gave her the proceeds, and I said to her, Here is your money, free your husband, but do not sin [by becoming a prostitute to raise the necessary funds]."
>
> They said to him, "You are worthy of praying and having your prayers answered."

Here the law of love is transcended, for love itself is now surpassed. Beyond love is the willing, uncoerced sacrifice of self: love of the other more than the love of self, love of the Other most of all. Feminine Judaism relates to God as lovers relate to one another: giving not in order to receive, receiving only in order to give.

What is asked of Israel and of the Israelite individual now is truly godly restraint, supernatural generosity of soul that is "in our image, after our likeness": that is what sets aside all rules. And, since as a matter of simple fact, that appeal to transcend the norm defined not personal virtue but the sainthood of all Israel, living all together in the here and in the now, we must conclude that, within Israel's society, within what the Greco-Roman world called its *polis*, its political and social order, the bounds of earth have now extended to heaven. In terms of another great system composed in the same time and in response to a world-historical catastrophe of the same sort, Israel on earth dwells in the city of God. And, it must follow, God dwells with Israel, in Israel: "today, if you will it."

Life in conformity with the rule, obligatory but merely conventional, did not evoke the special interest of heaven. Why should it? The rules describe the ordinary. But (in language used only in a later document) "the All-Merciful really wants the heart," and that is not an ordinary thing. Nor was the power to bring rain or hold up a tottering house gained through a life of merely ordinary sanctity. Special favor responded to extraordinary actions, in the analogy of special disfavor, misfortune deemed to punish sin. And just as culpable sin, as distinct from mere error, requires an act of will—specifically, arrogance—so an act of extraordinary character requires an act of will. But, as the mirror image of sin, the act would reveal in a concrete way an attitude of restraint, forbearance, gentility, and self-abnegation. A sinful act, provoking heaven, was one that one did deliberately to defy heaven. Then an act that would evoke heaven's favor, so imposing upon heaven a lien that heaven freely gave, was one that, equally deliberately and concretely, displayed humility.

Notes

1. Jacob Neusner, *The Incarnation of God: The Character of Divinity in Formative Judaism* (1988; repr. Binghamton, NY: Global Publications, 2000).
2. Yochanan Muffs, *Love and Joy: Law, Language and Religion in Ancient Israel* (New York: Jewish Theological Seminary of America, 1992), 4.
3. Mishnah Sotah 1:7.
4. The Fathers According to Rabbi Nathan 4:5.2.
5. Deuteronomy 6:4.
6. Leviticus 19:18.
7. Deuteronomy 6:5.
8. Hosea 2:19–20.
9. Song of Songs 1:2.
10. Abot 2:4.
11. Abot 3:10.
12. Jacob Neusner, *The Transformation of Judaism: From Philosophy to Religion* (1992; repr. Eugene, OR: Wipf and Stock, 2004).

Additional References

Borowitz, Eugene B. "Love." In *Encyclopaedia Judaica*. Jerusalem: Keter Publishing Co., 1971. 523–30.

Büchler, A. *Studies in Sin and Atonement in the Rabbinic Literature of the First Century*. London: Oxford University Press, 1928. 119–76.

Feldman, David M. *The Jewish Family Relationship*. New York: United Synagogue of America, 1975.

Glueck, Nelson. *Hesed in the Bible*. Translated by Alfred Gottschalk. Cincinnati: Hebrew Union College Press, 1967.

Gordis, Robert. *Love and Sex: A Modern Jewish Perspective*. New York: Farrar Straus Giroux, 1978.

Neusner, Jacob. *Vanquished Nation, Broken Spirit: The Virtues of the Heart in Formative Judaism*. New York: Cambridge University Press, 1987.

———. *Androgynous Judaism: Masculine and Feminine in the Dual Torah*. 1993; repr. Eugene, OR: Wipf and Stock, 2003.

———. *The Components of the Rabbinic Documents: From the Whole to the Parts: V. Song of Songs Rabbah. Part I. Introduction and Parashiyyot One through Four*. 1997; repr. Lanham, MD: University Press of America, 1997.

———. *The Components of the Rabbinic Documents: From the Whole to the Parts: V. Song of Songs Rabbah. Part II. Parashiyyot Five through Eight and a Topical and Methodical Outline of Song of Songs Rabbah*. 1997; repr. Lanham, MD: University Press of America, 1997.

4 Wisdom into Compassion

Buddhism in Practice

Ruben L. F. Habito

"Divine love" appears to be a problematic term from a Buddhist viewpoint, considering both components, "divine" and "love." First, the Buddha's central teaching is about overcoming the dissatisfactoriness (Pāli: *dukkha*) of the human condition, in understanding and uprooting its causes and thus attaining enlightenment and ultimate liberation. Given this thrust of his basic religious message, the Buddha set aside speculative questions about the origins of the world, about continuance or noncontinuance of existence after death, and so on, as irrelevant to the matter at hand, that is, eliminating *dukkha* and realizing ultimate liberation through the wisdom of enlightenment.[1] In this context, the question of a Creator God as a divine power who controls human destiny and to whom humans need to submit is a nonissue[2] in the religious worldview of the different forms of Buddhism that developed in history.[3]

Second, words translatable as "love" in Sanskrit (*preman*, *sneha*, *kāma*, *rāga*, *anurāga*, *abhilāsa*, *priya*) appearing in non-Buddhist as well as Buddhist texts refer to a variety of human relations and emotions that easily give way to an attitude of grasping or clinging (that is, to the "object" of one's "love"). The mind of awakening to be cultivated by Buddhist followers, in contrast, entails an inner freedom to "see things just as they are," without clinging or attachment. The kind of "love" as referred to by the terms listed above leads to or aggravates dissatisfactoriness and suffering, and is thus considered among the obstructions to be overcome by those in the path of awakening.[4]

With these reservations from a Buddhist standpoint in mind, we first need to clarify our terms in order to proceed. For this we take our cue from Sir John Templeton, who wrote, "Unlimited love was called *agape* by the ancient Greeks to distinguish the divine love from earthly emotions."[5] What interests us is this *agapeic,* or altruistic, kind of attitude and action—a pure, unlimited, "divine" kind of love that is to be distinguished from "earthly emotions."[6] Our task in this essay then is to map out and highlight this altruistic kind of attitude and action, and understand its place within the context of the religious praxis and worldview of the adherents of various forms of Buddhism in history and in our contemporary global scene.

The first part of this essay takes a panoramic view of early, Mahāyāna, and Tantric Buddhism, to examine the place of altruistic attitudes leading to concrete action as found within doctrinal, ethical, praxeological, and ritual expressions of this family of religious traditions.[7] The second part considers three contemporary forms of Buddhism with communities of adherents in different parts of the world, highlighting the pivotal place of compassion in their respective forms of religious praxis and worldviews. The concluding section offers reflections on tasks and challenges for Buddhists vis-à-vis their own stated religious ideal, which may have some relevance for adherents of other religious traditions as well.

Altruistic Attitudes in Early, Mahāyāna, and Tantric Buddhism

An intentful reading of Buddhist scriptural texts including Pāli, Sanskrit, Chinese, Tibetan, and other historical sources spanning many centuries provides solid ground for affirming that an altruistic, or *agapeic,* kind of attitude and action occupies a central place in the religious teachings of the Buddha as received and further developed by his followers through the ages. The very fact that there are such teachings at all is said to be due to the Buddha's resolve out of compassion for all sentient beings to convey what he realized in his experience of Enlightenment under the Bodhi tree, fully realizing that the profound liberating truth (*dharma*) could never be adequately expressed in words.[8]

Scriptural sources reflecting early Buddhist teaching, practice, and worldview emphasize the importance of cultivating lovingkindness (Pāli: *mettā*) and compassion (*karuṇā*) for followers of the Awakened One, both as a condition for arrival at the ultimate state of nirvana (Pāli: *nibbāna*) described as a "place of peace" (*santam padam*) and as a natural outcome or outflow of having arrived at that state.[9] *Mettā*, also variously translated as "benevolence," "kindliness," or "friendliness," is a word that implies affinity, kinship, filiality, friendship, and involving an active intent in willing another's well-being and happiness, whereas *karuṇā* involves sharing in and empathizing with the pain and suffering of another, with the active intent of seeking the removal of this pain and suffering.[10]

The Buddha himself, having attained that place of peace and who thereby teaches the way to its attainment to others, is described as full of empathy (*anukampā*) and pity (*dayā*), with a compassionate mind and heart (*mettā-citta*) that seeks the alleviation of suffering of others. His resolve to teach the *dharma* (liberating truth) to others arises out of compassion, as he opened his awakened eyes and gazed at the world, seeing all beings caught in the web of dissatisfactoriness and suffering. His entire teaching career, from the time of his awakening at the age of thirty-five until his death at the age of eighty, is motivated by this lovingkindness beyond measure (*mettā-appamānā*) and by great compassion (*mahākarunā*) for all beings.[11] The Buddha, the "World Honored One," is so honored precisely because of his magnanimous spirit and boundless heart that embraces all beings. In the Sanskrit text *Buddhacarita*, an account of the Buddha's life and career in verse that extols his many virtues, he is above all the Compassionate One, "one whose being is compassion itself" (*karunā-ātmaka*), whose birth in this earthly realm is precisely for the sake of liberating all sentient beings from suffering.[12]

A notable passage that underscores lovingkindness toward all beings as a characteristic of those on the path of awakening is found in the aptly titled *Mettā-sutta* (Short Treatise on Lovingkindness), in a collection said to belong among the earliest strata of textual compilations of the Buddha's teaching.[13]

> Even as a mother protects with her life her only child, her only child, so with a boundless heart should one cherish all beings. Radiating kindness over the entire world, spreading upwards to the skies, and downwards to the depths, outwards and unbounded, freed from hatred and ill will, whether standing or walking, sitting or lying down, free from drowsiness, one should maintain this recollection. This is said to be the sublime abiding.[14]

Mettā is one of the four aspects of a boundless mind known as the Sublime Attitudes (*brahmavihāra*), the Four Immeasurables (*cattaro-appamānā*) that characterize the state of mind of those on the path of awakening. The other three in this quartet are compassion (*karunā*), sympathetic joy (*mudithā*), and equanimity (*upekkhā*). These four are described in later commentaries in the following way:

> Loving-kindness is the state of desiring to offer happiness and welfare with the thought "May all beings be happy" and so forth. Compassion is the state of desiring to remove suffering and misfortune, with the thought "May they be liberated from these sufferings," and so forth. Sympathetic joy is the state of desiring the continuity of [others'] happiness and welfare, with the thought "You beings are rejoicing. It is good that you are rejoicing. It is very good," and so forth. Equanimity is the state of observing [another's] suffering or happiness and thinking "These appear because of that individual's own past activities."[15]

These Four Immeasurables are cultivated specifically in the context of meditative practice and become ingrained in the practitioner's worldview and behavior as one deepens in this meditative path.[16] They also serve as guideposts that indicate how persons on the path of awakening have come to embody its fruits in their daily lives. They arise in conjunction with, and presuppose the cultivation of detachment from, those things that cause sorrow and dissatisfactoriness.[17] These sublime attitudes that characterize those well on the path of awakening are thus to be clearly demarcated as from the "earthly emotions" (such as those associated with various kinds of human "love") that only serve to reinforce or aggravate clinging and attachment, and which thus obstruct those on the path laid out by the Awakened One.

With the spread and transmission of Buddhist teaching through the first few centuries, the image of the Buddha came to be further glorified and idealized: the Awakened and the World Honored One was regarded as having extraordinary and suprahuman characteristics, and often referred to as embodying Great Compassion (*mahākarunā*), with a heart reaching out to all beings in the universe. This idealization of the Buddha into a supramundane kind of being with a mind and heart of Great Compassion goes in tandem with historical developments that gave rise to the Mahāyāna, or

Great Vehicle. Mahāyāna scriptural texts depict the Buddha as one who, out of compassion for all sentient beings, chooses not to enter into final nirvana, but instead continues to work actively toward the liberation of all beings from their pain and suffering in this *samsāric* realm of birth and death.

The *Saddharmapundarīka*, also known as the Lotus Sutra, a Mahāyāna text that became widely influential in East Asia through centuries and remains so today, describes the Buddha as having attained enlightenment and ultimate liberation eons ago and, rather than entering into Final Nirvana, continuing to abide in this earthly realm out of Great Compassion for all beings. With fatherly love, he watches over sentient beings as his own children in their various situations of suffering and dissatisfactoriness, using skillful means to guide them to awakening and ultimate liberation. A well-known narrative in this sutra is the Parable of the Burning House, wherein sentient beings in this earthly realm are depicted as like children lost in their play inside a big house that is burning and crumbling down, oblivious of the imminent danger about to befall upon them. The Buddha is depicted as their wise father who, himself being already in a safe place outside of the house, uses all manner of skillful means to catch the attention of his children so they would notice the burning house and find their way to safety.[18]

Along with other Mahāyāna scriptural texts, the Lotus Sutra also highlights the notion of the bodhisattva, literally, a "being [on the path] of awakening," who traverses this path for the sake of liberating all beings from suffering. The term "bodhisattva" primarily referred to the Buddha in his previous lives, as narrated in popular lore and handed down in the *Jātaka* tales.[19] Having accumulated merit throughout countless lifetimes (human, as well as animal) through performing various acts of selflessness and compassion, he was finally reborn as Siddhārtha Gautama, the last rebirth before becoming a fully Awakened One. In the Mahāyāna, the bodhisattva ideal came to replace the earlier Buddhist ideal of the Arhat, or "Worthy One." An Arhat, as depicted in earlier monastic and scholastic texts, is one who has advanced in spiritual practice to the point of having destroyed the roots of the three poisons (greed, ill will, and delusion), and no longer bound by any ties to this *samsāric* world (this cyclic realm of birth and death), is now ready to enter nirvana. In contrast, a bodhisattva is one who, having attained liberating wisdom, foregoes final deliverance and instead deliberately seeks to reenter this world of birth and death for the sake of liberation of all beings still caught in this web of suffering. A bodhisattva is thus the embodiment of great compassion, having made a vow not to enter into nirvana until all other beings have done so, and to work tirelessly and selflessly toward this goal.[20]

The bodhisattva's vow to give oneself, over many lifetimes, toward the alleviation of the suffering of all, came to be regarded as a meritorious source of power that works for the liberation of all beings.[21] This power of the vow was embodied in the figure of the Bodhisattva Avalokiteśvara (*Kuan-yin* in Chinese, *Kannon* in Japanese, *Kwan-um* in Korean), literally, "Regarder of the Cries [of the World]." The twenty-fifth chapter of the Lotus Sutra describes in detail the effects of this power in liberating devotees from different kinds of situations of suffering and disaster in this earthly life. Depicted as a male figure in Sanskrit texts, Kuan-yin was transgendered as a female bodhisattva in East Asia, and came to be a widely popular figure of devotion throughout history up to the present time.[22]

The doctrinal core that underlies Mahāyāna Buddhism revolves around the notion of Emptiness (*śūnyatā*), a key term pointing to the horizon realized in the path of awakening. Mahāyāna emphasizes how the term "Emptiness" is not a "concept" (in the ordinary sense of the word meaning "an object of thought"), but is rather a term of soteriological or transformative import, with concomitant prescriptions for religious praxis for a whole lifetime of engagement.[23] In realizing Emptiness, one sees into the Selfless (*anātman*) nature of reality, and realizes the intimate interconnectedness ("dependently co-arising," *pratītya-samutpāda*) of all things in the universe. As such, one directly realizes that the pain and suffering of all sentient beings is no other than one's very own pain and suffering: this is the heart of *com-passion*, the state of mind of suffering-with all beings. In short, "realizing Emptiness" involves a transformation of one's entire mode of thinking and being, from one preoccupied with self-centered goals and projects, to one that opens up to a boundless horizon that embraces all beings in the universe in a magnanimous mind and heart of compassion.[24] This intimate connection between realizing Emptiness and embodying the Great Compassion is described in the *Bodhicaryāvatāra* ("Entering into the Bodhisattva Path"), a well-known treatise in verse by Śāntideva, an eighth-century Indian monk who wrote from the standpoint of the Mādhyamika school.[25] Delineating the steps involved in treading the way of the bodhisattva in meticulous detail, and expounding on the dimensions involved in the attainment of the Wisdom of Emptiness, in the eighth chapter the poem prescribes a meditative exercise called "exchange of self and other" as a direct way of realizing Emptiness qua Great Compassion.[26]

The notion of Emptiness that underlies all phenomena, together with the notion of Buddha as a transhistorical and metacosmic figure with a mind and heart of Great Compassion toward all beings, and the notion of the bodhisattva who selflessly and tirelessly gives oneself in service to all beings and set forth as the ideal to be aspired for by Buddhist followers, are three key features of Mahāyāna Buddhism. In reflecting on these three notions and their interplay, Buddhist systematic thinkers arrived at the formulation of the *Trikāya*, or the view of the three bodies of the Buddha.[27] This *Trikāya* theory offers a framework that masterfully integrates the three key notions of the Mahāyāna and articulates the inseparable connection between the Wisdom that realizes the truth of Emptiness and the Great Compassion that issues forth from this Wisdom in an intellectually coherent way.[28]

The teaching on Emptiness was taken to a new level with the advent of Tantric/Esoteric forms of Buddhist teaching and practice in China and Tibet. The term "Tantra," contrasted with Sūtra, is used to refer to those scriptural texts that contain not only doctrinal formulations, but also ritual, devotional, and practical prescriptions to be observed in the path of awakening. The performance of these prescriptive ritual acts, in addition to leading to ultimate enlightenment, was also regarded as bringing about different kinds of worldly benefit, such as healing from illnesses, avoidance of calamities, the acquisition of power, and so on. These ritual features were taught in secret and handed down from teacher to disciple, and are thus also referred to as esoteric forms of Buddhist practice.

In Tibet, schools of Tantric teaching developed with their distinctive ways of guiding disciples in this form of Buddhist practice toward realizing the Wisdom of Emptiness. A key feature of the Buddhist path of awakening as taught in Tantric traditions is the unleashing of the power of Great Compassion,[29] and the iconic figure often invoked for this power in Tibetan Buddhism is Chenrezig (Avalokiteśvara), the Bodhisattva of Compassion.[30]

In China, an esoteric form of practice consisting of recitation or chanting of a *dhāraṇī* (sacred formula) understood as a verbal expression of the power of compassion of Kuan-yin spread among the populace. This was the *Tapei-chou*, or *Great Compassion Dhāraṇī*, a formula in eighty-four syllables contained in a seventh-century Chinese translation of a text entitled *The Dhāraṇī Sūtra of the Vast, Perfect, Unobstructed, Great Compassionate Heart of the Thousand Handed, Thousand-Eyed Bodhisattva Avalokiteśvara.*[31] In this text, Kuan-yin is depicted as having a thousand eyes and a thousand arms, which emanate from the bodhisattva's vow to offer oneself for the benefit of all sentient beings. The thousand eyes represent the wisdom that sees throughout all realms of the universe, and the thousand arms and hands represent her activity using all varieties of skillful means to help sentient beings in different situations of suffering.

Kuan-yin, an "object" of popular devotion on one level, is described in treatises as an internal and dynamic reality, a soteriological power that issues forth from the bodhisattva's vow of compassion. Commenting on the *Great Compassion Dhāraṇī*, eleventh-century monk Chih-li writes, "You have to understand that the Great Compassionate Kuan-yin is our original nature. Because we want to return to our origin now, we invoke the origin and say the vow. This is the reason why the vow is the powerful use of our original nature."[32] Reciting the *Dhāraṇī* immerses one's whole being into this power of the bodhisattva vow, thus cultivating and bringing forth in oneself the activity of Kuan-yin to help all beings in their various situations of pain and suffering.

In sum, our panoramic survey above shows how an altruistic or *agapeic* kind of attitude and action, expressed in the terms "lovingkindness" and "compassion," is upheld as a keynote theme and developed in various ways in doctrinal, practical, and ritual expressions throughout the stages of development of Buddhist history. Schools of thought and practice arose through the centuries through the different cultures and societies of Asia, offering varying systematized formulations of Buddhist worldviews centered on the cultivation of liberating wisdom that generates boundless compassion, with their own prescriptions for religious praxis, ritual, and ethical behavior.[33]

Great Compassion in Practice: Lotus, Pure Land, and Zen Buddhism

Let us now examine three contemporary forms of Buddhism with active and growing communities of adherents both in the Eastern and Western hemispheres.[34] Here we focus attention on their particular forms of praxis to situate the place of compassion within their religious life and worldview, and refer the reader elsewhere for more detailed descriptions of these particular traditions of Buddhism.[35]

The Lotus Buddhism of Nichiren

A form of contemporary Buddhism that continues to win new adherents in different parts of the world takes the Lotus Sutra as primary scriptural text and as a religious icon. These are the Buddhist communities of followers who derive inspiration from the life and teaching of Nichiren, a thirteenth-century Japanese mystic and prophet. Nichiren lived during a tumultuous and religiously fertile epoch of Japan's history, and his major teachings arose in the context of his experiences of persecution by the authorities of his time, due to his relentless critiques of the political and religious establishment from a religious standpoint based on his reading of the Lotus Sutra.[36]

The central Buddhist practice taught by Nichiren is the recitation or chanting of the august title of the Lotus Sutra (*daimoku* in Japanese), in five characters pronounced in Japanese as *Myō-hō-ren-ge-kyō* (preceded by two characters, *Namu*, which comes from a Sanskrit word meaning "Homage to . . ."). A noted passage from Nichiren's writings provides background for the importance of this practice.

> Arousing Great Compassion for those who cannot comprehend the doctrine of three thousand realms in a single thought- moment, the Buddha wrapped this gem within the Five Characters, which he then hung around the necks of the childish people of the Age of the Latter Days. The Four Great Bodhisattvas will protect those who embrace the Five Characters faithfully.[37]

The "doctrine of three thousand realms in a single thought-moment" is a centerpiece in Nichiren's own teaching, referring to the boundless mind of enlightenment. This is a highly systematized rendition of the notion of Emptiness in its relation to the world of Form, as developed by the Chinese Master Chih-li, founder of the T'ien-tai school, and whose systematic philosophical exposition of the teachings of the Lotus Sutra Nichiren had studied. The doctrine of "three thousand realms in a single thought-moment" refers to the entire cosmic realm wherein every element in the cosmos is mutually interdependent and interpenetrating with every other element, and contained in every single spatiotemporal unit in every human being's earthly life.

The Buddha here is a supramundane, Abiding (or "Eternal") Buddha who appears in the fifteenth chapter of the Lotus Sutra, described as omniscient and omnipresent to sentient beings in this earthly realm. This Abiding Buddha, referred to as Śākyamuni Master of the Dharma (*Kyōshu-Shakuson*) is depicted as a caring father who continually acts to liberate these sentient beings who are his own children from their different situations of suffering, using all sorts of skillful means in this endeavor, a Buddha whose seed is embedded in the hearts and minds of all sentient beings.[38] In Nichiren's teaching, this is no other than the Buddha of the Three Bodies integrated as One, transcending time and space, and yet immanently present and embedded in the heart and mind of each and every sentient being, continually working in boundless compassion toward the awakening and liberation of all beings.[39]

To attain the Buddha Way in Nichiren's teaching is to experience the "three thousand realms in a single thought-moment," whereby one's being in a single instant pervades the entire universe and the realm of phenomena. It is to activate the seed of Buddhahood lying within our hearts and minds, and enable it to throw light on one's thoughts, words, and actions in this earthly life. This is to awaken to the Buddha's boundless compassion, which works ceaselessly for the liberation of all beings. Nichiren's simple prescription for bringing about this awakening is the reverential recitation of the august title of the Lotus Sutra: *Namu-Myō-hō-ren-ge-kyō*. Nichiren describes his own life and religious career as centered on the propagation of this practice:

> Now since the twenty-eighth day of the fourth month of the Kenchō year (1253) until now, the twelfth month of the year of Kōan (1280), for a period of twenty-eight years, Nichiren has devoted his life to none other than this cause: to do all that is possible to put these seven or five characters (*Na-mu*) *Myō-hō-ren-ge-kyō* into the mouths of all sentient beings of Japan. It is just as a mother, in her compassion, would do all that is possible to put milk into the mouth of her infant child.[40]

The above passage indicates how the very practice of chanting the august title of the Lotus Sutra is a manifestation of the boundless compassion of the Abiding Śākyamuni Buddha pervading throughout the universe. Nichiren's own personal testimony intimates how he himself has come to realize and embody this compassion in his own life, empowering him to dedicate himself entirely to propagating this practice of chanting the august title. Testimonies of contemporary Buddhists who have taken on this practice also describe their own transformation in doing so, enabling them to turn their lives around, and live and act on behalf of and at the service of others in the concrete contexts of their families, workplace, and society in general.[41]

Among the groups of followers of the Lotus Buddhism inspired by Nichiren, the Sōka Gakkai International and the Risshō Kōseikai, and Nipponzan Myōhōji are religious organizations with international outreach.[42] The last mentioned, founded by Fujii Nichidatsu (1885–1985), a Japanese monk inspired by Mahatma Gandhi in the 1930s, has been active in the peace movement for many decades, with a visible presence in peace marches in different parts of the world through their monks and nuns beating Dharma Drums and chanting the august title of the Lotus Sutra.[43] The former two are known for their professed commitment to socio-ecological healing, peace and justice, and interreligious dialogue. The leaders of these organizations continue to encourage their individual members and local congregations to engage in these causes as an aspect and outcome of their central religious praxis of chanting, as an effective way of unleashing the power of compassion in a practitioner's life.

Pure Land Buddhism

Pure Land Buddhism revolves around the religious practice known as *Nembutsu* (literally, "calling to mind" or "recollection," "visualization" of the Buddha), or recitation/chanting of the name of Amitābha Buddha. In scriptural texts known collectively as the Three Pure Land Sutras,[44] Amitāyus (Immeasurable Life) or Amitābha (Immeasurable Light) Buddha (pronounced *Amito-fo* in Chinese, *Amida* in Japanese) is depicted as reigning over the Land of Bliss (*Sukhavati*) or Pure Land. This Buddha has attained this status through the infinite merit generated by forty-eight vows he made in a previous existence as a monk named Dharmākara. The eighteenth vow in particular is highlighted as manifesting his magnanimous heart and great compassion:

> If, upon my attaining Buddhahood, the sentient beings of the ten quarters with a sincere mind, joyful trust and aspiration for birth in my land and saying my Name perhaps even ten times, should not be born there, may I not attain the supreme Enlightenment.[45]

This eighteenth, called the Primal Vow, together with the nineteenth, to the effect that he will appear before those who call upon him at the moment of death and will escort them across to the Land of Bliss, became the foundation stones for the devotional practice of Pure Land Buddhism.

Shin (True) Pure Land Buddhists, those who follow the teachings of Shinran (1193–1282), constitute by far the largest number of devotees of this tradition, with communities of adherents in different parts of the world. Shinran's teacher Hōnen (1133–1212) taught his followers to recite the name of Amida frequently in their day-to-day lives, as this would ensure that Amida will meet them at the point of death and they will be welcomed into the Pure Land. In contrast, Shinran, who had a profound religious experience of the power of Amida's compassion while still a young monk at Mount Hiei, a center of Buddhist monastic training for centuries in Japan, taught that even a single recitation of Amida's name, done with a pure and entrusting heart and mind, is sufficient and fully efficacious in assuring a person of rebirth in the Pure Land. With this inner assurance and peace of mind (*anjin*), a devotee thus no longer has to worry about her own fate after this earthly life, and can thus dedicate one's entire being to works of compassion toward all beings, empowered by the boundless compassion of Amida.[46]

The following passage from the *Tannishō*, a collection of sayings of Shinran as transcribed by his disciple Yuien, and widely used among Shin Buddhists, describes the understanding of the role of compassion in the practice of *Nembutsu*:

> There is a difference in compassion between the Path of Sages and the Path of Pure Land. The compassion in the Path of Sages is expressed through pity, sympathy, and care for all beings, but

> it is rare that one can help another as one completely desires. The compassion in the Path of Pure Land is to quickly attain Buddhahood, saying the *Nembutsu*, and with a true heart of compassion and love save all living beings completely as we desire. In this life no matter how much pity and sympathy we feel for others, it is impossible to help another as we truly wish; thus our compassion is inconsistent and limited. Only the saying of *Nembutsu* manifests the complete and never ending compassion which is true, real and sincere.[47]

The "Path of Sages" refers to the forms of Buddhism that emphasize the individual's earnest efforts in observing the precepts, ascetic discipline, and meditative, ritual, and other forms of religious praxis toward the realization of enlightenment. This is also called the path of Self-Power (*jiriki*), as contrasted with the Pure Land path, which relies utterly on Other Power (*tariki*)—that is, the boundless and all-encompassing compassion of Amida Buddha that gushes forth from the Primal Vow. Shinran's own personal experience of this overwhelming power of Amida's compassion, opened up through a total entrustment of mind and heart (*shinjin*) to this Power, is in the background of and is the motivation and source of inspiration for his entire religious career.[48] The passage above affirms his core teaching, expressed in a different way in his voluminous writings, that the very saying of the *Nembutsu* with a totally entrusting mind and heart assures the devotee of rebirth in the Pure Land in the next life and therefore of the ultimate realization of Buddhahood. This total entrustment is what brings inner assurance and total peace of mind, freeing the devotee from anxieties about one's own destiny in the afterlife, thus enabling one to dedicate one's life to the service of others, not out of one's own individual feelings of "pity and sympathy," but as a manifestation and embodiment of Amida's boundless compassion on this earth.

Zen Buddhism

Zen (*Chan* in Chinese, *Son* in Korean) is a school of Buddhism whose main prescriptive practice is that of seated meditation (*zazen*).[49] Tracing its origins to a legendary monk named Bodhidharma, said to have traveled from "the west" (India) to China sometime around the sixth century, the school took root in China and was subsequently transmitted to Korea and

Japan, and, since the twentieth century, to the rest of the world. Professing to offer a simple form of Buddhist practice centered on seated meditation and the cultivation of mindfulness in daily life, the Chan/Son/Zen school developed as a thriving tradition that upheld monastic discipline and ritual observance, branching off into schools with differing emphases on doctrinal issues as well as styles of meditative practice and ritual observance.[50]

Contrasted with Pure Land Buddhism, whose doctrine, praxis, and ritual revolve around devotion to the All-Compassionate Amida Buddha as an "Other Power," Zen is sometimes said to be a form of Buddhism that relies on "Self Power," that is, on the practitioner's own efforts in regulating one's life and focusing one's mind in the here and now in seated meditation. This categorization of Zen as a self-relying form of practice is reinforced by dicta attributed to this tradition, such as, "If you meet the Buddha, kill him!" However, a closer examination of the deeper and wider dimensions involved in Zen practice puts such a simplistic classification into question.

Formal seated meditation (*zazen*), the central practice of Zen Buddhism, involves an opening of one's entire being, with each breath, each thought, each word, each action, in every present moment, to a boundless horizon. This is the horizon of a "Selfless Self" that realizes the Wisdom of Emptiness and activates Compassion as arising out of that realization. To engage in the sustained practice of seated meditation is to allow this boundless horizon of Wisdom and Compassion to shed light on the entirety of one's life from day to day.[51]

In addition to formal seated meditation, an aspect of Zen practice is the chanting in common of scriptural texts and various verses handed down in tradition from Zen ancestors. The Four Bodhisattva Vows are also included as a regular item recited in common, usually as the concluding chant, followed by a call to "all Buddhas and Great Bodhisattvas throughout space and time," invoking their infinite merits and directing all this toward the enlightenment and liberation of all beings. Among the scriptural texts also included in the chanting are the Heart Sutra and a short form of the Kanzeon Sutra.[52]

The former is a central Mahāyāna sutra expounding the crux of enlightenment as the realization that "Form is Emptiness, Emptiness is Form."[53] It opens with the line, "Avalokiteśvara Bodhisattva, practicing the profound Perfection of Wisdom, realized the Emptiness of all phenomena, and was freed from *dukkha*." Avalokiteśvara or Kuan-yin (Kannon, or Kanzeon in

Japanese) is the subject of this chant, and the ritual effect of the chanting is to enable the practitioner to experience oneness with Kannon, in realizing Emptiness.

With these dimensions of Zen Buddhist practice in better view, we can affirm that Zen is not about a one-sided reliance on "self-power," but is a form of praxis with an underlying religious worldview that transcends this "self-versus-other" distinction. Taking the path of Zen, a practitioner immerses oneself in a realm of cosmic compassion, symbolized by the figure of Kannon. Bolstered by the support of a community of practitioners who sit in *zazen* and chant together, as well as by countless Buddhas and bodhisattvas of the past, present, and future, this religious praxis comes to bear fruit and effect a transformation in one's life. Three fruits of the practice of seated meditation are described as (a) deepening and enhancement of the power of *samadhi* or concentration and absorption; (b) the experience of seeing into one's own true self, or (Awakened, or Buddha) nature; and (c) the actualization of this awakened nature in one's day-to-day life.[54]

In short, Zen practice centered on seated meditation and mindfulness in one's daily life is about awakening to this "Selfless Self," which is one's own Buddha nature, and activating it in daily life. This Selfless Self finds its iconic representation in Kanzeon, Hearer of the Sounds of the World, with a thousand eyes (of wisdom) and a thousand arms and hands, activating boundless compassion and working ceaselessly on behalf of all sentient beings in the concrete contexts of one's life in society.

Concluding Reflections: The Two-Directional Structure of Buddhist Praxis

The picture of the Buddhist family of religious traditions conveyed in this essay, as placing central emphasis on lovingkindness and compassion in their doctrinal, ethical, ritual, and praxeological expressions, is in stark contrast with some images that have been circulated about Buddhism, even in recently published literature. There is a widespread impression of Buddhism as a pessimistic religion, with the view that this human life is impermanent and full of pain, and as advocating an escape from this world of suffering. The noted book *Crossing the Threshold of Hope*, published in the name of the late Pope John Paul II, for example, portrays Buddhism as espousing a nihilistic view of the world, as an "atheistic system" with a "negative soteriology."

> The "enlightenment" experienced by the Buddha comes down to the conviction that the world is bad, that it is the source of evil and of suffering for man [*sic*]. To liberate oneself from this evil, one must free oneself from this world, necessitating a break with the ties that join us to external reality—ties existing in our human nature, in our psyche, in our bodies. The more we are liberated from these ties, the more we become indifferent to what is in the world, and the more we are freed from suffering, from the evil that has its source in the world. . . . We liberate ourselves only through detachment from the world, which is bad. The fullness of such a detachment is not union with God, but what is called nirvana, a state of perfect indifference with regard to the world.[55]

This portrayal created a furor and led to vehement protests from Buddhist adherents, leaders, and intellectuals throughout the world. This image of Buddhism, however, as advocating an escapist attitude with emphasis on "detachment from the world," may not be entirely baseless, if one reads through many passages in Buddhist texts, and in the works of Western scholars published in the late nineteenth and early twentieth centuries. It may also be the kind of image projected by some Buddhist followers themselves who pursue a religious goal that they take to be "a state of perfect indifference with regard to the world."

If we look back in Buddhist history, it was precisely the reaction to this kind of otherworldly attitude of detachment, as exhibited by followers of the Buddha who were one-sidedly engrossed in their own ascetical efforts toward individual purification and liberation, that led to the rise of the Mahāyāna movement in the early centuries of the common era. The rallying call of its proponents was the recovery of the dimension of compassion toward all beings as an integral component in the path of awakening. They sought to convey the heart of the Buddha's message in likening it to a Great Vehicle that can ferry all beings toward the other shore of liberation.[56] This was set in contrast with the attitude of those who sought only their own liberation without concern for others, which they looked upon and criticized as an "inferior vehicle" (Hīnayāna) that can take only one individual (oneself) across.[57]

And if we look at the sociological picture of Buddhist institutions in Asia and other areas of the world where Buddhist communities have established themselves, and if we also examine the psychological portrait projected by some individual practitioners of different forms of Buddhism in our contemporary world, we cannot dismiss this phenomenon of being preoccupied with one's own narrow religious circle, or being self-engrossed in one's individual religious practices to the neglect of compassion or concern for others, as only a phenomenon of the past. We do not go into specifics of this point here, and simply note that this is a pitfall to which any group or institution held together by shared religious ideals, or any individual who undertakes a religious pursuit, can readily succumb.

In an insightful essay on the structure of Buddhist praxis titled, "Ascent and Descent: Two-Directional Activity in Buddhist Thought,"[58] the late and renowned scholar Gadjin Nagao describes two movements in the Buddhist path of awakening. Briefly put, the *ascending phase* refers to the "aspect of going forth" toward the attainment of the religious ideal, whereby one pursues the path of religious praxis in following the precepts, engaging in sustained meditative practice, and so on. This path leads to Wisdom, which, in Mahāyāna terms, is the realization of Emptiness and its corollary, the interconnectedness of all phenomena. The *descending phase* is "the aspect of coming back," as the practitioner, moved by Great Compassion, returns to the world of living beings to help liberate sentient beings from their suffering, using all modes of skillful means appropriate to different situations. In this regard, the word "*Tathāgata*," an appellation often used referring to the Buddha, is highly significant, as it involves the two directions of *tathā-gata*, "thus gone" (to the other shore of liberation and of wisdom), and *tathā-āgata*, "thus having returned" or "thus come" (back to this side of the shore, moved by compassion, to help all sentient beings across). The notion of the bodhisattva, as one who foregoes entering into nirvana and remains in this earthly realm so as to be able to help alleviate the suffering of other sentient beings, set forth as the ideal of the Buddhist follower, enshrines Compassion as the dynamic core of Buddhist worldview and religious praxis.

Nagao concludes his essay with the observation that "unless religion contains the 'aspect of return,' it is still incomplete and imperfect. Unless concern is directed to the world once more, the ultimate goal of religion cannot be fulfilled."[59] Followers and leaders of the world's rich variety of religious traditions may also take this as a call for self-examination and reflection regarding their own role, and the role of their respective religious communities, vis-à-vis our contemporary global society. Adherents and practitioners of the different traditions of Buddhism may be able to make a significant contribution toward healing our fragile Earth community, wounded on many levels and further fractured by divisions reinforced by our religious differences, as they reclaim and activate this dynamic two-directional structure of their own religious praxis.[60]

Notes

1. This attitude is enshrined in the well-cited parable of the poisoned arrow, and the fourteen metaphysical questions on which the Buddha remained silent. See Ruben L. Habito, "The Silence of the Buddha," in *Experiencing Buddhism: Ways of Wisdom and Compassion* (Maryknoll, NY: Orbis Books, 2005), 62–66.
2. Buddhism is considered a nontheistic religion. It must be noted, however, that the Hindu cosmological framework inherited by the Buddha and his followers acknowledged or took for granted the existence of various kinds of divinities (*devā* or *devatā* in Sanskrit), entities said to inhabit a realm above the human, endowed with long life spans and wondrous superhuman powers. These divinities were regarded as deluded beings nonetheless, caught within the cycle of birth and death (*samsāra*) and thus in need of liberation just as humans and other forms of sentient beings.
3. Pure Land Buddhism, which we consider in the course of this essay, comes close to a theistic worldview with its central doctrine of the Buddha Amitābha as a universal savior. However, it does not regard the latter as a creator god, but as one who also exists as codependently arisen with all other beings, albeit one who has realized the fullness of enlightenment and has thus come to embody boundless compassion in action.
4. Pace Harvey Aronson, *Love and Sympathy in Theravāda Buddhism* (Delhi: Motilal Banarsidass, 1980), who translates *mettā* (Sanskrit: *maîtrī*), an *agapeic* or altruistic attitude, as "love."
5. John Templeton, *Pure Unlimited Love: An Eternal Creative Force and Blessing Taught by All Religions* (Philadelphia: Templeton Foundation Press, 2000), 3.
6. John Templeton, *Agape Love* (Philadelphia: Templeton Foundation Press, 1999), 1.
7. For this general survey, in the first section I rely on several excellent treatments on the theme of compassion in Buddhism, including Royal W. Weiler, "The Buddhist Act of Compassion," in *Indological Studies in Honor of W. Norman Brown*, ed. Ernest Bender (New Haven, CT: American Oriental Society, 1962), 238–50; Hajime Nakamura, *Jihi (Lovingkindness and Compassion)* [Japanese] (Kyoto, Japan: Sara Sosho, 1975); Aronson, *Love and Sympathy*; Tsong-ka-pa, *Compassion in Tibetan Buddhism*, ed. and trans. Jeffrey Hopkins (London: Rider, 1980); Elizabeth Harris, *Detachment and Compassion in Early Buddhism* (Kandy, Sri Lanka: Buddhist Publication Society, 1987), available online at http://www.accesstoinsight.org/lib/authors/harris/bl141.html (accessed May 1, 2009); Ok-Sun An, *Compassion and Benevolence: A Comparative Study of Early Buddhist and Classical Confucian Ethics* (New York: Peter Lang, 1998); Moti Lal Pandit, *Transcendence and Negation: A Study of Buddhist Compassion and Christian Love* (New Delhi: Munshiram Manoharlal, 1999); Gadjin M. Nagao, "The Bodhisattva's Compassion Described in the *Mahāyāna-sutrālamkāra*," in *Wisdom, Compassion, and the Search for Understanding*, ed. Jonathan Silk (Honolulu: University of Hawaii Press, 2000), 1–38; John W. Schroeder, *Skillful Means: The Heart of Buddhist Compassion*

(Honolulu: University of Hawaii Press, 2001); Taigen Leighton, *Faces of Compassion: Classic Bodhisattva Archetypes and Their Modern Expression* (Somerville, MA: Wisdom Publications, 2003); and others.

8. This refers to the story whereby, upon attaining enlightenment, the Buddha remained rapt in silence, in awe at the profundity of the experience, and, recognizing that ordinary beings could never comprehend this subtle and wondrous dharma, wanted to remain in that silence. Thereupon, it is said, the god Brahma Sahampatti appears and entreats the Buddha to reconsider, otherwise the dharma would then be lost to humanity forever. The Buddha then surveys the world of sentient beings with his awakened eyes, and, seeing their suffering, agrees to embark on the impossible task of conveying in words that which is ultimately beyond words. For a detailed treatment, see Gadjin M. Nagao, "The Silence of the Buddha and Its Madhyamic Interpretation," in *Mādhyamika and Yogācāra: A Study of Mahāyāna Philosophies*, trans. Leslie Kawamura (Albany: State University of New York Press, 1991), 35–49.
9. See Aronson, *Love and Sympathy*, for a detailed study on the theme; see also Ruben L. F. Habito, "Compassion and Wisdom: Buddhist Perspectives from the Past toward the Human Future," in *Altruism and Altruistic Love: Science, Philosophy, and Religion in Dialogue*, ed. Stephen Post, Lynn G. Underwood, Jeffrey P. Schloss, and William B. Hurlbut (New York: Oxford University Press, 2002), 362–75; see 363–65.
10. Nakamura, *Jihi*, 20.
11. The *Mahāprajnāpāramita-sāstra* (*Tachitu-lun*), an encyclopedic work that provides a compendium of Buddhist doctrine written in the early centuries of the common era, makes the summary statement that "Lovingkindness (Pāli: *mettā*; Sanskrit: *maîtrī*) and compassion (*karuṇā*) are the basis (Sanskrit: *mūla*, "root," "cause," "origin," "foundation") of the Buddha Way." See Etienne Lamotte, *La Traite de la Grande Vertu de Sagesse*, vol. 3 (Louvain, France: Bureau au Museon, 1970), 1711; and Nakamura, *Jihi*, 1.
12. *Life of the Buddha by Aśvaghosa. Buddhacarita. English and Sanskrit*, trans. Patrick Olivelle (New York: New York University Press, 2008), 402 (14:4, 9).
13. *The Sutta Nipāta, a Collection of Discourses Being One of the Canonical Books of the Buddhists*, trans. from the Pāli by V. Fausboll (New York: Scribner's, 1901), vv. 143–52.
14. Translation from the Pāli by the Amaravati Sangha, English Sangha Trust, 1994, http://www.accesstoinsight.org/tipitaka/kn/snp/snp.1.08.amar.html (accessed May 22, 2009).
15. Cited in Aronson, *Love and Sympathy*, 63–64.
16. B. Alan Wallace, *Boundless Heart: The Cultivation of the Four Immeasurables* (Ithaca, NY: Snow Lion, 1999).
17. Harris, *Detachment and Compassion in Early Buddhism*.
18. Gene Reeves, trans., *The Lotus Sutra* (Boston: Wisdom Publications, 2008), 103–39.
19. Peter Khoroche, trans., *Once the Buddha Was a Monkey: Ārya Śūra's Jātakamālā*, with a foreword by Wendy Doniger (Chicago: University of Chicago Press, 1989).
20. Har Dayal, *The Bodhisattva Doctrine in Sanskrit Literature* (1934; repr. Delhi: Motilal Banarsidass, 1970); and Leighton, *Faces of Compassion*.
21. The heart of the bodhisattva is given succinct expression in what came to be formulated and handed down as the Four Bodhisattva Vows, recited even today by Buddhist practitioners all over the world:

    Sentient beings are numberless. I vow to liberate them all.
    Delusions are inexhaustible. I vow to end them all.

The Dharma-gates are innumerable. I vow to master them all.

The Awakened Way is unsurpassable. I vow to accomplish and embody it.

22. Chün-fang Yü, *Kuan-yin: The Chinese Transformation of Avalokiteśvara* (New York: Columbia University Press, 2001).
23. Frederick Streng, *Emptiness: A Study in Religious Meaning* (Nashville: Abingdon Press, 1967); and C. W. Huntington Jr., *The Emptiness of Emptiness: An Introduction to Early Indian Madhyamika* (Honolulu: University of Hawaii Press, 1989).
24. The notion of Emptiness is a central theme expounded upon and further developed by Buddhist thinkers since Nāgārjuna (second to third century CE) and others after him, developed in the Mādhyamika and Yogācāra schools. The former pursued further the logical implications of Emptiness, and the latter made explicit the unfolding of Emptiness into Compassion. See Nagao, *Mādhyamika and Yogācāra*, 34.
25. Kate Crosby and Andrew Skilton, trans., *Śāntideva: The Bodhicaryāvatāra*, with a general introduction by Paul Williams (Oxford: Oxford University Press, 1996).
26. Geshe Yeshe Tobden, *The Way of Awakening: A Commentary on Shantideva's Bodhicaryavatara* (Boston: Wisdom Publications, 2005), 201–37.
27. Ruben L. F. Habito, "The Trikāya Doctrine in Buddhism," *Buddhist Christian Studies* 16 (1986): 53–62.
28. The first, Dharma Body (*Dharmakāya*) or Body of Truth, is Emptiness itself, unfathomable, immeasurable, beyond all form and shape, beyond and yet pervading all time and space, and realizing itself as Infinite Wisdom generating Boundless Compassion for all beings. The second, Enjoyment Body (*Sambhogha-kāya*) is the glorified form taken by this Wisdom flowing into Compassion, personified in the celestial and transhistorical Buddhas and bodhisattvas depicted in various Mahāyāna scriptures. These innumerable Buddhas and bodhisattvas ceaselessly work on behalf of all living beings throughout the universe from their respective Buddha-realms. The third, Transformation Body (*Nirmāna-kāya*), refers to the earthly emanations and manifestations sent forth from the first and/or second body, employing all kinds of skillful means to assist and liberate sentient beings in their various situations of suffering. From this threefold Buddha-body framework, the prince of the Śākya clan who renounced his status to become a wandering ascetic, who awakens to the Dharma and out of compassion goes on to teach it to others, is considered as one form of the Transformation Body who appeared in this earthly realm in the appropriate historical epoch and geographical region (that is, fifth-century northern India) as an emanation of Great Compassion. Many other beings on the path of enlightenment who work selflessly on behalf of others, the bodhisattvas and saints who inspire others to lead lives of similar dedication and service, are also considered as forms of this third kind of Buddha-body. In short, the Mahāyāna doctrine of the *Trikāya* is a highly systematized way of articulating the intimate connection between the Wisdom that has realized the truth of Emptiness, and the dynamic Great Compassion that arises out of this realization, working ceaselessly through all epochs of history and through all regions of this earthly realm toward the ultimate liberation of all beings.
29. See Tsong-ka-pa, *Compassion in Tibetan Buddhism*; and Guy Newland, *Compassion: A Tibetan Analysis—A Buddhist Monastic Textbook* (London: Wisdom Publications, 1984). This intimate connection between realizing Emptiness and the unleashing of compassion is conveyed in the following verse, cited in Newland, *Compassion*, 19:

If you and the world wish to gain the highest enlightenment

Its roots are an altruistic aspiration to enlightenment

That is firm as the king of mountains,
Compassion reaching in all directions,
And a wisdom consciousness not relying on duality.

30. The Dalai Lama is regarded by Tibetan Buddhist followers as an incarnation of Chenrezig.
31. Maria Dorothea Reis Habito, *Die Dhāraṇī des Grossen Erbarmens des Bodhisattva Avalokiteśvara mit tausend Händen und Augen*, Monumenta Serica Monograph Series 27 (Nettetal, Germany: Steyler Verlag/Sankt Augustin, 1990).
32. Cited in Maria Reis Habito, "Putting on the Armour of Great Compassion and Becoming Buddha in This Very Body: Compassionate Love in East Asian Esoteric Traditions," in *Love in Esoteric Traditions*, Eranos Conference Papers, ed. Lawrence Sullivan (forthcoming).
33. Habito, *Experiencing Buddhism*, highlights these two elements of Wisdom and Compassion and their interplay in the historical development of Buddhist traditions.
34. Five major forms of contemporary Buddhism are Theravāda, Tibetan/Tantric, Lotus, Pure Land, and Zen. The second part of this essay devotes attention to the last three mentioned. Theravāda and Tibetan Buddhism deserve much more detailed treatment than can be offered here. For further treatment of Theravāda Buddhist practice in contemporary context as transmitted to the West in the form of Insight or Vipassana meditation and as related to our theme, see Wallace, *Boundless Heart*, and Jack Kornfield, *A Path with Heart: A Guide through the Spiritual Path with Its Perils and Promises* (New York: Bantam Books, 1993), among many others. For Tibetan Buddhist practice, see Tsong-ka-pa, *Compassion in Tibetan Buddhism*; Newland, *Compassion*; Tenzin Gyatso (The Fourteenth Dalai Lama), *The Compassionate Life* (Boston: Wisdom Publications, 2001); Tobden, *Way of Awakening*; and John Makransky, *Awakening to Love* (Boston: Wisdom Publications, 2007).
35. For concise chapter-length descriptions of Lotus, Pure Land, and Zen Buddhism, with bibliographical listings, see Habito, *Experiencing Buddhism*, chaps. 8, 7, and 5, respectively.
36. Ruben L. F. Habito, "Bodily Reading of the Lotus Sutra," in *Readings of the Lotus Sutra*, ed. Stephen F. Teiser and Jacqueline I. Stone (New York: Columbia University Press, 2009).
37. From the *Showa Teihon Nichiren Shōnin Ibun* (critical edition of Nichiren's writings, henceforth, *Teihon*) (Tokyo: Risshō Daigaku Nichiren Kyōgaku Kenkyūsho, 1968), 1:720 (my translation).
38. The notion that "All sentient beings are endowed with Buddha nature," which became a key feature in the development of major forms of East Asian Buddhism, finds its backgrounds in this notion of the seed of enlightenment as embedded in all sentient beings, and the depiction of all sentient beings as children of the Buddha as seen in the Lotus Sutra.
39. *Teihon*, 1:712. "The Śākyamuni within our hearts and minds is the Ancient Buddha since beginningless time manifested as the Three Bodies."
40. Ibid., 2:1844.
41. See David Machacek and Brian Wilson, *Global Citizens: The Soka Gakkai Buddhist Movement in the World* (New York: Oxford University Press, 2000); see also issues of *Dharma World*, a quarterly published by the Rissho Kosei Kai for international distribution.
42. For an excellent treatment of these three groups, see Jacqueline Stone, "Nichiren's

Activist Heirs—Sōka Gakkai, Risshō Kōseikai, Nipponzan Myōhōji," in *Action Dharma: New Studies in Engaged Buddhism*, ed. Christopher Queen, Charles Prebish, and Damien Keown (London: Curzon, 2003), 63–94. Other groups include the traditional Nichiren-shū and its tributaries in Japan; the Reiyūkai; and the small group of activist Buddhist priests who joined the International Network of Engaged Buddhists headed by Ven. Maruyama Teruo, among others. For the latter, see Habito, *Experiencing Buddhism*, 156.

43. Nichidatsu Fujii, *Buddhism for World Peace*, trans. Yumiko Miyazaki (Tokyo: Japan-Bharat Sarvodaya Mitrata Sangha, 1982).
44. Hisao Inagaki, trans., *The Three Pure Land Sutras, translated from the Chinese*, in collaboration with Harold Stewart (Kyoto, Japan: Nagata Bunshodō, 1994).
45. Cited in Taitetsu Unno, *River of Fire, River of Water: An Introduction to the Pure Land Tradition of Shin Buddhism* (New York: Doubleday, 1998), 22–23.
46. Alfred Bloom, ed., *Living in Amida's Universal Vow: Essays in Shin Buddhism* (Bloomington, IN: World Wisdom, 2004).
47. *Tannishō* No. 5, trans. Taitetsu Unno, available online at http://www.livingdharma.org/Tannisho/TannishoChaptersI-X.html (accessed May 22, 2009).
48. Shinran's pivotal religious experience is associated with the Bodhisattva Kannon (Kuan-yin), who appeared to him in a dream and gave him an overwhelming assurance of being embraced in Great Compassion. Shinran considers the feminine figure of Kannon to be an emanation of Amida Buddha himself, following a popular tradition to this effect. See Donald W. Mitchell, *Buddhism: Introducing the Buddhist Experience* (New York: Oxford University Press, 2002), 254–62.
49. "Zen" is the Japanese pronunciation for a Chinese ideogram pronounced *Ch'an*, in turn used to render the Sanskrit word *dhyāna*, or *dhyān*, referring to a state of deep absorption in meditative practice. We use the Japanese term "Zen" for this essay.
50. There are now a good number of scholarly treatments of this form of Buddhism, elucidating its historical developments and demythologizing some of its triumphal claims. Among those deserving mention are Bernard Faure, *The Rhetoric of Immediacy: A Cultural Critique of Chan/Zen Buddhism* (Princeton, NJ: Princeton University Press, 1991), and John McRae, *Seeing through Zen: Encounter, Transformation, and Genealogy in Chinese Chan Buddhism* (Berkeley: University of California Press, 2003).
51. Ruben L. F. Habito, *Healing Breath: Zen for Christians and Buddhists in a Wounded World* (Boston: Wisdom Publications, 2006), 19–89.
52. *Emmei Juku Kannon-gyō* (in English translation):

    Kanzeon, Homage to Buddha
    Buddha directly endowing Buddha, Buddha indirectly endowing Buddha
    Buddha, Dharma, Sangha in a Circle of Perfection
    Pure, Blissful, True Self, Abiding
    Morning Mind Kanzeon, Evening Mind Kanzeon
    This very moment Mind Kanzeon, Never let it go.

53. Tenzin Gyatso, *Essence of the Heart Sutra* (Boston: Wisdom Publications, 2002).
54. Habito, *Healing Breath*, 30–35.
55. John Paul II, *Crossing the Threshold of Hope*, ed. Vittorio Messori (New York: Alfred A. Knopf, 1994), 85–86.
56. Mitchell, *Buddhism*, 96–125.
57. As noted earlier, it was in this context of reacting to the narrow view of those intent only on their individual liberation and thus becoming self-absorbed in the process that

the Buddha's own life and teaching came to be seen in a new light. Having been preceded by countless rebirths through many lives as a bodhisattva, a being on the path of enlightenment motivated by compassion, Siddhārtha Gautama's birth in this earthly realm came to be regarded as a manifestation of Great Compassion that flows out of the wisdom of enlightenment attained in aeons past. See Patrick Olivelle, trans., *Life of the Buddha by Asvaghosa: Buddhacarita—English and Sanskrit* (New York: New York University Press, 2008), Canto 14, 402–13.

58. Nagao, *Mādhyamika and Yogācāra*, 201–7.
59. Ibid., 207.
60. What is referred to as "socially engaged Buddhism," a recently coined term but now acknowledged as having continuities to movements and traditions across epochs and across continents in the different forms of Buddhism, provides concrete historical examples wherein this two-directional activity in religious praxis is embodied. See Fred Eppsteiner, ed., *The Path of Compassion: Writings on Socially Engaged Buddhism* (Berkeley, CA: Parallax Press, 1988); Christopher Queen and Sallie King, eds., *Engaged Buddhism: Buddhist Liberation Movements in Asia* (Albany: State University of New York Press, 1996); Mary Evelyn Tucker and Duncan Williams, eds., *Buddhism and Ecology* (Cambridge, MA: Harvard University Press, 1997); David Chappell, ed., *Buddhist Peacework: Creating Cultures of Peace* (Boston: Wisdom Publications, 1999); Christopher Queen, ed., *Engaged Buddhism in the West* (Boston: Wisdom Publications, 2000); Queen, Prebish, and Keown, *Action Dharma*; Ken Jones, *The New Social Face of Buddhism* (Boston: Wisdom Publications, 2003); David Loy, *The Great Awakening: A Buddhist Social Theory* (Boston: Wisdom Publications, 2003); David Chappell, ed., *Socially Engaged Buddhism: Essays in Honor of Sulak Sivaraksa on His 70th Birthday* (Bangkok: Sathirakoses-Nagapradipa Foundation, 2003); Susan Moon, ed., *Not Turning Away: The Practice of Engaged Buddhism* (Boston: Shambhala, 2004); among others.

5 God as Infinite Love

A Roman Catholic Perspective

David Tracy

Infinite Love in the New Testament: A Catholic Theological Reading[1]

The New Testament renders the Invisible God visible for Christians through the words, deeds, and destiny—that is, the passion, cross, and Resurrection—of Jesus of Nazareth proclaimed to be the Christ. Through Jesus Christ and in the Spirit, Christians are led to experience and understand God as Infinite Love. The culmination of that New Testament proclamation is the first letter of John 4:7–8: "Beloved, let us love one another, because love is from God; everyone who loves is born of God and knows God. Whoever does not love does not know God, for God is love."[2]

As we shall see below, this famous Johannine proclamation, "God is love," gives rise to many diverse Christian theologies, philosophies, and spiritual and mystical ways of life focused on God's Infinite Love. It is essential, therefore, to understand that 1 John's "God is love" is not an abstract statement, although many theologies have rightly emerged over the centuries from John's "God is love." First John is best read as a commentary on the Gospel of John, the gospel of love. John's Gospel—the most meditative, at times mystical, the most symbolic and theological of the four Gospels—can itself be read as a meditation in the Wisdom tradition on the life and destiny of the Jesus portrayed less symbolically in the more realistic narrative genres in Mark, Matthew, and Luke.

The Synoptic Gospels, each in a distinct way, portray Jesus' love over and over—especially Jesus' love for the rejected and marginalized of his society. In all three Synoptics the love of Jesus and the love Jesus commands and empowers is love as excess. God's infinite love is excessive. God's infinite love empowers human beings to love excessively not only one's family, one's own people, but everyone, anyone—the neighbor. Nietzsche was entirely correct to insist that the Christian love of neighbor (which he considered both humanly impossible as well as nonaristocratic, i.e., for the weak, not the strong), was *the* transvaluation of all ancient values. As Aristotle, for example, makes clear, friendship (*philia*) with one's equal is the highest form of love (*eros*) for the Greeks. Hence, following the Greeks, Nietzsche's Zarathustra declares (to paraphrase), "I preach the friend not the neighbor."[3] On the contrary, Jesus preaches love of the neighbor.

The understanding that God is love and the resultant double command to love God and neighbor is, of course, already present in the Hebrew Bible itself: implicitly in its basic narratives, God's loving covenant with Israel, and in central passages on the love command in Deuteronomy, Leviticus, Jeremiah, Second Isaiah, the Song of Songs, and elsewhere. As a Jew, Jesus already knew the ancient command to love God and neighbor.

Jesus, in all three Synoptics, commands and empowers love as excess—the love of every neighbor, at the limit, the love of enemy. By contrast, the Gospel of John is the Wisdom Gospel where divine *Logos* becomes incarnate as Love. Wisdom yields to Love in John because in the life, words, and destiny of the Incarnate One, Jesus the Christ, one finally understands clearly what we all sense inchoately and hesitantly: God is love and thereby we now can become capable through God's grace to be those commanded and empowered to love.

In the Gospel of John, God's love is portrayed principally as relational and reciprocal. This Johannine reading of love as profoundly relational is in no way a lessening of the Synoptic understanding of love as excess. Rather, the love of Jesus Christ, the Incarnate One in John, frees one to understand that "God so loved the world that he gave his only Son, so that everyone who believes in him may not perish but may have eternal life."[4] In the Incarnation, John's *Logos* becomes Incarnate Love and, by that means, John implicitly joins the more explicitly excessive—that is, kenotic—language of the great hymn in Paul's Philippians:

> Let the same mind be in you that was in Christ Jesus,
> who, though he was in the form of God,
> did not regard equality with God as something to be exploited,
> but emptied himself, taking the form of a slave,
> being born in human likeness.
> And being found in human form,
> he humbled himself and became obedient to the point of
> death—even death on a cross.[5]

It is important to consider, too, how markedly different each Gospel account of the love of Jesus is. In Mark, one finds an often troubled but fiercely loving Jesus as apocalyptic prophet in a strange and unsettling narrative. Mark's Gospel, almost like a postmodern text, is more fragmentary than continuous; it seems to end in fear and deep confusion as the women flee the tomb in what is the first ending: "So they went out and fled from the tomb, for terror and amazement had seized them; and they said nothing to anyone, for they were afraid."[6] Mark's Gospel alone portrays the disciples as seeming to understand Jesus far less than the marginal figures do—the poor and the rejected. Even the demons in Mark's Gospel sense the terrifying uniqueness of the love preached and lived by this disturbing Markan apocalyptic Jesus more than his own disciples. Everything in Mark seems fragmentary, disjointed, paratactic, unnerving. In Mark, Jesus' love is fierce and excessive.

The Gospel register shifts almost completely with the Jesus of the Gospel of Luke. Luke's Jesus is portrayed not as an apocalyptic figure, but as a prophet who acts and speaks with clarity. In Luke, for example, unlike Mark, the disciples of Jesus understand that a new reality has arrived in their midst—the reign of God preached by this Jesus through his words and actions. Luke, more like John than Mark, shows the reign of God as not yet fully here but already begun in the words and deeds of this prophet Jesus. Luke's Jesus speaks and acts with clear speech, like such classical prophets as Amos, Hosea, and Isaiah. The Lukan Jesus both speaks lucidly and acts with directness. Luke's Jesus shows a sense of purpose that no one can miss. Moreover, in the parables of Luke's Jesus, one finds some of the greatest parables of love, such as the Good Samaritan and the Prodigal Son. In Luke, God's love for us—like the love of the Father for the prodigal's return—is overwhelming and without limit, that is, infinite. In Luke, the

Good Samaritan (a paradoxical choice for true neighbor-love for an ancient Jew) displays the kind of love for *any* other, any and every neighbor.

Moreover, Luke, unlike Mark, wants and achieves a more continuous, more Greek, and less fragmentary narrative. This does not mean that Luke wrote a sanguine narrative. His Jesus, like the ancient prophets, is clear but deeply unsettling. For example, as a creative narrator, Luke does not hesitate to change even the geography of ancient Palestine for the purposes of his narrative—that is, Jesus must fulfill his destiny by moving steadily and ineluctably to his "fated place," Jerusalem, no matter the geography involved.

In Luke, moreover, one finds the clearest portrayal of Jesus' actions for the poor. This will later become what modern Catholics call the "option for the poor." The International Synod of Bishops, in 1970, insisted that the option for the poor is not an addition to the Christian gospel of love but is at the very heart of the Christian Gospels. This is a modern version of a Lukan emphasis. The modern Catholic is called not just to love interpersonally, but to love by means of changing unjust structures that so damage the poor. Christians are called not simply to "charity" but are called to love by attempting to change unjust social structures and to aid in the development of a more just society. The contemporary Catholic recognition that charity cannot be separated from justice, nor justice from love, is a major modern development of Luke's option for the poor. Furthermore, in Luke's Acts, one also discovers that love is also social, communal, and ecclesial, never merely individualistic. In Acts, one finds a radical communal sharing of goods in the ancient Christian community—an almost forgotten tradition of communal love through justice. The new Christian base communities, especially in Latin America and Africa, are renewed attempts at a more communal Christianity, especially like that described in Acts. The call of Vatican II to replace the very hierarchical "perfect society" model for the church and to develop the "people of God" model was encouraging. Certainly, much more needs to be done in terms of reform of Roman Catholic institutional structures (still, in my judgment, too hierarchical, clerical, and reified) to embody a more communal church of loving *koinonia*. This need for institutional reform is especially so when one observes the role of women in the church. Here the contrast between the prominent role of women in the ancient church and today is stunning—and clearly calls for radical reform of present structures.

In the Gospel of Matthew, the social and communal, even institutional, character of Christian love is central. It is no surprise to discover that Matthew was the most influential Gospel for the early centuries of Christianity. Only in Matthew (the most Jewish of the Gospels) does one find such insistent attention to the needs of the early Christian community for institutional forms, legal regulations, and shared doctrines. In Matthew, Jesus is sometimes portrayed as the new Moses, teaching the prospective leaders of the new community. Matthew's Jesus preaches his Sermon on the Mount to the disciples alone. This is in direct contrast to Luke's portrayal of the Sermon on the Plain as preached not only to the disciples on a mountain but to everyone who can come and hear him on an open plain. Throughout his Gospel, Matthew provides the new community with needed institutional, legal, and doctrinal guides.

Matthew's institutional interests, although prominent, are not determinative of his Gospel. The heart of Matthew's Gospel is God's excessive love for us as disclosed in Jesus Christ and continued in the new community. Catholic love is always also social, thus ecclesial. Catholic communal love must also precisely as the community of love have just structures and laws, thus the need for never-ending ecclesial reform (Vatican II). Matthew's Gospel is structured around the role of his "great discourses." Each of those discourses in Matthew is followed by the increasing misunderstanding by the listeners until the tragically inevitable passion and cross. The Sermon on the Mount[7] is such an extraordinary text that Tolstoy was right to insist that it exposes forever the delusions and lies in our intractable egotisms. From the Sermon on the Mount to the last great discourse[8] just prior to Jesus' passion and death, Matthew presents discourse after discourse as Jesus tries unsuccessfully to reach the people—from the enormous optimism in the Sermon on the Mount to the resigned and angry cry of Matthew 25 and its call for actions for the poor, the sick, and outcasts.

Matthew 25 is even more striking coming from Matthew himself, the evangelist most concerned with ecclesial structures and doctrines. Matthew clearly does not yield on his structural and doctrinal concerns, but he does insist with a passion as moving as it is surprising in all the great discourses structuring his Gospel that the final Christian word is love.

The word-action, discourse-rejection structure of Matthew's Gospel is rather similar to the word-action structure of Dostoevsky's *Brothers Karamazov*.[9] Every great Jesuanic discourse in Matthew is followed by an increasingly tragic failure of response by his listeners until the final discourse whose word is action.

To sense the amazing mixture of discourse and action in Matthew, compare Matthew's Sermon on the Mount with the almost desperate call to help the poor, the imprisoned, the sick, and the naked that seems to suggest that the great idealistic and optimistic hopes of the Sermon on the Mount seem smashed at this point in the Matthean narrative by the rejection of that hope by so many then and now. To read both the Sermon on the Mount and Matthew 25 is to begin to grasp the fuller dialectic of Christian calls to love.

The Gospel of John has been justly called the Gospel of love.[10] As Augustine said about the Gospel, give me a lover and she or he will understand. In reading John, we can understand why John is a unique Wisdom text where wisdom yields to love without ever ceasing to be wisdom. In the prologue itself, Wisdom-*Logos* has become incarnate. For John, the incarnate *Logos* is manifested in a symbolic narrative disclosing the words, deeds, and destiny of the Incarnate One as love.

This iconic text employs motifs of light-darkness and love-hate in a rhythmic movement that becomes like a musical oratorio. John is unlike the realistic narrative of Luke, unlike the fragmentary apocalyptic narrative of Mark, unlike Matthew's discourse-action narrative. In the Gospel of John—in both the first thirteen chapters of the book of signs and the passion-cross-Resurrection final chapters of the book of glory—every historical action and word of Jesus can be read as disclosing an underlying motif: God's love as triune. Love in John is not so much excess but love as mutually reciprocal relationality among persons in the new community. These new reciprocal human loves are, for John, implicitly grounded in trinitarian mutual and reciprocal relations of Father, Son, and Holy Spirit. Precisely because God *is* love (as 1 John renders explicit for the Johannine community), God, in John, is implicitly trinitarian: Lover-Beloved and the Love uniting them—what the later tradition will name three divine persons as distinct relations of love to the other two.

Only John would see the cross so differently. Ordinarily the cross is the inexplicable and terrifying mystery of the self-sacrificial love of the crucified God proclaimed by Paul, the other great New Testament theologian. But, unlike Paul, even the lifting up of Christ on the cross, mysterious and painful—that stark torturous reality—is in John a manifestation of God's glory. For John, the lifting up of Jesus on the cross displays God's Infinite Love as the glory of the Incarnate Crucified One. Moreover, as many later mystics (like Angela of Foligno) and later theologians (like Pope Benedict

XVI in his splendid encyclical *God Is Love*[11]) note, even the piercing of Christ's side on the cross in John releases an overflowing love.

Like Paul in the hymn of Philippians (cited earlier), John's portrait of God can also be read as a kenotic, loving Christ emptying himself of the forms of God and taking on the form of a slave even unto death on the cross. So great is God's Infinite Love for John as for Paul that despite their very different theologies of the cross they finally harmonize. John and Paul, the first great Christian theologians, show not a dialectical clash but a coincidence of opposites on God's manifested Infinite Love in Jesus the Christ the Incarnate One (John) and God's love excessively manifested in the terrifying scandal of the crucified God (Paul).

What unites John and Paul in this New Testament coincidence of opposites is their joint conviction of God's Infinite Love manifested decisively (John) and dialectically (Paul) in Jesus Christ from his kenotic Incarnation to his kenotic passion and crucifixion until, for both of them, one witnesses the very triumph of love in Resurrection.

The four Gospels as well as Paul (along with some of the noncanonical gospels and other early Christian texts) are good news announcing and disclosing the impossible: the final truth about reality is love and God's infinite love disclosed in all in excessiveness in the self-sacrificing love of the Synoptic accounts of the words, action, and destiny of Jesus the Christ. That same truth is displayed as the mutual reciprocity of the relations of Infinite Love of the Trinity moving like a haunting refrain beneath and within all the icons and rhythms of the symbolic, meditative, and at times mystical text of the Gospel of John. In Paul's two letters to the Corinthians, moreover, we learn the next truth: neither faith nor hope, central as they are for Christian life, lasts forever. Only love is eternal:

> Love never ends. But as for prophecies, they will come to an end; as for tongues they will cease; as for knowledge, it will come to an end. For we know only in part; but when the complete comes, the partial will come to an end. When I was a child, I spoke like a child; when I became an adult, I put an end to childish ways. For now we see in a mirror, dimly, but then we will see face to face. Now I know only in part; then I will know fully, even as I have been fully known. And now faith, hope, and love abide, these three; and the greatest of these is love.[12]

This amazing New Testament vision of the ultimate reality as infinite, overflowing, personal love (not only the impersonal Good of the Platonist philosophers) can still stun any sensitive reader or listener. Such a vision is a vision of what some contemporary philosophers and theologians call the Impossible—the Impossible rendered not merely possible but actual in this unsubstitutable Jesus the Christ, the decisive manifestation of the infinitely loving God.

The infinite love of God narrated in the life of Jesus of Nazareth is seen for what it is: a fascinating, at times terrifying, love narrative. The Gospels proclaim in different narrative forms the good news that, despite all appearances to the contrary, God is love. In that gospel light, Christians embrace anew through Christ the love of God and neighbor earlier manifested in the Hebrew Bible. Christians read the Hebrew Bible in love as their First or Old Testament by reading over the shoulders, as it were, of their Jewish mentors. Both traditions are later joined by the third great monotheistic tradition, Islam, with its splendid call, "*Allah akbar*"—God is great, God is the all-merciful One. All three traditions try to live by the love of God and neighbor grounded in the Infinite Love of the God whose worship they share. All three hear the cry of Jeremiah's God: "'I have loved you with an eternal love."[13]

Such divine Infinite Love unnerves one as one realizes that in such light one's own egotism has been exposed in all its unlovely, unloving actuality.

In that sense, the first letter of John sums up not only John but the whole Bible. In fact, unlike 2 John and 3 John, 1 John is not really a letter but a commentary somewhat haphazardly composed. First John contains rather obscure and unattractive polemics against a secessionist community (part one of the letter) alongside the most amazing grace-filled and sublime statements in the whole Bible. A sample of the latter:

> Beloved, let us love one another, because love is from God; everyone who loves is born of God and knows God. Whoever does not love does not know God, for God is love. God's love was revealed among us in this way: God sent his only Son into the world so that we might live through him. In this is love, not that we loved God but that he loved us and sent his Son to be the atoning sacrifice for our sins. Beloved, since God loved us so much, we also ought to love one another. No one has ever

> seen God; if we love one another, God lives in us, and his love is perfected in us.[14]

Human Love: Augustine's *Caritas* Synthesis and the Catholic Tradition of Love[15]

For all Christians, the Bible is the foundation of all genuinely Christian reflection. Karl Rahner aptly named the Bible "*norma normans sed non normata*" (the norm that norms all other norms and is not normed by them).[16] Furthermore, for Augustine in *On Christian Doctrine*, the principal norm for interpreting the Bible is love of God and love of neighbor.[17] Indeed, Augustine, more than any other theologian in Western Christianity, is the great proponent of the major Catholic model for human love gifted by the grace of God: love as *caritas*.

Augustine's description of love or *caritas* is not uncontroversial among Christian theologians. For example, in the twentieth century, the Lutheran theologian Anders Nygren in his famous book *Agape and Eros* insisted against Augustine that God's love as divine *agape* (pure gift from God) could not but be in conflict with love as *eros* (for Nygren an acquisitive and therefore egocentric love; for Augustine a yearning for happiness and the good).[18] Augustine related *agape* to *eros* in his *caritas* synthesis. For Nygren, that Augustinian understanding of *caritas* was deeply wrong. On one empirical fact, Nygren is right: when Catholics (including the present writer) speak of Christian love they speak of *caritas*. For example, Benedict XVI's encyclical in the official Latin text is not entitled *Deus est Agape* but *Deus est Caritas*. This is a revealing choice. It suggests that Benedict XVI, like the early Greek fathers, like Augustine and practically the entire Catholic tradition, understands that God as Infinite Love is also both *agape* and *eros*—that is, *caritas*.

What, then, does the Augustinian understanding of love as *caritas* mean? For Augustine, *caritas* is the transformation of *eros* by God's gift-grace of unearned *agape* to become *caritas*—that is, a Christian love that affirms our basic drive-will-desire for truth, happiness, and the good while transforming our graced natural desire with the overwhelming unexpected gift-grace of God's Infinite Love disclosed in Jesus Christ. *Caritas* can help heal our twisted egotistical desires and turn them to love of God and neighbor. Such turning perfects our natural desire to love and to know. In Augustine, the

Catholic emphasis on nature-grace ("Grace does not destroy nature, but perfects it"[19]) is not divided from the Reformation emphasis on sin-grace. Both traditions rightly appeal to Augustine. The Catholic tradition does so by accepting Augustine's transformative model of love as *caritas*.

Augustine is also central in Western philosophy. Indeed, Augustine is the first philosopher to elaborate a concept of will as the central reality for understanding the self. And yet there is not really a systematic definition of will in this philosopher of will. Like Augustine's own famously restless will as self-described in the *Confessions*,[20] Augustine's understandings of will move here and there depending on context: sometimes straight ahead, more often restlessly digressing in its exact meaning as different issues come forward—consent, free will, the double command of love of God and neighbor, the two loves (*caritas* and *cupiditas*) defining individuals and whole cultures (the two cities of his *City of God*[21]).

Some discussion of Augustine on the will has too often been distracted by attempts to render into a single coherent statement his differing, highly contextual reflections on free will. The fact is Augustine shifts his views on will from his early work *De Libero Arbitrio*[22] to his later, more pessimistic anti-Pelagian writings. To be sure, Augustine maintained in his late *Retractions*[23] that Pelagius and Julian had no right to appeal to his early discussion of free will as evidence against his later, much bleaker reflections on free will. But in fact Pelagius and Julian of Eclanum did have a point. At the same time, their point becomes at best minor because of their fatal failure to understand Augustine's profound philosophical and theological reflections on the will. Augustine's reflections on will move into a dimension of the self that Pelagius's relatively untroubled, moralistic notion of the self's will and our moral faults (sins), rather than our fundamental disorientation, cannot grasp. In modern psychoanalytic terms, there is no unconscious in Pelagius, whereas the unconscious in all its conflictual, teeming, fierce actuality is everywhere in Augustine. Augustine speaks, like Freud, of the reality of infant greed, not innocence; of slips of the tongue; and, above all, of the importance of dreams. Dreams for Freud are the royal road to the unconscious; dreams for Augustine (here very much a North African of his period) are the royal road to some glimpse of an affect-laden experience of that other power, the unconscious will, that drives all our desires, will, love.

"*Pondus meum, amor meus.*" My love is my weight. Love draws me up like the flame or pulls me down like the falling rock. Love attracts me irresistibly forward like a magnet. We "fall" in love. We "are" in love. Even more than Plato in his *Symposium*, Augustine emphasized the power of beloved objects to attract us like a magnet: the fleshly bodies of others, the spirited intellects of beautiful souls, the night sky, the North African sun, the breeze from the sea into his seaport city of Hippo. At the same time, the wrong kinds of love—possessive, egocentric loves—trap us. As Luther, following Augustine, insisted, our self-love tries to escape our ego but cannot. Without grace, the ego curves back upon itself and finds no exit from itself: the ego is "*curvatus in se*" constantly curved in upon itself.[24] For this ego there is no genuine other, no genuine God, no actual neighbor, no authentic self. Yet it is important here to insist that for Augustine there are also real human loves: the satisfaction of understanding driven by the *desire* to know, the beauty present like a magnet in nature and the arts, especially music. Indeed, for Augustine, a kind of proto-Romantic on music, music affected him so deeply that he allowed it in church rituals but always feared its power to move him so deeply. Above all, for Augustine there are the four great loves that constitute the self: love of God, love of neighbor, love of self, and love of body. All four are grounded in the grace of the Infinitely Loving God revealed in Jesus Christ.

For Augustine we do not even rightly understand unless we love. Understanding is ultimately driven by desire, by love. Love's affections are central dimensions to all understanding. The affections, therefore, are not a pleasant addition to nor a distraction from understanding. Love, like faith and hope, is driven to understand: *Fides quaerens intellectum* is also *amor quaerens intellectum*. Augustine could easily have said what his later disciple, Gregory the Great, said so well: "*Ipse notitia amor est*" (Love is itself knowledge).[25]

In Augustine, the will does not merely choose and consent. The will wills. The will, ever active, cannot but will. The will—both as conscious love as well as preconscious and unconscious desire and drive—cannot help willing. If the will has been transformed by grace into *caritas* love, the will then wills with true freedom for Augustine. The will drives to a proper understanding of the really real. Without affections, understanding is paper-thin.[26] If faith does not work through love,[27] then the fundamental trust and understanding of faith becomes merely cognitive belief. As Martin Luther insisted, even Satan believes in God.[28] But Satan does not believe-trust-love-hope in God. Without love, there is no real understanding. With love as in ordinary human loves, we see better—more clearly, understandably, charitably. For Augustine, as for the earlier Plotinus whom Augustine revered, we understand the ultimately Real by turning inward into the self.

On his journey within, Augustine did not find the serene, divinelike self discovered by Plotinus. Instead Augustine found a self that was a fascinating and terrifying abyss. The abyss of the self for Augustine was alive with intelligence and love as well as seething with disordered passions, disturbing affections for false beloved objects, and ever-shifting, unceasingly restless moods. "The human heart is an abyss";[29] since "the human being is a vast deep . . . the hairs of our heads are easier far to number than are our feelings, and the movements of the heart."[30]

By his highly original reflections on will and the self, Augustine seems less a conversation partner to his fellow ancient philosophers than he is a contemporary of Schopenhauer and Nietzsche. If the Ultimately Real is will (for Schopenhauer) or will to power (for Nietzsche), one can also say that the Ultimately Real for Augustine is also will: not Nietzsche's will to power driving all reality without beginning or end or purpose (the void). Will, for Augustine, is, to be sure, before and beyond intelligence as driving energy. However, the fundamental energy of will displayed in God's Infinite Love in the Incarnation and cross is the will to love. The Augustinian will to love possesses a created beginning, an eschatological future, and a tense present. Will has purpose given as gift from God who is Infinite Love and Intelligence, creating, sustaining, and redeeming all.

Not surprisingly, Nietzsche's every reference to Augustine is negative, yet Augustine is Nietzsche's unwanted predecessor on the centrality of will in life and understanding. Nietzsche could easily have said of Augustine what he said about one of the most brilliant and satisfying of Augustinians in the West, Blaise Pascal: "He is in our blood."[31] Augustine, the master of the centrality of will, has himself become one of the driving forces of Western philosophy and theology of any understanding of the power of our affections, desire, loves, and will for knowledge itself. "*Ama et fac quod vis,*" Augustine dared to say. "Love, and do what thou wilt."[32] Augustine's influence on Catholic thought on love as *caritas* is unmatched: Gregory the Great, William of St. Thierry, Bernard, the Victorines, Angela of Foligno, Mechtild of Magdeburg, indeed all love mystics; Bonaventure ("*bonum diffusivum sui*"), Dante ("*L'amor che muove il sole et l'altre stelle*"), the Love-saturated Teresa of Avila who called Augustine's *Confessions* her second scripture, John Donne ("Lord, lest thou enslave me I can ne'er be free, nor chaste unless thou ravish me"), Pascal ("*Le coeur a ses raisons que la raison ne connait point*"). The list could easily be expanded. The Augustinian synthesis on love is the Catholic *caritas* synthesis—that is, *agape* transforming but not rejecting *eros*.

The will wills. Desire drives intellect forward. Love cannot but love. Love as gift cannot be caught in the economy of exchange. Intelligence-in-act and will as love: these two realities are so interwoven in Augustine that they can be distinguished but never separated. However, another reality—sin—enters the Augustinian interweaving of intelligence and love to darken and becloud knowledge and to twist the will away from its natural desire to love the Good. Sin, both personal and original, invades the Augustinian self. The will becomes not only weak and fragile (as will always was for Augustine), but twisted and hardened by false desires, calcified addictions, and sick habits. Long before the Pelagian controversy, Augustine began to fear that something was disturbingly awry about the self—however intelligent, however loving the self naturally is: no wonder his youthful attraction to Manicheanism and its focus on the issue of evil. Reading Paul focused this discontent for the convert Augustine in words he felt directly addressed to him: "The good that I would do that I do not; the evil I would not do, that I do."[33]

Why does this Pauline portrait of our state become Augustine's obsession? Without ever abandoning the Platonic model of an intelligent-loving self we have described thus far, another Augustinian self surfaced in his attempts to understand the abyss of the self. That tragic Augustinian self is related not in a community of neighbor love and love of God but a community that shares a solidarity-in-sin (Augustine's "original sin"). We are a *massa peccati*. On this matter the older Augustine was sometimes driven to extremes in his fierce polemical exchange with Julian of Eclanum. At one point, he even endorsed double predestination—a theological position so harsh and, to me, unreal that Augustine was forced (unlike his Greek Christian contemporaries) to deny any literal meaning to biblical hopes of universal salvation proclaimed in 1 Timothy 2:14. Read Augustine's tortured reading of that text: the kind of desperate reading of a clear scriptural passage that he earlier mocked in the Manicheans and Donatists on other texts. One finds with sorrow that Augustine, this brilliant reader of texts, was at times himself driven by conflicting feelings, passions, emotions, and motives that both helped and, at times, hindered his readings. So are we all.

Any Christian can easily become overwhelmed by the massive personal and social sin in our history: consider the evils of the last century alone. We also cannot avoid the sufferings caused by tragic necessities in nature. The saving, healing faith in God as Infinite Love is ultimately a Christian's basic faith. That basic faith is always challenged by the evil and sin in history and the intense sufferings caused by nature (earthquakes, tsunamis, diseases of all kinds). With Augustine, Christians do not claim, as the Manicheans did, to solve the mystery of evil, the tragedy of innocent suffering with some theoretical theodicy. Christians ultimately flee to the cross of Christ—the revelation of the loving, kenotic God. For a Christian, the cross-Resurrection is the final manifestation of Infinite Love's defeat of death itself. Theoretical exercises in theodicy, including Augustine's, are one and all futile. God's "kenotic," excessive, Infinite Love revealed in creation, covenants, and Incarnation is more than enough. For the Christian, God's Infinite Love has been revealed as the excess of self-sacrificial love in Christ's words, deeds, passion, crucifixion, and Resurrection. The final word is joy: "We are an Easter people and our song is Alleluia."[34] God's Infinite Love is further revealed as God's own trinitarian mutual, reciprocal, relational love in the Gospel of John to ground our own love. Unsurprisingly, Augustine's commentaries on the Gospel of John and 1 John are among the greatest tractates on love in the Christian tradition.

What other Christian Platonist prayed for more feelings and passions? What other ancient philosopher insisted so strongly on the philosophical-cognitive weight of emotion, mood, and passion? Most ancient philosophers strove for serenity as freedom from all passions. Not Augustine. He prayed for more passions to illuminate his understanding. Above all, Augustine understood the graced self as capable through grace of *caritas*: the understanding-loving, the intelligent-willing, the erotic and agapic—that is, the self of Augustinian *caritas*. This Augustinian understanding of *caritas* is his singular gift to Catholic Christianity. The Catholic hope is through agapic grace to transform but never reject *eros* in order to live a graced life of *caritas*. *Deus est Caritas*.

Infinite Love among Medieval Theologians: Love Mysticism, Trinitarian Mysticism, Creation Mysticism[35]

Bernard of Clairvaux: Theologian of Love

There is no more puzzling figure in the history of Christianity than Bernard of Clairvaux.[36] He was beloved as gentle, gracious, and loving by those who knew him best, his fellow monks. And yet, as he himself said to his former student, Pope Eugenius III, he was a "chimaera" and a paradox. Bernard was at once deeply committed to his austere reform of Cistercian monastic life, yet also too committed as a monk to public life in church and state. His public record was mixed. For example, he admirably defended Hildegard of Bingen even as he relentlessly hounded both Abelard and Gilbert de la Porrée. A second example among many: he helped launch the failed and disgraceful second crusade even as, at the same time, he tried with all his strength to try to stop the horrors of the persecution of the Jews by the Crusaders traveling through Europe to the Holy Land.

About his writings, however, there is little debate:[37] Bernard of Clairvaux wrote in a medieval Latin both lucid and lyrical. His writing, in both form and content, makes him the greatest interpreter of love mysticism in Christian history. His greatest works, *De diligendo deo* (*On Loving God*) and especially his extraordinary and lengthy commentary-sermons on the Song of Songs, have never been equaled for their passion, lyricism, and insight into the Christian understanding of love as experience of God. That experience of love was constituted by Bernard through his highly personal journey within—through the liturgy, sacraments, service to others, and an experienced loving contemplation.

For Bernard, love is all. Love explains God as Pure Creative Goodness or—as in this essay, words Bernard did not use but would gladly accept—Infinite Love. For Bernard, the Christian must intensify her experience of love by purifying it through austere asceticism and then by allowing it to illuminate all knowledge of God and self. Even more than Augustine, although deeply influenced by him, Bernard insisted that love was the key to true knowledge (wisdom), not the reverse.

For Bernard, love is primary for two principal reasons.

First, the confusion and sinfulness of our lives is ultimately not due to our ignorance but our wills. Our sinfulness is tied to the way we have, through our disordered lives and reified habits, twisted our wills away from God to the willful ego as its own center without intrinsic relationships to God and neighbor. The self as will has trapped itself into an ultimately unloving ego. Only God's graced love can liberate it.

Second, Bernard's emphasis on personal experience is not an early arrival of modern, purely subjective spirituality. Bernard's experience is, to be sure, highly subjective (more exactly, personal) but his love is always objectively focused on a clear object: the life of Jesus Christ. By Bernard's meditation and contemplation, the events of Christ's life gradually become the beloved contemplated object that can lead one to experience and understand the God who is Love. Moreover, one learns to experience God's love in the Spirit. Indeed, the accurate Christian meaning of "spirituality" for Bernard is to live more and more in and through the Spirit. Bernard is, at once, highly subjective (the focus is on one's personal experience of God's love) and objective (that love becomes intensified and understood through meditation and, at the limit, contemplation of the humanity of the living, suffering, kenotic Christ as well as such classic scriptural texts as the Song of Songs).

In one of his most original and penetrating insights, Bernard insists that love alone engages a person at a deep enough level to allow true conversion to God and thereby true love of neighbor and of one's true self: "Love truly converts souls since it makes them willing";[38] "The more surely you know yourself loved [by the Infinitely Loving God as shown as kenotic love in the crucified Christ], the easier you will find it to love in return."[39]

Bernard's mysticism is often named an "affective love mysticism." It is a fitting title. Indeed, even more than his mentor Augustine, Bernard emphasizes the central role of the affects in the loving knowledge and knowing love of God. Bernard—anticipating Blaise Pascal by centuries—insisted that our sense of the Word's presence in us is less through our intelligence than through the affective and illuminating "warmth" of our hearts. Without the heart on fire, understanding God as Love becomes more and more dim, cold, and dead as ashes.

William of St. Thierry: Love Mysticism Becomes Trinitarian Mysticism

Although William of St. Thierry was ten years older than Bernard of Clairvaux, he was, in some important ways, Bernard's disciple. William wanted to help Bernard's Cistercian reform movement.[40] In fact he did help that reform exemplarily as abbot of St. Thierry. William was a reluctant abbot. He would have preferred to stay with Bernard at the monastery of Clairvaux. The redoubtable Bernard refused this request because more reform monasteries were needed. Alternatively, William would have preferred solitude to contemplate, study, and write. More a trained theologian and scholar than Bernard, William (partly because his lifelong illness made him useless for monastic manual work) devoted himself fully to the work of study in the midst of a monastic regular life of prayer, liturgy, and contemplation.[41]

William embraced the bridal love mysticism that Bernard so lyrically articulated in his classical commentary on the Song of Songs. William, like many love mystics, wrote his own commentary on the Song.[42] William's briefer commentary is far less lyrical and passionate than Bernard's, but William's commentary displays his theological genius with a critical acumen and erudition that Bernard did not possess.

Indeed, William's theological gifts[43] allowed him to make two moves in harmony with, but beyond, Bernard's experience and understanding of God's love and our love: first, a more exact understanding of the relationship of love and knowledge; second, a more exact theological understanding showing how love mysticism becomes trinitarian mysticism.

First, the relationship of love and knowledge. William gave more deliberate exactness to Gregory the Great's famous statement "*Amor ipse notitia est*" (Love itself is knowledge) by his own "*Amor ipse intellectus est.*" By this cryptic yet theologically exact statement William did not identify love and knowledge (as some interpreters mistakenly think). Rather he insisted that only by love do we come truly to *understand* the reality of God as Love and therefore Trinity. William, here more like Augustine than the love-obsessed Bernard, tried to restore the balance of love and knowledge as both realities are involved in knowing God as Love. It is through love alone (William even calls love the "method" to understand). The "method" of love for William is clear: first, by our service for others (especially one's brothers in the monastery) since it is in a community of the like-minded we can learn best what the Gospel of John called love as mutual, reciprocal, relational love. Second, we learn to know God and self by undertaking a loving, contemplative journey by the method of love and theological study of the beloved object, Jesus Christ.

For William (the influence of Augustine, Eriugena, and the Greek fathers is clear here), we are created with the image of God (our graced intelligence and gifted love). Thereby we are graced with a dynamic, driving capacity to participate in God's own life—God's life as the Infinite mutual Love of Father, Son, and Holy Spirit.

Especially in his brilliant *Golden Epistle*, William develops one of the great theologies of the spiritual life: a theology where love mysticism becomes trinitarian mysticism. For William, we move in our interior journey from the "region of unlikeness" to a gradual restoration of the image of God in us in love and therefore also in knowledge. Our capacity to participate in God (William, like the Greek fathers, believes in human divinization) is the dynamic force of our graced *eros* impelling us to live in God through love and understanding. Our *eros* is transformed by God's *agape* into *caritas*. For William, our divinizing participation through the method of love is both, with Bernard, an actual experience of God's love (and, therefore, affective love mysticism) and a deepened understanding of God's life as the Infinite Love of Father, Son, and Spirit (and therefore trinitarian mysticism as well). William's original theology here is one of the best theological understandings of the Christian claim that God is Triune precisely because God is Love.

But for William, as the soul moves through his version of the many classic stages of purification, illumination, and union with God, we experience and partly understand a remarkable vision: a gradually restored likeness to God in love and wisdom given to us by the Holy Spirit. The Spirit is Love—a love that brings us to the point where we begin to understand more and more of the God who is Infinite Love as the Trinity of mutually related love of Father, Son, and Spirit. For William, therefore, through love we begin to possess a new *ratio fidei* or theological understanding of faith's proclamation "God is Love" as faith's further proclamation that God is Father, Son, Spirit. At the highest level of the spiritual life for William, the soul is moved by the Holy Spirit alone to a transformative *ratio caritatis* (an understanding of the Trinity by means of the love that is the Spirit).

For William, our graced natural drive to know and love God becomes through love a new supernaturalized movement of loving knowledge and divinized participation in God's own life as Infinite Love and Intelligence, Infinite Beauty, Peace, and Joy in the mutual and reciprocal relationships of love of Father, Son, and Spirit. For William of St. Thierry, love mysticism became, through theological reflection and personal spiritual journey, a trinitarian mysticism.

William's trinitarian mysticism cannot but help Christians today who, although often open to love mysticism, find it difficult to understand that the experience of God's Infinite Love is also an experience of God's loving, relational, Triune reality. God as Trinity, for Christians, should not be just a doctrinal and theological mystery. God's mutually reciprocal Triune reality as Infinite Love can be, as William of St. Thierry shows, both an experience and an analogous understanding for any Christian.

Therefore, faith grounded in divine Love can illuminate a superior form of loving wisdom. Although William seeks conceptual exactness in his theological understandings of love mysticism as trinitarian mysticism, he is far more concerned to insist that we come, through love, to know God less in the way we know a philosophical theory than in the way we know a friend or a work of art.

After William, the great Victorines (especially Richard of St. Victor in his splendid text, *On the Trinity*[44]) would refine the understandings of both love and Trinity in a way closer to the emerging scholastic method. Present space limitations do not allow more than mentioning and encouraging the reader interested in further understanding God's Infinite Love as Trinity to read the great Victorines. Limited space also forbids a discussion of love-focused, voluntarist Franciscan scholastics: first, the incomparable Bonaventure (especially in *The Soul's Journey into God*[45]); second, the subtle, logically dazzling Duns Scotus for whom voluntarism was central to his scholastic understanding of God's Infinity (the central attribute of God for Scotus) and thereby for God's Infinite Love. Although we regrettably cannot analyze in depth these two great Franciscan thinkers (as well as other Franciscan thinkers, all of whom emphasize love[46]), we must pause only long enough to analyze the most radical love mystic who moves Christian love to include not only our human neighbor but all living creatures. Here one meets the too often sentimentalized but in fact very radical Christian and sophisticated theologian, Francis of Assisi.

Francis of Assisi[47]

There can be no doubt that Francis, *Il Poverello*, the Poor One who married "Lady Poverty," is one of the most beloved religious figures in the entire world. Certainly this is true in Western culture, Christian and non-Christian. For example, Muslims remember Francis fondly as the holy, compassionate saint who preached with love, not polemical argument, to the Sultan of Egypt. A second example: many contemporary Buddhists, with their focus on compassion for all living beings, regard Francis of Assisi as the most radical and most attractive religious genius in the West—radical because Francis is the only Western religious leader who broke out of Western religious anthropocentrism to a Buddhist-like compassion for all living creatures. Ecologists throughout the world today rightly honor Francis as an honored predecessor.

St. Francis of Assisi is a singular saint. However often he has been Disneyfied, his radical life and thought still always manage to break through. Scholars make clear that the search for the "historical Francis" is a difficult one. The great stories and legends about him (classically expressed in the moving film *Fioretti*, or *The Flowers of St. Francis*) do not always present historical facts so much as they brilliantly represent how contemporaries experienced and understood the spirit and power of this charismatic whose heart was more than good. The spirit of Francis has crossed borders and time to become almost everyone's embodiment of a genuine saint or a real religious genius. The best theological description of Francis's person is that by the greatest of Franciscan theologians, St. Bonaventure: Francis of Assisi was a manifestation of the Infinite Love of God for all creatures. Who else ever praised even "Sister Bodily Death"?

For the purposes of this essay, remember not only Francis's extraordinary person and life but his subtle theology of love. Francis left twenty-eight brief writings that articulated his theological vision with the directness and clarity of religious genius. Like so many in his period, Francis shared a christological focus on the humanity of Christ, especially the passion and cross. His famous marriage to "Lady Poverty" and his commitment to the poor and outcasts of his society, especially lepers, was uncompromising. Francis's option for the poor was theologically grounded in an understanding of God's love for all, especially the poor and outcast as revealed in the life and death of Jesus. God's love was infinite to the point of radical self-emptying (*kenosis*). For Francis, the kenotic Incarnation of the God-man was the empowering ground for the central Christian virtue of humility. Moreover, the passion and cross were empowering ground for the infinitely compassionate, self-sacrificing love that Francis believed the gospel of Jesus displays as a way of life open to all.

Francis's distinctive expressions of God's Infinite Love for all creatures are theologically grounded, as his writings demonstrate, in his christological and trinitarian visions. Francis of Assisi knew, in his thought as in his life, that God's love for all, especially the poor, the marginal, the outcasts—even the enemy—was infinite and therefore both excessive and incomprehensible. *Il Poverello* knew and lived the fact that God's Infinite Love was best understood through a radical following of Jesus in poverty and humility. From his never-ending meditations on the biblical accounts of the life of Christ, Francis knew that human beings, especially in an image-rich age like his own, are aided greatly by images and stories to guide their way. For example, Francis is the one who promoted the creation of the crib of the Christ-child at Christmas to aid every Christian's meditation and contemplation. Thus, too, many great legends exist about Francis. Such legends (as recounted in *The Flowers of St. Francis*) may often be grounded in the historical reality of Francis's highly original disclosure of God's compassionate love for all creatures, not only humans: the famous legend of the wounded wolf at Gubbio, Francis's preaching to the birds at Assisi, the insistence on a vegetarian life except when "courtesy" to a host demanded otherwise (Francis here was a successor of the troubadour tradition). Francis of Assisi's compassionate attitude to animals was a radical not sentimental extension of the range of Christian love (as Buddhists often see more clearly than Christians). In our present industrial and postindustrial society, with its often cruel and revolting treatment of animals, one can look to Francis's radical love, expressive of God's Infinite Love, to help us rethink and change our unloving ways toward our fellow animals and to Earth itself.

Near the end of his life, Francis experienced his vision of Christ and his famous stigmata at Mount LaVerna. In spite of suffering acute stomach ulcer pain and near blindness, Francis, in these final years, wrote his most famous and most joyful poetic hymn, "The Canticle of Brother Sun." This hymn is one of the greatest pre-Romantic poetic praises of God's Infinite Love manifested in all nature and in every creature, even "Sister Death." We are fortunate to have the many stories, some historical, some legendary, and the theological writings of this incomparable person. Bonaventure was correct: Francis of Assisi's life is a clear manifestation of the central Christian belief that the final word on reality is God's Infinite Love for all creatures.

Angela of Foligno[48]

Many of Francis's contemporaries were deeply influenced by his love mysticism. This was true above all in Clare of Assisi who further radicalized the Franciscan "privilege of poverty" for a community of contemplative women that she founded at San Damiano.

Moreover, Francis deeply influenced theology. As noted above, Bonaventure was the best theological exponent of Francis's unique creation-mysticism. Among others inspired by Francis, none is more striking than the amazing laywoman, Angela of Foligno (a town in Umbria near Assisi).

The two most important developments in religious life in the thirteenth and fourteenth centuries were, first, the emergence of women as the prominent vernacular theologians; second, the birth of the new mendicant orders—the Dominicans (the Order of Preachers) and the Franciscans (which could have been named the Order of Witnesses to God's Infinite Love). In Catholic theology, the greatest Dominican theologians have always stood for an emphasis on intellect, wisdom, and a strong intellectualism (e.g., Albert the Great, Thomas Aquinas, Meister Eckhart). The Franciscan theologians (e.g., Alexander of Hales, Bonaventure, Duns Scotus) have emphasized love and therefore a strong voluntarism. The Franciscan theologians began a new insistence on the primacy of will rather than intellect even in the highly intellectualist Scholastic theology and philosophy. For the Franciscans, God's wisdom became Love in God's kenotic Incarnation, cross, and Resurrection. Of course, neither Franciscan nor Dominican ignored the alternative: Thomas Aquinas wrote brilliantly of Love as *eros* and *agape*—that is, *caritas*—and of love as the "virtue of all virtues";[49] Bonaventure employed the sharp logical and metaphysical tools of contemporary intellectualist, university-based Scholasticism very well indeed. However, the emphasis of each order is clear: intellect for the Dominicans, love for the Franciscans. Since the concern of this essay is love, our attention is properly focused on the Franciscans, always keeping in mind that love and knowledge, for all the Scholastics, as earlier for such monastic theologians as William of St. Thierry, are to be distinguished but never separated. Love and knowledge are both grounded in God's Infinite Love as also Unbounded Wisdom.

As mentioned above, even more important than the birth of the great mendicant orders was the emergence in the thirteenth and fourteenth centuries of women mystics and theologians such as Mechtild of Magdeburg (who also recalls one of the greatest twelfth-century theologians, Hildegard of Bingen), Hadewych of Antwerp, Marguerite Porete, and Angela of Foligno. Bernard McGinn, the great scholar of Western mysticism, even "provocatively" calls these four remarkable vernacular theologians—Mechtild, Hadewych, Porete, and Angela—"the four women evangelists" of the age.[50] Angela, for example, was known by many male theologians of the period as "*Magistra theologorum*" ("teacher of theologians"). In sum, in the thirteenth and fourteenth centuries we find a new emergence of vernacular theologies (as distinct from monastic and Scholastic theologies, which are written in Latin). Even more surprising, in this period one finds a new prominence of women mystics and theologians usually writing in the vernacular. There are affinities between many of the lay Beguine theologians of northern Europe and the Italian laywoman and "third-order" Franciscan, Angela of Foligno. However, on love as excessive, the remarkable Angela of Foligno has no rival. This highly intelligent and educated woman expressed her thoughts on her many visions in texts dictated to her cousin and conversation partner, Brother Arnaldo.

Angela, following the example of Francis, gave up her considerable wealth and served the poor and outcasts. Again like Francis, Angela first served the many lepers in her society. Lepers in medieval society were the most outcast of all societal outcasts who were forced by law to live outside the city walls (literally society's outcasts). Eventually Angela became more and more committed to the interior life without ever abandoning her commitment to the poor. Her great work—*The Book of the Blessed Angela of Foligno: The Memorial and the Instructions*[51]—is one of the classic texts on the stages of a spiritual journey ending in contemplative loving union.

What is most striking about Angela is her note of Christian love as excess and God's love as excessive-infinite. Her writings express with striking force the intense excessive love of the crucified Christ, especially his wounds on the cross. The resounding note of God's Infinite Love is so clear to Angela that she experienced both intense visions and an equally intense intellectual theology of love.

What is also striking is the originality of Angela's unique and characteristically excessive *dual* understanding of the metaphor of "mystical darkness" in the soul's interior journey. Darkness for Angela is, first of all, positive darkness as radically apophatic (an unusual emphasis for a love mystic). God's Infinite Love is apophatically incomprehensible. At the same time, the metaphor of "darkness" (here like the later John of the Cross on the "dark nights" of the soul) also, for Angela, bears a negative note: the soul's "dark" and suffering lack of understanding of the abyss of God now experienced in the "second abyss," the abyss of the soul as a terrifying darkness. Angela of Foligno's stark originality—in her thought as much as in her life—is one of the greatest theological expressions in the whole tradition of God's Excessive Love as that Love may be discovered by human beings by their active service to others, especially the outcasts in every society as well as by their disciplined loving contemplation of God's Infinite Love. Love as infinite excess in God and finite excess in the self has never found a more brilliant exponent than Angela of Foligno.

Summary and Conclusion: Catholic Thought Today—God's Infinite Love; Human Finite *Caritas*[52]

In this essay, we have been able to relate only some basic forms of the Catholic understandings of "God is love." Correlatively we have related some basic Catholic understandings of human love (theological and spiritual). Human *caritas* is made possible by the Infinite Love of God revealed decisively for Christians in Jesus Christ.

In relationship to the wider Christian tradition on divine Infinite Love and human finite *caritas*, I have, as on all major issues, become convinced that any serious Christian theologian today is exactly that: a Christian theologian with a nonexclusive personal center of gravity in one of the major Christian traditions: Orthodox, Catholic, or Protestant. Therefore, a responsible contemporary Christian theologian should study and articulate (of course, when necessary, critically) as much of the entire pluralistic Christian tradition as is personally possible in a single lifetime.

However, given the enormity and complexity of the Christian tradition (like all the great traditions) the editors were wise to ask various Christian authors to focus on one of the Christian traditions within the great tradition. Hence, I present here only my own Christian center of gravity, the Roman Catholic tradition on divine and human loves. Any one of the other Christian traditions on understanding Infinite Love and finite loves is also rich, pluralistic, and complex. Moreover, no tradition, no text, and no reading (including this one) is innocent. For example, even in the love-saturated text, 1 John, one can find both "God is love" as well as Christian love sometimes portrayed as exclusive to only orthodox communities. A second example: even the incomparably loving Francis of Assisi seems at times not to have freed his great creation theology from some unfortunate earlier spiritual traditions of "hating" as well as "loving" the body.

These problems of ambiguity in the Catholic tradition on love are overshadowed by the prominent Catholic traditions on God's Infinite Love commanding and empowering human beings to love all creatures, even themselves. In this essay, we have witnessed only a few of those rich Catholic traditions starting with the New Testament. There we found three classical love motifs on both God and human beings. These biblical models of love have been both retrieved and refashioned throughout the two thousand years and many cultures touched by Catholic Christianity.

First, the biblical model of love as excess is expressed principally in the Synoptic accounts of love: first, in the words of Jesus (especially the Markan apocalyptic sayings, the Lukan parables, and the Matthean discourses); second, the Jesuanic deeds of excessive love, especially Jesus' healings and privileging of the poor, the ill, the marginal, and the outcasts of his society; and third, the ultimate loving excess of Jesus Christ's self-sacrifice on the cross. Christ's self-sacrificial love is followed in the Resurrection with the triumph of Infinite Love over death itself. From this follows in Acts, an account of the new community of the Spirit released at Pentecost. Christian love is excess: first, God's Infinite Unbounded Love disclosed in the unsubstitutable Jesus the Christ; second, God's grace rendering human beings capable of love toward the neighbor even the enemy.

The second biblical model of love is their mutually reciprocating relational love of the Trinity. In interpreting the Gospel of John, one finds Christian love is illuminated as Christian mutual, reciprocal, relational love grounded in trinitarian love—that is, Infinite Love is the mutually and reciprocally related Infinite Love of Father, Son, and Spirit. Such relational love drives all Catholic social and communal love, especially in the many services for others demanded by a loving justice. Trinitarian love also empowers many spiritual interior journeys in communal settings.

The third biblical model of love is Paul's model of Infinite Love as *kenosis*. To understand the New Testament on love we should join the Synoptic model of Christian love as excess, especially for the poor and marginal, to John's communal trinitarian and Eucharistic understanding of Christian love as loving reciprocal relationships in community. By this union of love as excess and love as mutual relationships we arrive at the dialectical formulations of Paul in love: love is so excessive and so trinitarian-relational to be renamed kenotic love—that is, the self-emptying of God in the Incarnation leading to the ultimate *kenosis* of the crucified God.

These three New Testament models of God's Infinite Love also become the clues to the graced possibilities of human love: first in Augustine and his synthesis of *eros* and *agape* into *caritas*; second, in the experienced love of God and neighbor as the key to understanding God as Infinite Love and the self as loving every neighbor in Bernard of Clairvaux; third, this Bernardine love mysticism as completed by William of Thierry's theological understanding showing how love mysticism is also trinitarian mysticism and theology. Catholic human love is individual (better, personal) but never individualistic. Catholic love is principally communal: best witnessed in the communal celebration of the agapic feast of the Eucharist, and for Catholics in the model for love among the redeemed: the Virgin Mary. The Marian devotion of Catholics is human love mysticism made humanly concrete by focusing on the exemplary strength and love of Mary, mother of Jesus and *theotokos* (mother of God).

Fourth, in Francis of Assisi, one witnesses how Christian love should not be confined to the human neighbor but extended to others, all God's creatures, all the animals, all living creatures, the Earth itself. Fifth, in Angela of Foligno, one finds one of the greatest Catholic mystical understandings focused above all on how every love like Christ's love inevitably involves both suffering and joy. One finds in Angela of Foligno the working out and a remarkable putting together of two classic Catholic traditions for understanding love: first, Infinite Love is incomprehensible—that is, God's kenotic Love revealed in Christ's self-sacrificial love is Infinite and thereby Incomprehensible in a positive mode of apophatic darkness (as earlier described in Gregory of Nyssa and Dionysius). At the same time, Christian love also brings another kind of darkness: the frightening and suffering experience of a dark night in the soul (as later in John of the Cross's "dark nights of the soul"). Angela's position unites these two contrasting models of darkness. One can sense why she expressed so powerfully both great sorrow and even greater joy in her experiences of Christ's self-sacrificial love on the cross.

In fact, Angela radicalizes both the Bernadine and the Franciscan traditions of love by highlighting the horrifying details of ancient crucifixion on the cross: the wounds, the outpouring of blood from Jesus' pierced side, his nakedness, his crying out, "My God, my God, why have you abandoned me?"[53] Nevertheless, it is an error to read Angela's attention to the intense sufferings of Jesus as dolorism, much less masochism. Rather Angela faces, like so many mystics (including Francis and Clare), the omnipresent presence of both joy and suffering in human existence as that suffering is illuminated as God's own suffering in the self-sacrificial love of Jesus. Once faced, such Christian suffering does not end in sorrow but in resurrection/joy.

Today, too, these classical understandings of love (and others not discussed here) continue in ever new forms.

In modernity, first, love as excess is best seen today among Catholics in the Catholic option for the poor: that is, the now official Catholic position that our prime attention in love should be given to the oppressed, forgotten, marginalized ones of our modern globalized world where justice transformed by love often seems a lost memory. This modern Catholic option for the poor is present in the Catholic social justice tradition articulated in the social papal encyclicals from Leo XIII[54] to Benedict XVI.[55] This option for the poor also lives dramatically in political, feminist, and liberation theologies of our day. These modern theologies rethink the relationships of love and justice. For example, Gustavo Gutiérrez (in his classic *A Theology of Liberation*[56]) rethinks the relationships of action and contemplation and love and justice as a new theology of liberation. Many modern Catholic feminist theologians make analogous theological and spiritual moves on the crucial issue of justice for women in both church and society. Nowhere has this option for the poor been expressed more powerfully than in the lifelong work of Dorothy Day for the truly forgotten ones of society, the poorest of the poor whom even modern welfare societies do not locate in order to serve.

Other contemporary Catholic philosophers and theologians have continued the speculative theological traditions of understanding the mysteries of the Incarnation and Trinity as the central theological-spiritual clues to God's Infinite Love and God's Infinitely *kenotic* love in Incarnation and cross. Catholic philosophers like Edith Stein, Simone Weil, Jean-Luc Marion, and many others have developed in modern philosophical terms the classical Catholic philosophical traditions on love. Many Catholic spiritual leaders, moreover, continue to express love as the central vision driving and directing their remarkable lives and thoughts—for example, Mother Teresa of Calcutta, Jean Vanier, and countless others. In many modern Catholic theologians, one finds the same love-centeredness for understanding God, self, and neighbor: Henri de Lubac, Teilhard de Chardin, Karl Rahner, Bernard Lonergan, and Hans Urs von Balthasar (in his fine little book *Love Alone*[57]).

In this essay, therefore, we have studied several but by no means all or even the majority of the classical Catholic thinkers on God's Infinite Love and human *caritas*. I can only hope that readers use the occasion of this essay to make up this loss by means of their own readings. For example, to understand Catholic *caritas*, one can profitably reread or read for the first time the brilliant *Pensées* of Blaise Pascal.[58] There Pascal insists that the "order of charity" is not merely distinct but separate from both the "order of flesh" (the world of power) and the "order of intelligence." In an acute observation, Pascal argues that we know that those who have dedicated their lives to the "order of intelligence" (scientists, scholars, critical theorists, philosophers, theologians—indeed all those named "intellectuals") are a mystery to those who live principally in the worlds of business, power, or sensuality (the latter of whom he calls the "order of the flesh"). In the same way, it is just as difficult for those in the "order of intelligence" to understand those in the order of love or charity. Pascal's "order of charity" describes very well the intense life of service to others like Mother Teresa's. The "order of charity" also describes well those who live deeply in an interior spiritual journey of increasing participation in God's infinite Love.

Moreover, it is not just these extraordinary types of human beings who experience the order of charity. We all have experienced this order at times in those moments in ordinary life that seem outside of time in the deep love of one human being for another. These moments give each of us "hints and guesses"[59] of what the order of charity is. The order of charity transforms but does not reject either the order of flesh or the order of intelligence, both of which orders we must also live in. But these extraordinary moments in our ordinary lives do help us to understand that love is the ultimate clue to God's own life and to our lives at their most true.

The most important fact of all about modern Catholic charity is that Catholicism is no longer just a European religion but now a global one. In this accelerating pluralism of world Catholicism, all Catholics in Europe and North America must learn from Asian Catholics, African Catholics, and South American Catholics. These peoples have found and are finding new cultural ways to express a Catholic understanding of God's Infinite Love and human finite love. For example, Catholic Asian theologies are exploring the relationship of Christian *caritas* to Buddhist compassion and Hindu *bhakti*. A second example: the teaching of the love of God and love of neighbor is now the major focus for a global Christian-Muslim dialogue just as the covenant remains the major focus for Christian-Jewish dialogue.

One reality about the future is clear: the already existing pluralism of Catholic life and thought will surely increase in this new global world. Indeed, more Catholics now live in the Southern Hemisphere than in the Northern Hemisphere. New theologies and spiritualities from non-European cultural and intellectual traditions arrive every year. Given the finite limits of space and the limits of my own competence, in this essay I have not analyzed the new models for love in global Catholicism. But clearly these new understandings are the future of Catholic Christianity. That future is likely both to continue to develop and to change the classical theologies of love discussed in this essay. One example: Dorothy Day was a Catholic thinker and activist who both lived among and learned from the poorest of the poor in the United States. The poor whom Day served her whole life were so marginalized in rich American society that even the admirable social services of the state and the religions could not find them, much less help them. But Dorothy Day did find and help them. By founding the Catholic Worker Movement, Day served and learned from these forgotten ones. She was often asked by the press and others what strange kind of Christian love had driven her on this task day after day, year after year. Her answer over and over again was to quote these words from Dostoevsky's *Brothers Karamazov*:

> Love in action is a harsh and dreadful thing compared with love in dreams. Love in dreams is greedy for immediate action, rapidly performed and in the sight of all. Men will even give their lives if only the ordeal does not last long but is soon over, with all looking on and applauding as though on the stage. But active love is labour and fortitude. . . . Just when you see with horror that in spite of all your efforts you are getting further from your goal instead of nearer to it—at that very moment . . . you will reach it and behold clearly the miraculous power of the Lord who has been all the time loving and mysteriously guiding you.[60]

Notes

For the purposes of this essay, I have confined references to Anglophone books and English translations.

1. The readings of the New Testament are my own "theological" readings. For a recent analysis of historical-critical work in the Synoptics, see Pheme Perkins, *Introduction to the Synoptic Gospels* (Grand Rapids: Wm. B. Eerdmans, 2007).
2. 1 John 4:7–8 (NRSV).
3. Friedrich Nietzsche, *Thus Spake Zarathustra*, trans. Thomas Common (Mineola, NY: Dover Thrift, 1999 [1891]), 39.

4. John 3:16.
5. Philippians 2:5–8.
6. Mark 16:8.
7. Matthew 5–7.
8. Matthew 25.
9. Fyodor Dostoevsky, *Brothers Karamazov*, trans. Constance Garnett (New York: Random House, 1933 [1879]).
10. For a now classic historical-critical reading of the epistles of John, see Raymond E. Brown, *The Epistles of John* (Garden City, NY: Doubleday, 1982), *The Gospel According to John* (Garden City, NY: Doubleday, 1966, 1970), and *An Introduction to New Testament Christology* (New York: Paulist Press, 1994).
11. Pope Benedict XVI, *God Is Love: Deus Caritas Est* (San Francisco: Ignatius Press, 2006).
12. 1 Corinthians 13:8–13.
13. Jeremiah 31:3.
14. 1 John 4:7–12.
15. Augustine, *Confessions*, trans. Henry Chadwick (New York: Oxford University Press, 1991); *On Christian Doctrine*, trans. D. W. Robertson (Indianapolis: Bobbs-Merrill, 1981); *Homilies on the First Epistle of John (Tractus in Epistolam Joannis ad Parthos)*, trans. Boniface Ramsey (Hyde Park, NY: New City Press, 1990); and *City of God*, trans. H. Bettenson (New York: Penguin Classics, 1984).
16. Karl Rahner, "Scripture and Theology," in *Theological Investigations*, vol. 6 of *Concerning Vatican Council II* (Baltimore: Helicon Press, 1969), 89–97.
17. Augustine, *On Christian Doctrine*.
18. Anders Nygren, *Agape and Eros: A Study of the Christian Idea of Love*, trans. A. G. Hebert (London: SPCK, 1932). See also John Burnaby, *Amor Dei: A Study of the Religion of St. Augustine* (London: Hodder & Stoughton, 1947); and Hannah Arendt, *Love and Saint Augustine* (Chicago: University of Chicago Press, 1996).
19. From Thomas Aquinas, *Summa Theologica*, trans. Fathers of the English Dominican Province (New York: Benzinger Brothers, 1947), first part, question 1, article 8.
20. Augustine, *Confessions*.
21. Augustine, *City of God*.
22. Augustine, *On Free Choice of the Will*, trans. Thomas Williams (Indianapolis: Hackett, 1993).
23. *Fathers of the Church: St. Augustine: The Retractions*, trans. Mary Inez Bogan (Washington, DC: Catholic University of America Press, 1999).
24. Martin Luther, *D. Martin Luthers Werke: Kritische Gesamtausgabe* (Weimar, Germany: Verlag Hermann Böhlaus Nachfolger, 1883–), Band 56:304.26, 365.5. Published in English as *Lectures on Romans: Glosses and Scholia* in *Luther's Works*, XXV (St. Louis: Concordia Press, 1972), 291.
25. Gregory the Great, *Homelia in Evangelium* 27.4, in *Patrologia Latina*, vol. 76 of *Patrologiae Cursus Completus*, ed. Jacques-Paul Migne (Paris: Apud Garnier Fratres, 1878), 1207.
26. Bernard Lonergan, *Method in Theology* (New York: Seabury, 1982), 30–31.
27. Galatians 5:6.
28. Luther, *D. Martin Luthers Werke*, Band 39/1:46.
29. Psalm 16:13.
30. Augustine, *Confessions*, 4.14.22.

31. Friedrich Nietzsche, *Nachlass*, contained in *Krisische Gesamtausgabe: Werke*, ed. G. Colli and M. Montinari (Berlin and New York: deGruyter, 1975), XII, 217.
32. Augustine, *Homilies on the First Epistle of John*, Homily 7:8.
33. Romans 7:19.
34. Widely attributed to Augustine.
35. Of the many excellent books on the medievals, for the purposes of this essay, see especially Jean Leclercq, Francois Vandenbroucke, and Louis Bouyer, *The Spirituality of the Middle Ages* (New York: Seabury, 1968); Bernard McGinn, *The Foundations of Mysticism: Origins to Fifth Century* (New York: Crossroad, 1991), *The Growth of Mysticism: Gregory the Great through the Twelfth Century* (New York: Crossroad, 1994), and *The Flowering of Mysticism: Men and Women in the New Mysticism: 1200–1350* (New York: Crossroad, 1998); Bernard McGinn, John Meyendorff, and Jean Leclercq, eds., *Christian Spirituality: Origins to the Twelfth Century* (New York: Crossroad, 1992); Jill Raitt, ed., *Christian Spirituality: High Middle Ages and Reformation* (New York: Crossroad, 1987); G. R. Evans, ed., *The Medieval Theologians* (Oxford: Blackwell, 2001); and Louis Dupré and James A. Wiseman, O.S.B., eds., *Light from Light: An Anthology of Christian Mysticism* (New York: Paulist Press, 1988).
36. Bernard of Clairvaux, *On Loving God* (Kalamazoo, MI: Cistercian Publications, 2005), and *Bernard of Clairvaux on the Song of Songs* (Kalamazoo, MI: Cistercian Publications, 1971–80).
37. On Bernard, see Bernard McGinn, "Bernard of Clairvaux: 'That Contemplative' (Quel Contemplante)," in McGinn, *The Growth of Mysticism*, 158–223; G. R. Evans, *The Mind of St. Bernard of Clairvaux* (Oxford: Clarendon, 1983); Jean Leclercq, *A Second Look at Bernard of Clairvaux*, trans. Marie-Bernard Said (Kalamazoo, MI: Cistercian Publications, 1990); and Etienne Gilson, *The Mystical Theology of Saint Bernard*, trans. A. H. C. Downes (London: Sheed & Ward, 1940).
38. Bernard of Clairvaux, *On Loving God*, XII, 34.
39. Ibid., III, 7.
40. On the Cistercian movement, see Louis Bouyer, *The Cistercian Heritage*, trans. Elizabeth A. Livingston (London: A. R. Mowbray, 1958); M. Basic Pennington, O.C.S.O., *The Last of the Fathers: The Cistercian Fathers of the Twelfth Century* (Still Rivers, MA: St. Bede's Publishers, 1983).
41. William of St. Thierry, *The Golden Epistle* (Kalamazoo, MI: Cistercian Publications, 1971), and *On the Nature and Dignity of Love* (Kalamazoo, MI: Cistercian Publications, 1981).
42. William of St. Thierry, *Exposition on the Song of Songs*, trans. M. C. Hart (Kalamazoo, MI: Cistercian Publications, 1968).
43. On William of St. Thierry, see David Bell, *The Image and Likeness: The Augustinian Spirituality of William of St. Thierry* (Kalamazoo, MI: Cistercian Publications, 1984); and J.-M. Déchanet, *William of St. Thierry: The Man and His Work* (Kalamazoo, MI: Cistercian Publications, 1972).
44. Richard of St. Victor, *On the Trinity*, trans. Jonathan Couser, from *Richard de Saint-Victor: De Trinitate*, ed. Jean Ribaillier (Paris: Librairie Philosophique J. Vrin, 1958), available at http://pvspade.com/Logic/docs/StVictor.pdf.
45. Bonaventure, *The Soul's Journey into God, The Tree of Life, The Life of St. Francis*, trans. Ewart Cousins (New York: Paulist Press, 1978).
46. On Francis and the Franciscans there is a voluminous literature. For examples, see John Moorman, *A History of the Franciscan Order* (Oxford: Clarendon Press, 1968); David

Flood, *Francis of Assisi and the Franciscan Movement* (Quezon City, Philippines: FIA Publishing, 1989); Lawrence S. Cunningham, *Francis of Assisi, Performing the Gospel Life* (Grand Rapids: Wm. B. Eerdmans, 2004); Jacques LeGoff, *Saint Francis of Assisi*, trans. Christine Rhone (London: Routledge, 2004); and Edward A. Armstrong, *St. Francis: Nature Mystic; The Derivation and Significance of the Nature Stories in the Franciscan Legend* (Berkeley: University of California Press, 1973).

47. Regis J. Armstrong, ed., *Francis and Clare: The Complete Works* (New York: Paulist Press, 1982); and Marion A. Habig, ed., *St. Francis of Assisi: Writings and Early Biographies, English Omnibus of Sources for the Life of St. Francis* (Chicago: Franciscan Herald Press, 1983).
48. See Angela of Foligno, *Complete Works*, trans. Paul Lachance (New York: Paulist Press, 1993). See especially the fine introduction, Paul Lachance, *The Spiritual Journey of Blessed Angela of Foligno According to the Memorial of Brother A.* (Rome: Pontificium Athenaeum Antonianum, 1984), 15–119. It is also significant that the early postmodern thinker Georges Bataille, with his philosophy of excess, strongly affirmed Angela of Foligno. Bataille's postmodern reading has been continued by Amy Hollywood, *Sensible Ecstasy: Mysticism, Sexual Difference, and the Demands of History* (Chicago: University of Chicago Press, 2002).
49. Aquinas, *Summa Theologica*, Parts I–II, Question 62, Article 4.
50. McGinn, *Flowering of Mysticism*, 141–42.
51. Included in Angela of Foligno, *Complete Works*.
52. Among the works and persons mentioned here, see especially Blaise Pascal, *Pensées* (New York: Penguin Classics, 1995); Hans Urs von Balthasar, *Love Alone*, trans. Alexander Dru (New York: Herder and Herder, 1969); Edith Stein, *The Science of the Cross: A Study of St. John of the Cross* (Chicago: Regnery, 1960); Louis Dupré, *The Deeper Life: An Introduction to Christian Mysticism* (New York: Crossroad, 1981); Dorothy Day, *The Long Loneliness: The Autobiography of Dorothy Day* (New York: Image Books, 1968); Anne E. Carr, *Transforming Grace: Christian Tradition and Women's Experience* (San Francisco: Harper & Row, 1987); Lonergan, *Method in Theology*; and Pierre Teilhard de Chardin, *The Divine Milieu: An Essay of the Interior Life* (New York: Harper & Row, 1960).
53. Matthew 27:46.
54. Leo XIII, *Permoti Nos (On Social Conditions in Belgium)*, July 10, 1895.
55. Benedict XVI, *Caritas in Veritate* (*Charity in Truth*), June 29, 2009.
56. Gustavo Gutiérrez, *A Theology of Liberation: History, Politics, and Salvation* (Maryknoll, NY: Orbis Books, 1973).
57. Balthasar, *Love Alone*.
58. Pascal, *Pensées*.
59. From T. S. Eliot, "Dry Salvages," in *Four Quartets* (1943; repr. Orlando, FL: Harcourt, 1968), 44.
60. Dostoevsky, *Brothers Karamazov*, 60.

6 Divine and Human Love in Islam

William C. Chittick

Islam begins with the two-part Shahadah, the "bearing witness" that there is no god but God and that Muhammad is God's messenger. The second part acknowledges the historical reality of the religion established by the message known as the Qur'an. The first part, called the sentence that "asserts unity"—*tawḥīd*—declares the unique, ahistorical reality of the divine Being. In the Islamic perspective, this twin truth—the unity of God, and the specific, historical consequences that follow upon this unity—was taught by all prophets, traditionally said to number 124,000. To each of them God revealed the message, "There is no god but I, so worship Me."[1] God's unitary reality is everywhere and always the same, but "worship" or "service" (*'ibāda*) varies according to circumstances, for "God never sent a messenger save in the tongue of his people."[2]

Nowadays, discussions of Islamic teachings typically gloss over the ahistorical foundation of the message and focus instead on sorting out the social and political implications of the second part of the Shahadah. This is to say that both Muslims and outside observers stress the Shariah, the law that came to be established on the basis of the Qur'anic message, and neglect the Haqiqah, the Reality that gave rise to both the universe and prophetic guidance. Law, however, deals with activity and society; it has nothing to say about God Himself or His love for creation.[3] The jurists (*fuqahā'*)—the specialists in the Shariah—have never discussed love in their capacity as jurists; to speak of legislating or adjudicating love is ludicrous. Thus, in order to investigate the role of love in the tradition, we need to look at the writings of theologians, philosophers, Sufis, and poets.[4] It is they who look at the Haqiqah beyond the Shariah, the Reality that gave rise to the Law. It is they who explain that God's love for human beings animates the universe and guides people to live their lives in conformity with that love.[5]

When we look closely at the universal message of the prophets—"There is no god but I, so worship Me"—we can see that its two clauses correspond to the two parts of the Shahadah. The meaning is simply that all reality derives from the Real; human beings must therefore strive to accord with the Real. Muslim theologians sometimes unpack the implications of this message in terms of God's two "commands" (*amr*), one of which gave rise to the universe and the other to the moral realm. The first is commonly called "the engendering command" (*al-amr al-takwīnī*) and the second "the prescriptive command" (*al-amr al-taklīfī*). The first is addressed to all things and is mentioned in Qur'anic verses like, "His command, when He desires a thing, is to say to it 'Be!,' and it comes to be."[6] Notice here that God is motivated to issue this command by "desire" (*irāda*),[7] which the tradition takes as a synonym for creative love. The engendering command is rooted in *tawḥīd*, the basic sense of which can be understood in terms of the divine attributes: "There is no god but God" means that there is no life but God's life, no knowledge but God's knowledge, no truth but God's truth, no reality but God's reality, no love but God's love. All contingent reality—"everything other than God" (a common definition of the universe)—derives from God, who is the source of all, the sustainer of all, and the ultimate goal of all.

As for the prescriptive command, it follows on the authority established by the second part of the Shahadah, "Muhammad is God's messenger." The Qur'an presents this command as various dos and don'ts that provide the basis for worship, law, morality, and spiritual transformation.[8]

The engendering command brings the universe into existence, and it takes everything back to God. This dual movement is commonly called "the Origin and the Return" (*al-mabda' wa'l-ma'ād*), or the descending and ascending "arcs" (*qaws*) of the circle of existence. Likewise the prescriptive command implies two movements: the descent of guidance (*hudā*) from God, and the ascent of souls to God. These movements are expressed mythically in the defining "nights" of Islam's infancy, both of which received the shining of the divine light. During "the Night of Power" (*laylat al-qadr*),[9] God sent Gabriel, the angel of revelation, to deliver the message: "a Book We have sent down to you, so that you may bring forth the people from the darknesses into the light."[10] During "the Night of the Ladder" (*laylat al-mi'rāj*), Gabriel carried the Prophet to Jerusalem: "Glory be to Him who made His servant journey by night from the Holy Mosque [in Mecca] to the Furthest Mosque [in Jerusalem]!"[11] From there Gabriel took him up through the heavenly spheres to "the lote tree of the far boundary,"[12] on the outermost edge of paradise. Then Muhammad parted from the angel, left the created realm, and entered the Eternal Light.[13] On his return, he instituted the basic Islamic ritual, the daily prayers (*ṣalāt*). When asked if others could also climb the ladder to God, he responded, "The daily prayer is the believer's ladder."

Both Sufis and philosophers have taken the night journey as the archetype for the spiritual transformation that is the goal of praxis.[14] Sufism has produced a vast literature on the stages of the journey to God, as well as personal accounts by seekers who climbed the ladder in the Prophet's footsteps (accounts that may well have provided the literary models for Dante's *Divine Comedy*). The ascending steps were invariably explained as human virtues and character traits that need to be actualized if people are to escape from their own shortcomings. This is not to say, however, that the path can be traversed without God's help. The whole point of focusing on prophecy and the prescriptive command has been to show that divine grace provides the only means to reach the goal.

In short, there are two basic ways of looking at God's love. In terms of the engendering command, it is the motive force of both the Origin and the Return. In terms of the prescriptive command, it invites human beings to love God as he loves them.

The Divine Form

Muslim theologians speak of God in terms of names and attributes derived from Qur'anic verses or hadiths (sayings of the Prophet). The divine names are said to number ninety-nine, though many more are mentioned in the texts. Numerous commentaries were written on the names, always highlighting the fundamental reality of God and the derivative reality of everything else. The names and attributes are of course anthropomorphic, for human beings can think of God only in terms of themselves. The principle of *tawḥīd*, however, reminds us that God alone possesses true Being and its concomitant attributes. People conceive of God in terms of themselves because He conceives of them in terms of Himself. He is anthropomorphic because they are theomorphic. When the Prophet said,

"God created Adam in His form (*ṣūra*)," he was not simply reiterating the biblical statement, but also clarifying the Qur'anic designation of God as the Form-giver (*al-muṣawwir*),[15] who "formed you, and made your forms beautiful."[16] Indeed, Arab logicians employed the word *taṣawwur* (derived from the same root) to render the notion of "concept"; its literal meaning is "to give form to something within oneself." It is God who "conceives of" all things—who "gives form to them in Himself"—before saying "Be!" to them.

The Qur'an describes God as possessing "the Most Beautiful Names" (*al-asmāʾ al-ḥusnā*) and it calls Him "the Beautiful-doer" (*muḥsin*). It says, "He made beautiful everything that He created."[17] The Prophet said, "God is beautiful (*jamīl*), and He loves beauty." The notion that all love is directed at beauty (*jamāl*, *ḥusn*) permeates the tradition. As for man, God "taught him all the names" (Qur'an 2:31) and created him "in the most beautiful stature."[18] Among all existent things, man alone was created in the form of Him who is named by the Most Beautiful Names. Other creatures were created by the activities of specific names, so they can be "signs" (*āyāt*) of God's life-giving, His gentleness, His might, His beneficence; only human beings can be signs of the Beautiful per se, embracing all of the Most Beautiful Names without exception. This is why Rūzbihān Baqlī (d. 1209)—a prolific author of Arabic and Persian books that gave love a high profile—tells us that human beauty is differentiated from every other sort of created beauty because it displays the radiance of the divine Essence, whereas other creatures manifest only the activities of God's attributes.[19]

When the Qur'an says that God created man in the most beautiful stature, it goes on to say that God "sent him down to the lowest of the low."[20] This can be read as a reference to Adam's fall, though Muslim scholars have rarely understood the fall as pointing to moral corruption. Rather, it demonstrates both human election and human need. After all, at the very beginning of the Qur'an's retelling of the myth, God announced to the angels that He would be appointing a vicegerent in the earth.[21] Having created Adam, He placed Adam in paradise. Then, by issuing the command, "Fall down!"[22] He sent His newly appointed vicegerent to the realm for which he was created. Adam's "sin" was a onetime act of disobedience,[23] quickly forgiven by God, who then made him a prophet to guide his children. Moreover, the Qur'an provides Adam with an excuse for disobeying the divine command not to approach the tree: "He forgot,"[24] which is hardly surprising, for "Man was created weak,"[25] and "There is none strong but God." Despite the divine form of human beings, they are contingent on the Form-giver, so they are forgetful and heedless. They remain forever needy toward the two commands, that is, the bestowal of being and the bestowal of guidance.

The secret of climbing the ladder to God is to empty oneself of self-centeredness and to open oneself up to the divine light, which has appeared most clearly in prophetic guidance. The process is never-ending, for the light is infinite and the human form finite. Teachers have described the steps on the ladder in many ways, often enumerating them in archetypal numbers—7, 40, 100, 1001. They also say that the journey "to God" is only the prelude to the journey "in God." Many discuss a third journey "from God" back to the world, and a fourth journey "with God" in the world. In the posthumous realms as well, journeying can have no end, for God is endless.

The more theoretical analyses of human transformation focus on "character" (*khuluq*), not least because the Qur'an says, addressing Muhammad, "Surely you have a tremendous character."[26] The plural of this word, *akhlāq*, was used by philosophers to translate the Greek notion of "ethics" and "morals." Using either of these terms to translate the Arabic word back into English, however, obscures *khuluq*'s shared etymology with *khalq*, "creation." In the normal, unvoweled script, the two words are written exactly the same way. Their common source indicates that a person's character is intimately tied to God's creative act and that character traits (*akhlāq*) are not so much moral qualities or ethical principles as the modalities of a person's being. Morals and ethics pertain primarily to objective reality, not to subjectivity. This does not imply, however, that character traits are fixed—far from it. In Islamic theology, calling God "Creator" is tantamount to saying that He is creating the universe always and forever, so everything undergoes constant change and transformation. To climb the ladder to God is to harness the ongoing flow of creation in order to transform "base character traits" (*safsāf al-akhlāq*) into "noble character traits" (*makārim al-akhlāq*). Hence Muhammad used to pray, "O God, Thou hast made my creation beautiful, so make my character beautiful too!" He also said, "The most beloved of you to God is the most beautiful of you in character."

Theologians often speak of the character traits of God, meaning not His ethics, but His names and attributes. It is these that God instilled into Adam when He created Adam in His form and taught Adam the names. The Prophet is quoted as having said, "Become characterized by God's character traits!" (*takhallaqū bi-akhlāq Allāh*). The famous theologian Muḥammad al-Ghazālī (d. 1111) dedicates the last section of the introduction to his book on the divine names to "clarifying that the servant's perfection and salvation lie in becoming characterized by God's character traits and adorned by His attributes and names to the extent conceivable."[27] Al-Ghazālī and many others insist that people must strive to be God-like. Abu'l-Ḥasan al-Daylamī (d. ca. 1000), author of the first Arabic treatise on love from a largely Sufi perspective, says that when someone loves God,

> God beautifies his character traits, for He bestows upon him a robe of honor from His love and character traits from His character traits. He dresses him in a light from His light, a beauty from His beauty, a splendor from His splendor, a generosity from His generosity, a forbearance from His forbearance, a kindness from His kindness, a munificence from His munificence, and so on with the other attributes. Thus he becomes characterized by God's character traits.[28]

For their part, the philosophers speak of "becoming similar to God" (*al-tashabbuh bi'l-iāh*) or even "deiformity" (*ta'alluh*, from the same root as the word *Allāh*). The Ikhwān al-Ṣafā' ("Brethren of Purity"), a group of highly influential tenth-century sages, explain in these terms why people should search for wisdom:

> The furthest goal of philosophy . . . is becoming similar to God in keeping with the capacity of mortal man. . . . It consists of four qualities: First, knowledge of the realities of the existent things; second, firmly knotted belief in sound views; third, becoming characterized by the beautiful character traits and praiseworthy tempers; and fourth, pure practices and beautiful acts.[29]

Avicenna (d. 1037), the greatest of the Muslim Peripatetics, agrees. In his "Book of Salvation" (*Kitāb al-najāt*), for example, he employs the term "deiformity" only once, but as the last word of the text.[30] He is referring to the station of Muhammad, but the implication is clear: Lovers of wisdom will never achieve ethical and moral perfection until they become God-like. Deiformity remained the underlying goal of the search for wisdom, which helps explain the title "Foremost of the Deiform" given to Mullā

Ṣadrā (d. 1640), whom many consider the greatest of all philosophers. Ibn ʿArabī (d. 1240), the "greatest teacher" of the Sufis and arguably the most influential theologian and philosopher of the second half of Islamic history, sums up the issue as follows: "The philosophers allude to the fact that the goal sought by the servant is becoming similar to God. The Sufis say 'becoming characterized by the traits of the names.' The expressions are different, but the meaning is the same."[31]

Mercy

To speak of God's love for creation, we need to say something about Qur'anic terminology. Several divine attributes have semantic fields that overlap with that of English "love," including friendship (*walāya*), munificence (*jūd*), gentleness (*luṭf*), and forgiveness (*maghfira*). In discussions of God's loving care for His creatures, however, the most prominent attribute is *raḥma*, typically translated as mercy, compassion, or benevolence. The word derives from the same root as *raḥim*, "womb," and designates the characteristics of a caring and compassionate mother. The etymological sense was lost on no one, even if theologians avoided stressing it, not least because of their antipathy toward the Christian notion of God as "father." The Prophet, however, had no such inhibitions, as illustrated by this hadith:

> God created a hundred mercies on the day He created the heavens and the earth, each mercy of which would fill what is between the heaven and the earth. Of these He placed one mercy in the earth. Through it mothers incline toward their children, and birds and beasts incline toward each other. When the day of resurrection comes, He will complete this mercy with those mercies.[32]

Among all divine attributes, mercy is most closely associated with the notion of "God" (*Allāh*). One of the most often cited proof-texts for this is the verse, "Call upon God, or call upon the All-Merciful—whichever you call upon, to Him belong the Most Beautiful Names."[33] Notice that the formula of consecration, which begins almost every chapter of the Qur'an and should initiate a Muslim's every action, contains two of the four Qur'anic divine names derived from the word *raḥma*: "In the name of God, the All-

Merciful (*al-raḥmān*), the Ever-Merciful (*al-raḥīm*)."[34] Ibn 'Arabī points out that this formula expresses God's nature. All divine names refer back to "God" and can be divided into two basic categories: the gentle and the severe (or the beautiful and the majestic, or those that stress immanence and those that stress transcendence). Thus, the word "God" designates the divine Reality not only as merciful but also as wrathful. Nonetheless, as the Prophet insisted (and various Qur'anic verses imply), "God's mercy takes precedence over His wrath." The formula's two names of mercy emphasize that every quality of existence, even wrath, serves the benevolent purposes of a wise and loving Creator.[35]

Ibn 'Arabī also explains that mercy is the Qur'anic equivalent of *wujūd*, "existence" or "being," the typical philosophical and theological designation for the absolute reality of the Real. He uses the term "Breath of the All-Merciful" (*nafas al-raḥmān*), taken from a prophetic saying, to designate the luminous divine Spirit, the effusion of Real Being that animates the universe as the result of the divine command "Be!" He develops an elaborate cosmology based on the Qur'anic notion that all creatures are divine words, articulated, as he says, in the All-Merciful Breath, which is the underlying substance of the universe. His foremost disciple, Ṣadr al-Dīn Qūnawī (d. 1274), commented on a series of sayings in which the Prophet tells us that "the womb" is attached to the divine throne (which encompasses the universe) and that it is a "branch of the All-Merciful." This is because the very existence of the universe is nothing but the mercy about which God says, "My mercy embraces everything."[36]

Given the Qur'anic notion of mercy as God's essential attribute, it is not surprising to find it highlighted as a key human virtue, not least because the Qur'an says that God sent Muhammad, whom it calls a "beautiful model,"[37] as "a mercy to the worlds."[38] Mercy, however, is not exactly love, for God has mercy on human beings, not the other way around. In Islamic languages, God can be the object of love (*maḥbūb*), but not the object of mercy (*marḥūm*).[39]

Divine Love

Two Qur'anic words are typically translated as "love." The first is *wudd* (or *mawadda*), from which we have the divine name *al-wadūd*,[40] which means both lover and beloved. The second is *ḥubb* (or *maḥabba*), which becomes much more prominent in the later literature. Although the Qur'an does not mention a divine name from the root, the later literature commonly refers to God by three names deriving from it: *muḥibb* (lover), *maḥbūb* (beloved), and *ḥabīb* (lover/beloved). A third word for love, *ʿishq*, is not used in the Qur'an but becomes at least as prominent as *ḥubb*. It is said to designate a more intense or an excessive love and is commonly used for erotic love, so the legitimacy of using the word in reference to God was much debated. Many authors considered it either a synonym for *ḥubb*, or as an even more appropriate designation for man's love of God, precisely because God's supreme reality demands the most intense love.[41] A fourth word, *hawā*—caprice, whim, or passion—is roundly condemned by the Qur'an and the hadiths, but is sometimes discussed as a generic word for "love" in later times.[42] Gradually an extensive literature appeared on what Western scholars have called "profane love," even though there is no clear demarcation between "sacred" and "profane" in the Islamic context.[43]

Numerous definitions and etymologies for the various "names and titles" of love are offered in the texts, though many authors, whether Sufis like ʿAyn al-Quḍāt Hamadānī (d. 1131) or theologians like Ibn Qayyim al-Jawziyya (d. 1350), insist that love is beyond definition and can only be known by way of "tasting" (*dhawq*).[44] The Ikhwān al-Ṣafāʾ, in their treatise "On the Quiddity of Love" (*Fī māhiyyat al-ʿishq*), suggest that the best definition is "intense yearning for unification,"[45] adding that "unification" (*ittiḥād*) pertains specifically to the soul and spirit, not to bodily things, where we should speak rather of contact, contiguity, and mixing.[46] The later literature often targets the word "unification" as inappropriate,[47] but everyone agrees that the goal of two lovers is to come together. The disputed issue was whether one can speak of the "coming together" of God and man.

The dispute over unification often circled around the most frequently discussed Qur'anic verse about *ḥubb*: "He loves them, and they love Him."[48] The apparent meaning of this verse is that God is a lover who takes man as His beloved, and man is a lover who takes God as his beloved. Hence God is both lover and beloved, as are human beings. When considered in terms of *tawḥīd*, the divine names Lover and Beloved mean "There is no lover but God" and "There is no beloved but God," so loverness and belovedness as human attributes gain their reality from God. Lest these two divine names suggest some sort of duality in God, authors often stress that God in His Essence is simply love. Al-Daylamī puts it like this:

> The root of love is that God is eternally described by love, which is among His abiding attributes. He is always gazing

> upon Himself for Himself in Himself, just as He is always finding Himself for Himself in Himself. In the same way, He loves Himself for Himself in Himself. Here lover, beloved, and love are a single thing without division, for He is Unity Itself, and in Unity things are not distinct.[49]

In his "Treatise on Love" (*Risāla fi'l-'ishq*), al-Daylamī contemporary Avicenna, provides a philosophical explanation of the same point. First he says that God is the Necessary Being and the Absolute Good, so all contingent being and relative good derive from His Reality. God is not only infinitely lovable, but also infinitely loving. Moreover,

> The First Good perceives Itself in act always and forever, so Its love for Itself is the most perfect and most ample love. There is no essential distinction among the divine attributes in the [Divine] Essence, so love is identical with the Essence and with Being, by which I mean the Sheer Good.[50]

The two most famous Persian prose classics on love also address the unity of love. The first is *Sawāniḥ* ("Apparitions"), written by Amid Ghazālī (d. 1126), the younger brother of the famous theologian, and the second *Lama'āt* ("Flashes"), by Fakhr al-Dīn 'Irāqī (d. 1289), a poet and second-generation student of Ibn 'Arabī. 'Irāqī tells us that he wrote his book in the style of *Sawāniḥ*, and he often expands on Aḥmad Ghazālī's famously allusive expressions. The latter wrote, for example, that the divine Essence "is Lover, Beloved, and Love," but "Lover and Beloved are derived from Love."[51] 'Irāqī put it this way:

> "Lover" and "Beloved" are derived from "Love," and, in the abode of Its exaltation, Love is pure of all specification; in the sanctuary of Its own entity, Love is too holy for nonmanifestation and manifestation. It wanted to manifest Its own perfection, which is identical with Its Essence and attributes, so It presented Itself to Itself in the mirror of Lover and Beloved. It disclosed Its own beauty to Its own gaze. Gazing and being gazed upon made apparent the names "Lover" and "Beloved," the description "Seeker" and "Sought."[52]

Despite the clear sense of the verse of mutual love—that both God and man are lover and beloved—most early theologians, including the mainstream Ash'arites (who are notorious for their abstracting mind-set), denied the apparent meaning, claiming that God's utter transcendence made love between Him and creation impossible. In contrast, many later theologians, such as the Hanbalites Ibn Taymiyya (d. 1328) and Ibn Qayyim al-Jawziyya, dedicated a good deal of attention to proving that the verse means what it says.[53] Among the many who rejected the Ash'arite position was Aḥmad Samʿānī (d. 1140), scion of a famous family of scholars from the city of Marv in eastern Iran. His only known book is a long Persian commentary on God's ninety-nine Most Beautiful Names. He points out that the verse of mutual love is the only place in the Qur'an where a divine quality is ascribed equally to God and man. He cites a series of verses stressing God's greatness and man's smallness, God's omniscience and man's ignorance, God's power and man's weakness. But, he says, "When God gave news of love, just as He affirmed it for Himself, so also He affirmed it for us."[54]

In the course of his commentary, Samʿānī is able to explain practically every one of the divine names in terms of mutual love, developing along the way an elaborate spiritual anthropology.[55] His language is extraordinarily poetic, and indeed, he articulates most of the themes that were soon to dominate the rich Persianate tradition of love poetry as represented by authors like ʿAṭṭār, Rūmī, Saʿdī, and Ḥāfiẓ, as well as a host of other poets in Persian, Turkish, and Urdu. In Samʿānī's view, "He loves them" is the determinant of human destiny, for God loves human beings always and forever. He imagines God as saying,

> "Do not suppose that Our business with you belongs to today, or Our talk with you pertains to right now. There was no world, and there was no Adam; there were no substances, and there were no accidents; there was no Throne and no Footstool, no paradise and no hell, no Tablet and no Pen—and I was talking to you without you."[56]

Aḥmad Ghazālī also stresses the eternal primacy of "He loves them":

> Is it not enough for man that his specific quality is to be a beloved before being a lover? Is this a small favor? "He loves them" threw

> so much food at the beggar before he ever showed up that he will enjoy himself into endless eternity, with plenty left over.[57]

Like the Ikhwān al-Ṣafā' and many early Sufi authors, Aḥmad Ghazālī speaks of unification (*ittiḥād*) as the goal of love, though he prefers the word "union" (*wiṣāl*). In the following, he alludes to the Qur'anic verse, "O people, you are the poor toward God, and God is the Rich, the Praiseworthy!"[58] which is the source of the term "(spiritual) poverty" (*faqr*), a synonym for "Sufism."

> The Beloved says to the lover, "Come, become Me! If I were to become you, then we would need a beloved. The lover would grow, and need and needfulness would increase. But if you become Me, the Beloved will grow—all will be Beloved, not lover, all will be unneedingness, not need, all will be riches, not poverty, all will be help, not helplessness."[59]

Khwāja 'Abdallāh Anṣārī (d. 1088), author of a classic Arabic text on the ladder to God, *Manāzil al-sā'irīn* ("The Way Stations of the Travelers"), often speaks of the mysteries of union in his Persian prayers, which are marvels of early prose. Among them is this: "O God, all love is between two, so there is no room for a third. In this love, all is You, so there is no room for me."[60]

God as Lover of Man

Tawḥīd tells us that there is no love but the Creator's love: His love is real and eternal, and it creates the universe and everything within it. Beginning around the twelfth century, the most commonly cited scriptural reference to creative love is a saying ascribed to the Prophet, according to which David asked God why He created the universe. God replied, "I was a hidden treasure, and I loved (*ḥubb*) to be recognized, so I created the creatures that they might recognize Me." In place of "love," some versions of this saying have "desire" (*irāda*), the attribute mentioned by the Qur'an when it speaks of the engendering command.

According to this hadith, the object of God's love is "recognition" (*ma'rifa*). In explaining the meaning, authors point out that the "Hidden Treasure" alludes to the divine Essence inasmuch as It embraces all possibilities of existence, possibilities whose general characteristics are designated by the divine names. In order to make Itself known, the Hidden Treasure "disclosed Itself." The word here, *tajallī* or "self-disclosure"—often translated as "theophany"—derives from a Qur'anic passage in which Moses asks God to show Himself, and God replies that Moses will not be able to see Him: "And when his Lord *disclosed Himself* to the mountain, He made it crumble to dust, and Moses fell down thunderstruck."[61]

If something is to recognize the Hidden Treasure when It discloses Itself, that something must already have knowledge of It. The only creature that fills this bill is the human being, who was "taught all the names" and created in the form of "God," the divine Reality inasmuch as It embraces all possibility. When man truly recognizes God, he is recognizing his own characterization by the divine names. God-recognition goes hand in hand with self-recognition. This is the message of the famous prophetic saying, constantly quoted in Sufi texts, "He who recognizes himself recognizes his Lord."

Creative love propels the universe both centrifugally and centripetally, that is, on both the descending and the ascending arcs. The centrifugal movement seems to contradict the definition of love as "yearning for unification," but unification is impossible without difference. If God's love is directed toward recognition, that can only come about when there are beings other than God who are capable of recognizing Him. Thus God's "self-disclosure as manifestation" (*tajallī-yi ẓuhūrī*) is the prelude to His "self-disclosure as consciousness" (*tajallī-yi shuʿūrī*),[62] the latter of which can only be actualized fully by human beings. They alone have the capacity to become characterized by all of His character traits. In the Qur'an the angels say, "None of us there is but has a known station,"[63] and, says Ibn ʿArabī, other creatures are the same, with the exception of human beings.[64] We alone are not fixed; we alone can rise in consciousness, and we alone can fall—this is precisely why the prescriptive command invites us to love God. It cannot force us to love Him, however, for that would fix us in a station and make us no different from angels. Samʿānī makes the point in these terms:

> God created every creature in keeping with the demand of power, but He created Adam and his children in keeping with the demand of love. He created other things in respect of being the Strong, but He created you in respect of being the Lover.[65]

The engendering command creates the universe: "Be!" says God, and all things come to be. The prescriptive command addresses those who are not fixed in station, providing instructions on how to love their own Creator and yearn for union with Him, how to act in a manner that will allow them to ascend in consciousness and achieve self-recognition. The texts refer to the ascent by many names, such as the "voluntary return" as contrasted with the "compulsory return." In Sufism, it is often called "dying before you die," a major theme of teachers like Rūmī. It is nothing other than giving up egocentricity and becoming characterized by the divine attributes. It is to follow the Prophet on the ladder to God.

By issuing the engendering command, God disclosed Himself through the properties and traces of His own Most Beautiful Names. Ibn ʿArabī writes,

> Know that the divine beauty through which God is named "Beautiful" and by which He described Himself in His messenger's words, "He loves beauty," is in all things. There is nothing but beauty, for God created the cosmos only in His form, and He is beautiful. Hence all the cosmos is beautiful.[66]

In loving the beauty of created things, God is in fact loving the manifestation of the Hidden Treasure. In other words, He is loving Himself. Al-Ghazālī, who summarized and systematized much of the earlier discussion of both "religious" and "profane" love in Book 36 of his classic *Iḥyāʾ ʿulūm al-dīn* (*Reviving the Sciences of the Religion*), explains that God's love for Himself is demanded by *tawḥīd* or the fact that, as he often puts it, "There is nothing in existence but God" (*laysa fi'l-wujūd illa'Llāh*).[67]

> He is the All, and nothing else [truly] exists. When someone loves only himself, his acts, and his compositions, his love does not transgress his essence and the concomitants of his essence inasmuch as they are connected to his essence. Thus, God loves only Himself.[68]

God issues the engendering command out of love for all things, for He is beautiful, and He loves His beautiful creation. In the same way, His love motivates Him to issue the prescriptive command, but in this case He loves human beauty, for man alone is capable of recognizing all of the Most

Beautiful Names, loving Him who is named by them, and actualizing the names as his own character traits. This is why the Qur'an frequently associates God's love with the moral and ethical perfections that are achieved by climbing the ladder to self-realization. It tells us that God loves those who do what is beautiful,[69] who repent,[70] who trust,[71] who are godfearing,[72] who are just.[73] It also tells us that God does *not* love wrongdoers,[74] workers of corruption,[75] transgressors,[76] the immoderate,[77] the treacherous,[78] the proud,[79] the boastful.[80] In short, the basic message of the prescriptive command—beneath the rituals, rules, and regulations—is the prophetic instruction, "Become characterized by the character traits of God!"

In his "Treatise on Love," Avicenna explains that love motivates the Absolute Good to create the universe and that "no entity is devoid of love."[81] He tells the tale of the Hidden Treasure's love to be recognized and Its creation of human beings in the rather complex philosophical style that typifies his writings. Along the way and contrary to his usual custom, he employs the favorite Sufi term "self-disclosure" to refer to God's creative activity.

> Each of the existent things loves the Absolute Good with an inborn love, and the Absolute Good discloses Itself to Its lovers. Their reception of Its self-disclosure and their conjunction with It, however, is disparate. The utmost limit of nearness to It is the true reception of Its self-disclosure, I mean, in the most perfect way possible. This is what Sufis call "unification." . . . If the Absolute Good did not disclose Itself, nothing would be received from It . . . , so Its self-disclosure is the cause of every existence. . . . The love of the Most Excellent for Its own excellence is the most excellent love, so Its true beloved is the reception of Its self-disclosure. This is the reality of Its reception by deiform souls, so it can be said that they are Its beloveds. To this refers what has been narrated in the reports that, when God's servant is such and such, "He loves Me, and I love him."[82]

Al-Ghazālī dedicates a good portion of Book 36 of the *Iḥyā'* to God's love for human beings, explicitly rejecting its denial by the Ash'arites. Nonetheless, he says that in God's case the word means something different from what it means in man's case. This is how he sums up his argument:

> God's love for the servant is that He brings him near to Himself by fending off distractions and acts of disobedience, purifying his inner self from the turbidities of this world, and lifting the veil from his heart so that he witnesses Him "as if"[83] his heart is seeing Him.
>
> As for the servant's love for God, that is his inclination to grasp the perfection without which he is destitute and lacking. So, he must yearn for what escapes him, and when he grasps something of it, he takes enjoyment. Yearning and love in this meaning are absurd for God.[84]

Although al-Ghazālī breaks with the excessive transcendentalism of his Ash'arite predecessors, he does not accept all the implications of divine immanence. In contrast, Ibn 'Arabī insists throughout his voluminous corpus that a true understanding of *tawḥīd* demands full acknowledgment of both transcendence and immanence—or "declaring incomparability" (*tanzīh*) and "asserting similarity" (*tashbīh*). He explains, for example, that a lover demonstrates his sincerity by taking on the attributes and qualities of his beloved, and that this is just as true of God as it is of man. To demonstrate his point, he cites a series of hadiths (the last of which parallels Matthew 25:41–45):

> The sincere lover is he who passes into the attributes of the beloved, not he who brings the beloved down to his own attributes. Do you not see that God, when He loves us, descends to us in His hidden gentleness by means of that which corresponds to us and above which His eminence and greatness are high exalted? He descends to "happily receiving" us when we come to His house in order to confide in Him; "joy" at our repentance and our return to Him after we turned away from Him; "wonder" at the young man who lacks sensual desire when he should be controlled by it, even though he has that by God's grace; being our deputies in our hunger, thirst, and illness, and placing Himself in our stations. When one of His servants is hungry, He says to the others, "I was hungry, but you did not feed Me." He says to another of His servants, "I was ill but you did not visit Me." When the servants ask Him about this, He replies to them, "Verily so-and-so was ill; if you had visited him,

> you would have found Me with him. So-and-so was hungry; if you had fed him, you would have found Me with him. . . ." This is one of the fruits of love, when He descends to us.[85]

'Abd al-Raḥmān Jāmī (d. 1492), a great Persian poet and master of philosophical prose, was highly influential in the later Persianate expression of Islamic teachings from Turkey to China. In his *Lawā'iḥ* ("The Gleams"), a classic summary of Ibn 'Arabī's teachings, he explains that *tawḥīd* demands the coming together of God and man in love:

> In respect of the Essence, the Unlimited has no need for the contingent. Nonetheless, without the contingent, the names of Divinity cannot become manifest and the attributes of Lordship cannot be realized.
>
> O You whose beauty has incited my yearning and seeking,
> Your soughtness is a branch of my seeking!
>
> If not for the mirror of my loverness,
> the beauty of Your belovedness would not have appeared.
>
> No, rather the lover is the Real and the beloved He, the seeker is the Real and the sought He. He is the sought and the beloved in the station of Unity's gathering, and the seeker and the lover in the level of differentiation and manyness.[86]

In his monumental description of the "four journeys" of human souls in their quest for perfection, the philosopher Mullā Ṣadrā, "Foremost of the Deiform," devotes a long section to the role of love in creation. The overall picture he provides resonates with the notion of the descending arc of manifestation and the ascending arc of realized consciousness. He sums it up when he says,

> Thus have we established that love pervades all existent things in the order of their existence. . . . All of them, in keeping with their appropriate perfections, seek the perfections of the Being that is necessary by Its Essence and become similar to It inasmuch as they actualize Its perfections. Thus the Author—holy are His names!—is the final goal of all existent things and the

> furthest limit of their levels. Love and yearning are the cause of both the existence and the continuity of the existent things in their possible perfections. Were it not for love and yearning, no newly arrived thing could arrive newly in the bodily world, and no being could enter into the world of generation and corruption.[87]

Human Election

Few people actualize their full potential to love God and to be loved by Him. Those who do are sometimes called "perfect human beings" (*insān kāmil*), an expression derived from the Prophet's saying, "Many among men have become perfect, and among women, Mary and Āsiya [the wife of Pharaoh]."[88] The tradition maintains that the most perfect of all human beings was the Prophet Muhammad, followed by the other prophets, such as Abraham, Moses, and Jesus, and then by the "friends" (*awliyā'*) of God, and finally by the believers generally. Given Muhammad's primacy, a good deal of the discussion of God's love for creation centers on his person—though it needs to be kept in mind that the whole point is to insist that everyone has the potential to climb the ladder by following in his footsteps. It is commonly said that God's specific love for Muhammad brought the universe into existence, and God is quoted as saying, "But for thee [O Muhammad!], I would not have created the spheres." Sa'īd al-Dīn Farghānī (d. 1296), who wrote both a Persian and an Arabic commentary on the 760-verse *Poem of the Way* of Ibn al-Fāriḍ (d. 1235), the greatest Arab poet of love, summarizes the theoretical discussion when he says,

> The root of love is the reality of "I *loved* to be recognized." The lover is the One Divine Essence, and the beloved is the complete appearance and total manifestation of the perfections of the divine names. The perfect mirror of this beloved as it is in itself can be nothing but the human reality, in both form and meaning. This is because the human reality has a perfect all-comprehensiveness and a complete correspondence and receptivity [vis-à-vis God], while all other creatures fall short of this. This point is alluded to in the often quoted divine words addressed to Muhammad: "But for thee, I would not have created the spheres."[89]

On the philosophical level, the notion of Muhammad as God's supreme beloved was explained in terms of "the Muhammadan Reality" (*al-ḥaqīqat al-Muḥammadiyya*), the uncreated prototype of creation, also designated by names such as "the Muhammadan Light," "the Reality of Realities," and "the First Self-Disclosure." This uncreated Reality is what many Christian theologians call the *Logos*, the divine self-expression *in divinis*, the prototype of both the universe and the divine form known as man.[90] One can see the notion lurking in these verses of Rūmī (as well as in the whirling dance of the dervishes, as practiced by his followers):

> Heaven circles round about love—
>   jump up, so that we also may circle.
> Look what God said: "If not for thee, I would not have created."
>   Muhammad the Chosen is the quarry of love.[91]

When the discussion focuses on the Muhammadan Reality, the Prophet is considered the only creature who was able to actualize God's full purpose in creating the universe, become totally characterized by all the divine character traits, and achieve the station of perfect deiformity. The mythic proof of this is that he was chosen to receive the Qur'an, God's plenary message. His wife 'Ā'isha, when asked after his death about his character (*khuluq*), replied, "His character was the Qur'an."[92] The Qur'an, we need to remember, is God's speech, the divine Logos in the form of a book, the culminating message of the line of prophecy, which extends back through 124,000 individuals to Adam. The word "Qur'an" (*qur'ān*) famously means "the recitation," but it also means "that which brings together." This second meaning was understood as a reference to the all-comprehensiveness of divine self-revelation in the final message. Ibn 'Arabī has this in mind when he writes, "The character of God's Messenger was the Qur'an and becoming characterized by the divine names as his own character traits."[93]

As God's beloved, Muhammad was able to act as the receptacle for God's Speech and to undertake the Night Journey. During the journey, he achieved the goal of every lover: union with his beloved. This helps explain why following his Sunnah—the beautiful model that he established—plays such an important role in the tradition. The Qur'an says, "Say [O Muhammad!]: 'If you love God, follow me, and God will love you.'"[94] In other words, if people want to actualize the full implications of the creative love that brought each of them into existence, they need to observe the prescriptive command by climbing the ladder in Muhammad's footsteps. Muhammad is a "mercy to the worlds" because God's light is too intense to allow access to Him without His chosen intermediary. As ʿAyn al-Quḍāt Hamadānī explains, "Seeing the sun of 'God is the light of the heavens and the earth' (Qur'an 24:35) without the mirror of Muhammad's beauty burns away the eyes. But, with that mirror, one can study the sun's beauty constantly."[95]

The fact that God loves us all—that He says "Be!" to the entire creation—does not mean that every human being will reap immediate benefit, nor does it demand posthumous felicity (*saʿāda*). As Samʿānī puts it, "When you say, 'He loves them,' your own shirt collar says, 'You've got nothing over me.'"[96] Even those who suffer the wretchedness (*shiqā'*) of hell are the objects of God's love, for He created them out of love and preserves them in existence for the same reason. Another way to think of this is in terms of the Qur'anic verse, "He is with you wherever you are."[97] God is Emmanuel, "God-with-us," but we are not necessarily with Him. The goal of our existence is precisely to recognize the Hidden Treasure and love God so that we can be with Him as He is with us. This is "unification," or rather, realized *tawḥīd*.

Lovers should follow Muhammad because, as we saw in the just-quoted verse, the fruit of following him is that God will love them in return: "Follow me, and God will love you." In a well-known hadith, the Prophet quotes God as saying, "When My servant approaches Me through good works [i.e., by following Muhammad], I will love him, and when I love him, I will be his hearing through which he hears, his eyesight through which he sees, his hand through which he grasps, and his foot through which he walks."[98] This again is the unification achieved by love.

Despite the emphasis of most texts on earning God's love by following the Prophet, many authors stress God's unconditional love. No matter how much credit God may give people for their efforts to achieve perfection, ultimately "There is no agent but He," as al-Ghazālī frequently reminds us. In His infinite mercy, He created people with all their imperfections, knowing full well that they would fall short of angelic purity. The Prophet made the point rather clearly: "If you did not sin, God would take you away and replace you with a people who do sin, and then He would forgive them."[99] The Qur'an also makes the point, in a verse that jurists and preachers sometimes prefer to ignore: "Despair not of God's mercy! Surely God forgives all sins."[100] The manner in which God's love for man trumps every other consideration plays a major role in Samʿānī's commentary on the divine names. For example, the Qur'an says that the angels objected when God told them that He was going to place a vicegerent in the earth. Sam'ānī explains God's answer:

> The angels said, "What, will You place therein one who will work corruption there and shed blood?" God did not reply that He was not doing that. He said, "I know what you do not know" (Qur'an 2:30). In other words, "I know that I will forgive them. You know their disobedience, but I know My forgiveness. In your glorification, you make manifest your own activity, but in My forgiveness, I make manifest My own bounty and generosity. 'I know what you do not know,' which is My love for them and the purity of their belief in loving Me. Although outwardly their good works are barefoot, inwardly their love for Me is pure. 'I know what you do not know,' which is My love for them. No matter what they are, I love them."[101]

Man as Lover of God

We saw that the first half of the verse of mutual love, "He loves them," can be read in terms of both the engendering and the prescriptive commands. In other words, it can refer to God's general, creative love and to God's specific love for human beings, which intensifies when they make themselves worthy by following the Prophet. In a similar way, the second half of the verse, "They love Him," can refer to both commands. By saying, "Be!" God bestowed on all creatures the energy of love, an intense desire to actualize the divine attributes and character traits through which they come to be what they truly are. And, by sending guidance, God teaches human beings how to acknowledge and actualize their innate love for Him. When He said, "I loved to be recognized," He knew full well that all human beings and indeed all creatures would love Him, but that does not mean that they would also recognize who it is that they love. Recognition of God along with the appropriate love is what characterizes prophets, saints, and believers in varying degrees. It is precisely this recognition and love that bring about differentiation among human individuals. Thus al-Ghazālī says, "Disparity of degree in people's love is the cause of the disparity of degree of their felicity in the afterworld. 'Surely the afterworld is greater in ranks and greater in preferment' (Qur'an 17:21)."[102]

The philosophers often explain that all things love God whether they know it or not. The Ikhwān al-Ṣafā' put it this way:

> It has been clarified that God is the First Beloved, and that all existent things yearn for Him and aim for Him. "And to Him the whole affair is returned" (Koran 11:123). For, in Him is their existence, their abiding, their subsistence, their continuity, and their perfection, because He is the Sheer Existent, and He has eternal subsistence and continuity and everlasting completeness and perfection.[103]

Suhrawardī (d. 1191), the founder of the Illuminationist school of philosophy, agreed with his predecessors on love's universal presence. He says, for example, "The First is the lover of His own Essence, and He is also the beloved of His own Essence and of everything else—all contingent things."[104] In summing up a long explanation of what he means, his commentator remarks, "So, all things are lovers and yearners—'He loves them, and they love Him.'"[105]

Ibn 'Arabī speaks of omnipresent love when he says, "None but God is loved in the existent things. It is He who is manifest in every beloved to the eye of every lover—and nothing exists that is not a lover. So, all the cosmos is lover and beloved, and all of it goes back to Him."[106]

Sam'ānī makes the point in a passage that reflects the positive Qur'anic evaluation of all prophetic revelation:

> If you go to the Sufi lodge—burning for Him. If you go to the lane of the taverns—the pain of not having found Him. If you go to a Christian church, everyone is on the carpet of seeking Him. If you go to a Jewish synagogue, all are yearning for His beauty. If you go to a Zoroastrian fire-temple, all are burned by His majesty. If you look at His familiars, all are wounded by His drunken eyes and the glances of His beauty. If you look at those estranged from Him, they are tied down by the bond of His exaltation and majesty.[107]

Ḥāfiẓ (d. 1390), typically considered the greatest poet of the Persian tradition, epitomizes universal love in this couplet:

Everyone's seeking a beloved,
whether sober or drunk,
everywhere's the house of love,
whether mosque or synagogue.[108]

Rūmī frequently talks about love's omnipresence. He also differentiates carefully between "real love" (*'ishq ḥaqīqī*)—that is, love for God based on recognition of Him—and "metaphorical love" (*'ishq majāzī*), which is love that has not yet reached the stage of true discernment. He compares the latter to a wooden sword that a warrior gives to his son. As people's character traits develop and mature, they find that all metaphorical love leads them back to true love, for, as the Arabic proverb has it, "The metaphor is the bridge to the reality" (*al-majāz qanṭarat al-ḥaqīqa*). 'Ayn al-Quḍāt takes the same approach when he says that God gave Majnūn, the most famous of mythic lovers, his intense love for Laylā in order to prepare him for climbing the path to God:

> Do you know why all these curtains and veils have been placed in the path? So that day-by-day the lover's vision may become mature and he may gain the ability to carry the load of encountering God without a veil.... God ordained that Majnūn's love for Laylā be made into a riding beast for his nature, so that love for her would mature him and give him the ability to carry the load of love for God.[109]

Throughout his writings Rūmī advises his readers to gain the capacity to look beyond the veils and curtains, to see through the metaphor and gaze upon the Reality that is disclosing Itself.

> In man there is a love, a pain, an itch, and an urgency such that, if a hundred thousand worlds were to become his property, he would still gain no rest or ease. These people occupy themselves totally with every kind of craft, artistry, and position; they learn astronomy, medicine, and other things, but they find no ease, for their goal has not been attained.... All these pleasures and goals are like a ladder. The rungs of a ladder are no place to take up residence and stay—they're for passing on. Happy is he who wakes

> up quickly and becomes aware! Then the long road becomes short, and he does not waste his life on the ladder's rungs.[110]

More than most teachers, Rūmī brings the theoretical discussion of love down to everyday experience. He is especially adept at showing that the pain, heartache, and suffering that characterize human existence follow directly on the engendering command, which results in the separation of lover and beloved. This is why he begins his famous *Mathnawī*, sometimes called "the Qur'an in the Persian language," with the verse, "Listen to the reed as it complains, telling the tale of separation."[111] The poem's twenty-five thousand couplets are dedicated to explaining that every hunger, thirst, desire, and longing is in fact love for the Source who, in loving us, brought us out from the Hidden Treasure and called upon us to love Him in return.

In one of his prose works Rūmī explains that before entering this world, we were like fish swimming in the ocean, unaware of the water. When the ocean wanted to be recognized, it threw us up on dry land. Now we flip and flop, suffering the pain of love for the ocean. Once we go back where we came from, we will have the same situation as we did at first, but we will live in the joy of recognition and union, a joy that we could never have actualized without our exile.[112] Fakhr al-Dīn 'Irāqī makes the same point in terms of the circle of existence, composed of the two "arcs" or "bows" (*qaws*) mentioned in the Qur'an's account of Muhammad's climb to God, when he was "two bows'-length away, or nearer."[113]

> Suppose that the lover and beloved are one circle, cut in half by a straight line, such that it appears as two bows. If this line that appears to be there, but is not, falls out of the diagram at the moment of meeting, the circle will appear as one, as it is. The secret of "Two Bows' Length" will become plain. . . . But, there is something more to say: You should know that, although the line falls away from the circle, the circle will not appear as it did at first. The property of the line will not vanish. Though the line will disappear, its trace will remain.[114]

Rashīd al-Dīn Maybudī (d. after 1126), who wrote one of the longest premodern Persian commentaries on the Qur'an, meditates throughout the book on the secrets of the mutual love between God and man. He, like

Rūmī's teacher Shams-i Tabrīzī, read the Qur'an as a love letter.[115] Take, for example, his remarks on the verse, "Satan made them slip therefrom":[116]

> Be careful not to suppose that Adam was taken out of paradise to abase him. It was not that. Rather, it was because of the grandeur of his aspiration. The petitioner of love came to the door of Adam's breast and said, "O Adam, the beauty of meaning has been unveiled, but you have stayed in the Abode of Peace." Adam saw an infinite beauty, compared to which the beauty of the eight paradises was nothing. His great aspiration tightened its belt and said: "If you ever want to be lover, you must be a lover of that." . . .
>
> The command came: "Now that you have stepped into the lane of love, leave paradise, which is the house of ease! What do lovers have to do with the safety of the Abode of Peace?" . . .
>
> Your love came to my door and knocked.
> I didn't open it, so it burnt it down.[117]

In several passages of his commentary on the divine names, Samʿānī refers to Adam's purposeful decision to leave Paradise. The "grain of wheat" in the following is the Islamic "apple"—the forbidden fruit:

> By God the Tremendous! They placed the worth of paradise in Adam's hand. There was no bride more beautiful than paradise among all the existent things—it had such a beautiful face and such a perfect adornment! But the ruling power of Adam's aspiration entered from the world of the Unseen Jealousy. He weighed the worth of paradise in his hand and its value in the scales. Paradise began to shout, "I cannot put up with this brazen man!"
>
> O noble youth! If tomorrow you go to paradise and look at it from the corner of your heart's eye, in truth, in truth, you will have fallen short of Adam's aspiration. Something that your father sold for one grain of wheat—why would you want to settle down there?[118]

Al-Ghazālī begins his long chapter on love in the *Iḥyā'* by saying that it is the highest rung on the ladder of spiritual ascent:

> Love for God is the furthest goal among the stations and the highest pinnacle of the degrees. After reaching love, later stations, like yearning, familiarity, and contentment, are among its fruits and consequences. And all the stations before love —such as repentance, patience, and abstinence—are introductions to it.[119]

In defining human love, al-Ghazālī says that it is "the inclination of one's nature toward a pleasurable thing,"[120] and he stresses that no one can love anything without knowing it first.[121] He then provides a long analysis of five basic causes of human love, which he summarizes as follows:

> (1) Man's love for his own existence, its perfection, and its subsistence. (2) His love for those who act beautifully [*iḥsān*] toward him in what relates to the continuity of his own existence, helping its subsistence, and protecting it from harm. (3) His love for those who act beautifully in general, whether or not they act beautifully toward him. (4) His love for all things that are beautiful in essence, whether these be outward or inward forms. (5) His love for those with whom he has a hidden, inner affinity [*munāsaba*].[122]

Al-Ghazālī then turns to an even longer discussion in which he applies the principle of *tawḥīd* to these five sorts of love, showing that the seeker needs to recognize who it is that he truly loves. Since there is no god but God, (1) there is no existence and no bestower of existence but God, (2–3) all beautiful activity goes back to God as the Beautiful-doer, (4) none is truly beautiful but God, and (5) man's deepest affinity is with God, in whose form he was created and by whose character traits he is characterized.[123] Later on in the same chapter, having cited many anecdotes about the pains and sacrifices that people willingly undertake because of love for other people, he again applies the principle of *tawḥīd*:

> These and similar things are acknowledged as true in love for fellow creatures, so it is even more appropriate that they be seen as true in love for the Creator. After all, inner insight is more truthful than outer eyesight, and the beauty of the Lordly Presence is

> more complete than any other beauty. Or rather, every beauty in the universe is a loveliness deriving from that beauty.[124]

Among the many authors who stress the importance of recognition and knowledge in loving God is Ibn al-Dabbāgh (d. 1296), author of one of the clearest and most systematic treatises on love in Arabic.

> Nothing allows people to reach complete love but recognition of the perfection and beauty of the Beloved.... Love is the fruit of recognition, and recognition is the cause and occasion of love. ... Every lover is a recognizer [*ʿārif*], but not every recognizer is a lover [*muḥibb*]—I mean, at the beginning of recognition. But, when recognition reaches perfection, and when love becomes continuous through recognition's continuity, then the lover is the same as the recognizer, and the recognizer is the same as the lover, with no difference. This is because, when recognition is firmly rooted, the attributes of the Beloved disclose themselves to the lover. This self-disclosure becomes constant through the constancy of the love, and love becomes constant through the constancy of the recognition. ... Through witnessing and self-disclosure, the recognizer's love and the lover's recognition are unified, and each of these two stations yields the other in succession.[125]

Ibn al-Dabbāgh also explains why the lover's journey to his Beloved must go on forever. He has in mind the Qur'anic commandment to seek increase in knowledge.[126]

> The many attributes witnessed from the Beloved are beyond count, and they cannot enter in upon the lover all at once. Rather, they follow one another in keeping with the increase in perception. Each attribute demands a trace in the soul, so the lover is always striving to seek increase. When a beautiful form of his Beloved appears to him, he yearns to perceive it so as to enjoy it. When he perceives it, he seeks to perceive what is higher, for the Beloved's self-disclosures have no end, and yearning drives the lover to embrace them all. In yearning to achieve

> them all, he suffers pain, and in gazing upon the beauty of what he witnesses from his Beloved, he lives in joy.[127]

The fact that God is the only true object of love does not lead our authors to conclude that human beings should abandon the world and become ascetics. The principle here is that man should love what God loves and dislike what God dislikes. Those who love God also love His beautiful creation. As al-Ghazālī says, "When love for God dominates over someone's heart, he loves all of God's creatures, for He created them."[128] Sa'dī, the great love-poet and moralist, makes the same point when he begins a *ghazal* with the line,

> I delight in the world
> because the world delights in Him,
> I love the whole cosmos
> because the whole cosmos comes from Him.[129]

Among the specific things that God loves is the prescriptive command, because it guides His creatures to love Him in return. Sahl al-Tustarī (d. 896), a famous early Sufi, explains this point in an aphorism. By "this world" (*al-dunyā*) he means not the cosmos as beautiful divine creation, but the fleeting preoccupations and misguided loves that prevent people from remembering and loving God. Thus the Prophet said, "This world is accursed—accursed is everything within it, save the remembrance of God."[130] When one remembers and loves God, this world is His self-disclosure, constantly displaying the divine beauty.

> The mark of love for God is love for the Koran, the mark of love for God and love for the Koran is love for the Prophet, the mark of love for the Prophet is love for his Sunnah, the mark of love for the Sunnah is love for the afterworld, the mark of love for the afterworld is hatred for this world, and the mark of hatred for this world is that you take nothing from it but the provisions that convey to the afterworld.[131]

As Annemarie Schimmel has illustrated copiously in her book on the manner in which the Prophet was understood in premodern Islamic culture, love for Muhammad was the most prominent of the lesser, praiseworthy loves, for it is he who is the beautiful model whose Sunnah guides people on the ladder to God.[132] Moreover, as this culture knew so well, his Sunnah embraces not only his acts and deeds, but also his inner attitudes and his union with God. This is why a saying was attributed to him, "The Shariah is my words, the Tariqah (path to God) is my deeds, and the Haqiqah (the Supreme Reality) is my inner state."

The Suffering of Love

Love demands pain. This is one of the great themes of the literature of love, so much so that many chapters and even a few books celebrate the "martyrdom" that is achieved by dying in the pain of unconsummated love, typically taking inspiration from a famous hadith: "He who loves, remains chaste, conceals the secret, and dies, has died a martyr."[133] At first sight, to say that love demands pain seems harsh—don't we imagine that love for God must be perfect bliss? But perfect bliss is promised for paradise, when people "shall have what their souls desire."[134] In the meantime they are faced with separation from what they love, and nothing is more painful. As Anṣārī points out, the problem is straightforward: "O God, what is more painful than that the beloved be rich, and the lover poor?"[135]

Not only that, but the prescriptive command calls for effort, exertion, and struggle. Why, after all, would a lovely woman accept a man's petitions simply on his say-so? Yes, the lover wants union, but the beloved does not pass out her favors so easily. Aḥmad Ghazālī explains why:

> The Beloved flees from the lover because union is not something small. Just as the lover must give himself over to not being himself, so also the Beloved must give Herself over to his being Her lover. As long as She has not consumed him completely from within and counted him as belonging to Herself, and as long as She has not received him totally, She will flee from him.[136]

The Qur'an frequently speaks of the trials and tribulations of love, though typically it poses them in terms of faith (*īmān*). When al-Ḥārith al-Muḥāsibī (d. 857) was asked about "the root love" from which all other love for God grows up, he replied, "It is the love of faith, for God bears witness that the faithful have love in the verse, 'Those who have faith love God more intensely' (Qur'an 2:165)."[137] Concerning faith, the Qur'an asks,

"Do people think they will be left to say, 'We have faith,' and they will not be tested?"[138] In explaining this verse, Maybudī cites the hadith, "The most severe in tribulation are the prophets, then the most excellent, and so on."[139] Rūmī frequently refers to the same hadith to demonstrate that Muhammad was the greatest lover of God. After all, he says, "Whoever is more awake has greater pain, whoever is more aware has a yellower face."[140] True lovers alone know the meaning of pain. Anṣārī wonders, "O God, since You had the fire of separation, why did You need the fire of hell?"[141] Along these lines, Aḥmad Ghazālī says, "In reality, love is affliction. In love intimacy and ease are foreign and borrowed. The truth is that in love separation is duality, and the truth is that union is oneness. All the rest is the fantasy of union, not its reality."[142]

Love, in short, demands separation. Through it, God acquaints His lovers with their true Beloved, teaches His fish about the ocean, instills human beings with His own character traits, and turns forgetful mortals into loving, compassionate, deiform souls. Thus, Ibn 'Arabī writes,

> The Beloved keeps Himself absent from the lover for the sake of imparting knowledge and teaching courtesy in love. For, if the lover is truthful in his claim when God tests him by the absence of what he loves, a movement of yearning to witness Him will appear in him, and thereby he will display his truthfulness. Then he will rise up in station, and his reward of bliss in his Beloved will be multiplied.[143]

In his commentary on the divine names, Sam'ānī is especially eloquent in describing the lover's pain. Typical is the following:

> The experienced lover, his heart given to the wind, steps out on the path and devotes his whole self to the quest, driven by the assaults of yearning, the heat of ecstasy's flames, and the burning fire of love. Wherever he looks, he sees nothing but the object of his quest. He intends nothing but that object and sees nothing but his desire. He inscribes the figure of reality across the face of imagination, but from the quarters of the Divine Majesty blows a wind that turns all his suppositions into scattered dust.[144]

In short, love for God burns away all the illusions of "the real world." It throws people into the fire of pain and suffering so that they may find their true Self. In explaining the meaning of the verse, "Those who have faith love God more intensely,"[145] Maybudī writes,

> The Lord of the Worlds says, "The love of the faithful for Me is not like the unbelievers' love for idols, such that every once in a while they incline toward another. Rather, the faithful never turn away from Me and never incline toward anyone else. If they turned away from someone like Me, they would never find themselves, no matter how hard they tried."[146]

According to 'Ayn al-Quḍāt Hamadānī, "Wherever love may be, it is a fire that does not let anything settle down. It burns whatever it reaches and makes it the same color as itself."[147] This fire of love is lit by *tawḥīd*, for there is no beauty but God, no beloved but God, no life but God, no joy but God. As Ibn al-Dabbāgh explains, "Love is a fire in the heart that burns away everything except the Beloved."[148] This is what lovers understand from the universal prophetic message, "There is no god but I, so worship Me." They see that pain and suffering will continue until love incinerates all transitory wants, desires, hopes, and fears and nothing is left but the true Beloved. Rūmī distills this teaching into the following verses, in which he compares the "No" of the Shahadah to a sword:

> Love is that flame which, when it blazes up,
> burns away everything except the Subsistent Beloved.
> It drives home the sword of "No" in order to slay other than God.
> Look closely—after "No" what remains?
> There remains "but God," the rest has gone.
> Bravo, O great, idol-burning Love![149]

A Final Word

I can sum up the picture of love drawn by Muslim lovers in these terms: Love is the very Reality of God Himself. It gives rise to the universe and permeates all of creation. God singled out human beings for special love by creating them in His own form and bestowing on them the unique capacity to recognize Him in Himself and to love Him for Himself, not for any specific blessing. The mark of this capacity is that they alone are addressed by the prescriptive command and offered the choice of loving Him or rejecting Him. The engendering command instills them with love, but He cannot force them to recognize who it is that they truly love without depriving them of their humanity. As the Qur'an puts it, "There is no coercion in religion,"[150] for coerced love is no love at all. Those who accept the call of the prescriptive command should not expect an easy road. Falling in love is the beginning of pain, not its end. Nonetheless, the more intense the pain, the greater the joy. This is why Rūmī tells us that lovers prefer the pain inflicted by the Beloved to anything else.

> Marvelous pain You stir up that becomes the cure of my pains!
> Marvelous dust You stir up that refreshes my eyes![151]

Tawḥīd, Islam's founding principle, negates false reality and presents God as the only Lover and the only Beloved. Prophecy, the first corollary of *tawḥīd*, explains that becoming characterized by the divine character traits provides the means to participate fully in God's love by loving Him and loving others as oneself. Compassion, brotherhood, ethics, morality, and justice can only be actualized if one receives a luminous robe of honor woven from the divine attributes; beautiful character traits, which are nothing but the embodiment of the divine names, are not, and cannot be, human possessions, for there is no beauty but God's beauty. Over Islamic history, the most popular spokespersons for virtue, goodness, and love have not been theologians and jurists, but rather those saintly souls who lived lives of loving-kindness and compassion. Among them were great poets who sang of love, figures like Ibn al-Fāriḍ in Arabic, Rūmī and Saʿdī in Persian, and Yunus Emre in Turkish. The intense love and compassion that radiates from their lives and poetry has inspired people for centuries to love "the whole cosmos," as Saʿdī put it, and it has helped them to understand that God's love for man is in fact the heart of the Qur'anic message.

Notes

1. Qur'an 21:25.
2. Qur'an 14:4.
3. Not only that, but in the past decades the Islamic legal tradition has to a significant degree been usurped by engineers and doctors, convinced that the Qur'an provides clear-cut, precise, even "scientific" instructions that can be imposed on any society, by force if need be. For a fine summary of the case against this puritanical and very modern "fundamentalism," see Khalid Abou El-Fadl, *The Great Theft: Wrestling Islam from the Extremists* (New York: HarperOne, 2007). Karen Armstrong summarizes in

her book *The Battle for God* (New York: Ballantine Books, 2001) the scholarly arguments showing that Jewish, Christian, and Muslim fundamentalists take a totally new approach to their religions.

4. By "theologians" I mean not only the representatives of Kalām (apologetic theology) but also other Muslim thinkers who unpacked the theoretical implications of God's unity, including philosophers and Sufis. By "philosophers" (*falāsifa*) I mean specifically those known by this term because of their respect for Greek philosophy, and by "Sufis" those whose primary concern was to establish a personal relationship with the divine Reality. These labels, however, are by no means mutually exclusive; many figures in Islamic history have simultaneously been theologians, philosophers, and Sufis. The best early text on love bringing together the views of these three approaches is by Abu'l-Ḥasan al-Daylamī (d. ca. 1000), *A Treatise on Mystical Love*, trans. Joseph Norment Bell and Hasan Mahmood Abdul Latif Al Shafie (Edinburgh: Edinburgh University Press, 2006). A great deal has been published specifically about Sufi views on love, and any overview of Sufism is likely to touch on the topic. The most detailed historical discussion is provided by Hellmut Ritter, *The Ocean of the Soul: Man, the World, and God in the Stories of Farīd al-Dīn 'Aṭṭār* (Leiden, The Netherlands: Brill, 2003), especially 360–614. For a quick scholarly survey, see Binyamin Abrahamov, *Divine Love in Islamic Mysticism: The Teachings of al-Ghazâlî and al-Dabbâgh* (London: RoutledgeCurzon, 2003); also Carl W. Ernst, "Stages of Love in Early Persian Sufism, From Rabi'a to Ruzbihan," *Sufi* 14 (1992): 16–23. Many of the Sufi poets were deeply rooted in theoretical teachings about love, a point that Ritter makes repeatedly. For Rūmī, see William C. Chittick, *The Sufi Path of Love: The Spiritual Teachings of Rumi* (Albany: State University of New York Press, 1983).
5. Among theologians, Ibn Qayyim al-Jawziyya (d. 1350) was especially explicit on this point, declaring that love for God is the foundation of all religion and all scripture. See Joseph Norment Bell, *Love Theory in Later Hanbalite Islam* (Albany: State University of New York Press, 1979), 209. Both Ritter, *Ocean of the Soul*, and Abrahamov, *Divine Love in Islamic Mysticism*, provide useful discussions of philosophy's contributions to love theory.
6. Qur'an 36:82.
7. Often this word is translated as "will" when God is the subject, and "desire" when others are the subject. This tactic, however, ignores the literal sense of the word and turns scripture into apologetic theology. Bell and Shafie, for example, object to Arberry's translation of the word as "desire" (in this verse and elsewhere in his *The Koran Interpreted*, trans. Arthur J. Arberry [London: Allen & Unwin, 1955]) and claim that translating it as "will" shows that it refers to "the totally free exercise of God's creative will (*irāda*), unfettered by want, lack, need, or purpose (*gharaḍ*)" (*Treatise*, 9).
8. For the two commands, see William C. Chittick, *The Sufi Path of Knowledge* (Albany: State University of New York Press, 1989), 291ff. Ibn Taymiyya, much interested in love despite his reputation as the grandfather of Muslim fundamentalism, called the two commands the "creative, engendering desire" (*al-irādat al-khalqiyyat al-kawniyya*) and "the religious, law-giving desire" (*al-irādat al-dīniyyat al-shar'iyya*); see Bell, *Love Theory in Later Hanbalite Islam*, 66. His student, Ibn Qayyim al-Jawziyya, calls them "the engendering command" (*al-amr al-kawnī*) and "the religious command" (*al-amr al-dīnī*); see *Rawḍat al-muḥibbīn* (Aleppo, Syria: Dār al-Shaw'ī, 1397/1977), 65.
9. Qur'an 97:1.
10. Qur'an 14:1.

11. Qur'an 17:1.
12. Qur'an 53:14.
13. For a graphic presentation of the light symbolism, see M.-R. Séguy, *The Miraculous Journey of Mahomet* (New York: George Braziller, 1977), which provides fifty-eight color reproductions from a fifteenth-century Turkish manuscript.
14. Avicenna, for example, wrote a treatise describing the Night of the Ladder as a model for achieving intellectual perfection. See Peter Heath, *Allegory and Philosophy in Avicenna (Ibn Sīnā), with a Translation of the Book of the Prophet Muḥammad's Ascent to Heaven* (Philadelphia: University of Pennsylvania Press, 1992).
15. Qur'an 59:24.
16. Qur'an 40:64.
17. Qur'an 32:7.
18. Qur'an 95:4.
19. *'Abhar al-'āshiqīn*, ed. Henry Corbin and M. Mo'in, in Ruzbehan Baqli Shirazi, *Le Jasmin des Fidèles d'Amour* (Tehran: Institut Franco-Iranien, 1958), 35. For Rūzbihān's views on love, see Carl Ernst, *Ruzbihan Baqli: Mysticism and the Rhetoric of Sainthood in Persian Sufism* (London: RoutledgeCurzon, 1996).
20. Qur'an 95:5.
21. Qur'an 2:30.
22. Qur'an 2:38.
23. Qur'an 20:121.
24. Qur'an 20:115.
25. Qur'an 4:28.
26. Qur'an 68:4.
27. For a translation of the book, see David Burrell, *al-Ghazālī on the Ninety-Nine Most Beautiful Names of God* (Cambridge: Islamic Texts Society, 1992).
28. Al-Daylamī, *Kitāb 'aṭf al-alif al-ma'lūf 'ala'l-lām al-ma'ṭūf*, ed. J. C. Vadet (Cairo: Institut Français d'Archéologie Orientale, 1962), 93. For Bell and Shafie's translation of this passage, see *Treatise*, 140.
29. *Rasā'il Ikhwān al-Ṣafā'* (Beirut: Dār Ṣādir, 1957), 3:30.
30. In Avicenna's *Shifā'*, this passage is found in a late chapter called, "On the Acts of Worship and Their Benefit in This World and the Next." See Michael E. Marmura, *The Metaphysics of the Healing* (Provo, UT: Brigham Young University Press, 2005), 370.
31. *al-Futūḥāt al-makkiyya* (1911; repr. Beirut: Dār Ṣādir, n.d.), 2:126, line 8.
32. Muslim, *Tawba* 21. In providing sources for the hadiths, I give the minimal information, recognizable to specialists, but little help to those without a knowledge of Arabic (there are no reliable English translations of the hadith collections). The numbering of the hadiths follows that established by A. J. Wensinck, J. P. Mensing, and J. Brugman in *Concordance et Indices de la Tradition Musulmane* (Leiden, Germany: E. J. Brill, 1936–69). The references that I give are by no means exhaustive.
33. Qur'an 17:110.
34. The other two are *al-rāḥim*, the Merciful, and *arḥam al-rāḥimīn*, the Most Merciful of the merciful.
35. See "The Hermeneutics of Mercy," in William C. Chittick, *Ibn 'Arabī: Heir to the Prophets* (Oxford: Oneworld, 2005), chap. 9, specifically p. 133.
36. Qur'an 7:156. On Qūnawī's discussion, see Sachiko Murata, *The Tao of Islam: A Sourcebook on Gender Relationships in Islamic Thought* (Albany: State University of New York Press, 1992), chap. 7, especially p. 220.

37. Qur'an 33:21.
38. Qur'an 21:107.
39. This word is used for a deceased person, like the English "late."
40. Qur'an 85:14.
41. Al-Daylamī addresses the arguments concerning the use of the word *'ishq* in *Treatise*, and Bell and al-Shafie discuss some of the historical context in their introduction.
42. Lois Anita Giffen, in *Theory of Profane Love among the Arabs: The Development of the Genre* (New York: New York University Press, 1971), part 2, chap. 3, finds that authors who attempted to be comprehensive in discussing love provided definitions for sixty to eighty "names and kinds" of love. In *Love Theory*, Bell dedicates a chapter to "Kinds and Stages of Love," including five tables comparing the terminology of fifteen different theologians and Sufis.
43. In *Theory of Profane Love*, Giffen points out that all twenty authors whose books she analyzes also deal with religious themes. She seems to have chosen "profane" so that she could exclude texts that she deemed to be "mystical," itself a problematic word.
44. For a good sampling of definitions, see Bell and Shafie, *Treatise*, chap. 4.
45. *Rasā'il Ikhwān al-Ṣafā'*, 3:272.
46. Ibid., 3:273.
47. For something of the debates over its use, see Bell and Shafie, *Treatise*, xxxix–xl.
48. Qur'an 5:54. This verse is almost invariably cited in this form, even though everyone who cited it knew perfectly well that these two clauses are part of a longer sentence. Some Western scholars, trying to be faithful to the Qur'anic context, add words to the translation and give us, for example, "a people whom He loves, and who love Him." But this obscures the sense in which the verse is being read.
49. Al-Daylamī, *Kitāb 'atf al-alif*, 36–37; and Bell and Shafie, *Treatise*, 59.
50. Ḥusayn al-Ṣiddīq and Rāwiyya Jāmūs, eds. *Risāla fi'l-'ishq* (Damascus, Syria: Dār al-Fikr, 2005), 54. Cf. Emil L. Fackenheim, "A Treatise on Love by Ibn Sina," *Medieval Studies* 7 (1945): 208–28, specifically 214.
51. N. Pourjavady, ed., *Sawāniḥ* (Tehran: Intishārāt-i Bunyād-i Farhang-i Īrān, 1359/1980), 10. On love as the Divine Essence, see Pourjavady's remarks in his translation of the work, *Sawāniḥ: Inspirations from the World of Pure Spirits* (London: KPI, 1986), 88–89.
52. Jawād Nūrbakhsh, ed., *Lama'āt* (Tehran: Intishārāt-i Khānaqāh-i Ni'matullāhī, 1353/1974), 5–6; for a translation, see William C. Chittick and Peter Lamborn Wilson, *Fakhruddin 'Iraqi: Divine Flashes* (New York: Paulist Press, 1971).
53. Bell, *Love Theory*, 74, 209.
54. Najīb Māyil Hirawī, ed., *Rawḥ al-arwāḥ fī sharḥ asmā' al-malik al-fattāḥ* (Tehran: Shirkat-i Intishārāt-i 'Ilmī wa Farhangī, 1368/1989), 519.
55. For a review of some of this theory, see "The Fall of Adam" in William C. Chittick, *Sufism: A Short Introduction* (Oxford: Oneworld, 2000), 111–36.
56. Hirawī, *Rawḥ*, 83.
57. Pourjavady, *Sawāniḥ*, 12.
58. Qur'an 35:15.
59. Pourjavady, *Sawāniḥ*, 16.
60. Cited in Maybudī, *Kashf al-asrār wa 'uddat al-abrār*, ed. 'A. A. Ḥikmat (Tehran: Dānishgāh, 1331–39/1952–60), 7:310.
61. Qur'an 7:143.
62. The terminology is from Lāhījī, *Mafātīḥ al-i'jāz fī sharḥ Gulshan-i rāz*, ed. Muḥammad-

riḍā Barzgar Khāliqī and ʿIffat Karbāsī (Tehran: Zuwwār, 1381/2002), 16. The general notion of God's creative activity as a darkening of awareness, and the human ascent to God as a reawakening of that awareness, is found in most schools of Islamic philosophy and Sufism. Historians of ideas like to point out the parallel with Neoplatonic notions (and one should not forget parallels with Hindu schools like Samkhya-Yoga).

63. Qur'an 37:164.
64. Strictly speaking the *jinn*, whom the Qur'an pairs with man as "the two weighty ones," are also not fixed. For a translation of Ibn ʿArabī's discussion, see Chittick, *Sufi Path of Knowledge*, 295.
65. Hirawī, *Rawḥ*, 223.
66. *Futūḥāt*, 2:542, line 19.
67. For a summary of this chapter and a survey of earlier views on love, especially those of Sufis like Shaqīq al-Balkhī, Abu'l-Naṣr al-Sarrāj, and the woman saint Rābiʿa, see Abrahamov, *Divine Love*. Al-Ghazālī himself wrote a version of the chapter in his abbreviation of his Arabic tome, *Kīmiyā-yi saʿādat*, [*The Alchemy of Happiness*], trans. Jay R. Crook (Chicago: Great Books of the Islamic World, 2002), specifically section 39; this was also published separately as *Al-Ghazzali on Love, Longing and Contentment*, trans. Muhammad Nur Abdus Salam (Chicago: Kazi Publications, 2003).
68. *Iḥyā' ʿulūm al-dīn* (Beirut: Dār al-Hādī, 1993), 4:474.
69. Qur'an 2:195.
70. Qur'an 2:222.
71. Qur'an 3:159.
72. Qur'an 3:76.
73. Qur'an 49:9.
74. Qur'an 3:140.
75. Qur'an 5:64.
76. Qur'an 5:87.
77. Qur'an 7:31.
78. Qur'an 8:58.
79. Qur'an 16:23.
80. Qur'an 31:18.
81. Al-Ṣiddīq and Jāmūs, *Risāla fī'l-ʿishq*, 54; Fackenheim, "Treatise on Love," 214.
82. Al-Ṣiddīq and Jāmūs, *Risāla fī'l-ʿishq*, 82, 87–88; Fackenheim, "Treatise on Love," 225, 228.
83. These two words allude to the famous hadith of *iḥsān* or "doing what is beautiful," according to which the Prophet said, "*Iḥsān* is to worship God *as if* you see Him, for if you do not see Him, He sees you."
84. *Iḥyā' ʿulūm al-dīn*, 4:476.
85. *Futūḥāt*, 2:596, line 6. For the sources of the hadiths, see Chittick, *Sufi Path of Knowledge*, 392n33.
86. *Abdorrahmân b. Ahmad Jâmi: Les Jaillissements de Lumière; Lavâyeh. Texte persan édité and traduit avec introduction et notes*, par Yann Richard (Paris: Les Deux Océans, 1982), 102. See also the English translation of the text in Sachiko Murata, *Chinese Gleams of Sufi Light* (Albany: State University of New York Press, 2000), 174.
87. *al-Asfār al-arbaʿa* (Tehran, 1282/1865–66), 679.
88. Bukhārī, *Anbiyā'* 32, 46; *Faḍā'il Aṣḥāb al-Nabī* 30; Muslim, *Faḍā'il al-Ṣaḥāba* 70.
89. Farghānī, *Mashāriq al-darārī*, ed. S. J. Āshtiyānī (Tehran: Anjuman-i Islāmī-yi Ḥikmat

wa Falsafa-yi Īrān, 1358/1979), 606–7. For translations of Ibn al-Fāriḍ's major poems on love, see E. Homerin, *'Umar Ibn al-Fāriḍ: Sufi Verse, Saintly Life* (Mahwah, NJ: Paulist Press, 2001). For a commentary on one of these poems by a fourteenth-century intellectual descendant of Ibn 'Arabī, see E. Homerin, *The Wine of Love and Life: Ibn al-Fāriḍ's al-Khamrīyah and al-Qayṣarī's Quest for Meaning* (Chicago: Middle East Documentation Center, 2005).

90. The discussion of the Muhammadan Reality has many variations, the earlier versions often taking a mythic form. See, e.g., Gerhard Böwering's study of al-Tustarī, *The Mystical Vision of Existence in Classical Islam* (Berlin: Walter de Gruyter, 1980), chap. 4.
91. B. Furūzānfar, ed., *Kulliyyāt-i Shams yā dīwān-i kabīr* (Tehran: Dānishgāh, 1336–46/1957–67), vv. 12295–96.
92. Muslim, *Musāfirīn* 139.
93. *Futūḥāt*, 3:61, line 2.
94. Qur'an 3:31.
95. 'Afif 'Usayrān, ed., *Tamhīdāt* (Tehran: Dānishgāh, 1341 [1962]), 103.
96. Hirawī, *Rawḥ*, 295.
97. Qur'an 57:4.
98. Bukhārī, *Riqāq* 38. Meditation on the full text of this hadith gave rise to an extensive discussion of two sorts of "nearness" (*qurb*) or union, one in which God is the servant's faculties, and the other in which the servant is God's faculties. See, for example, Chittick, *Sufi Path of Knowledge*, 325–31; also Chittick and Wilson, *Fakhruddin 'Iraqi*, 138–39, 142–43.
99. Muslim, *Tawba* 9, 11.
100. Qur'an 39:53.
101. Hirawī, *Rawḥ*, 224–25.
102. *Iḥyā' 'ulūm al-dīn*, 4:464.
103. *Rasā'il Ikhwān al-Ṣafā'*, 3:286.
104. Ghiyāth al-Dīn Manṣūr Dashtakī, *Ishrāq Hayākil al-nūr*, ed. 'Alī Awjabī (Tehran: Mīrāth-i Maktūb, 2003), 17.
105. Ibid., 368.
106. *Futūḥāt*, 2:326, line 19. Ibn 'Arabī has a great deal to say about love in various passages of his books. His most concentrated discussion is found in chap. 178 of the *Futūḥāt*, "Recognizing the station of love." This has a French translation by Maurice Gloton, *Traité de l'amour* (Paris: Albin Michel, 1986). For a few of these teachings, see Chittick, *Ibn 'Arabi,* chaps. 2–3.
107. Hirawī, *Rawḥ*, 35–36.
108. *Dīwān*, the ghazal whose first rhyming word is *sirisht*.
109. 'Usayrān, *Tamhīdāt*, 104–5.
110. B. Furūzānfar, ed., *Fīhi mā fīhi* (Tehran: Amīr Kabīr, 1969), 64. See also A. J. Arberry, *Discourses of Rumi* (London: John Murray, 1961), 75.
111. R. A. Nicholson, ed., *Mathnawī* (London: Luzac, 1925–40), book 1, verse 1.
112. Tawfīq Subḥānī, *Majālis-i sab'a* (Tehran: Intishārāt-i Kayhān, 1379/2000), 121–22; see also Chittick, *Sufi Path of Love*, 70–71.
113. Qur'an 53:9.
114. Nūrbakhsh, *Lama'āt*, 27; Chittick and Wilson, *Fakhruddin 'Iraqi*, 98.
115. See William C. Chittick, *Me & Rūmī: The Autobiography of Shams-i Tabrizi* (Louisville, KY: Fons Vitae, 2004), 156.
116. Qur'an 2:36.

117. Maybudī, *Kashf al-asrār*, 1:161–62.
118. Hirawī, *Rawḥ*, 90.
119. *Iḥyā' 'ulūm al-dīn*, 4:427.
120. Ibid., 4:431.
121. Ibid., 4:430.
122. Ibid., 4:436.
123. Ibid., 4:444.
124. Ibid., 4:507.
125. Hellmut Ritter, ed., *Kitāb Mashāriq anwār al-qulūb wa mafātiḥ asrār al-ghuyūb* (Beirut: Dār Ṣādir, 1959), 11–12.
126. Qur'an 20:114.
127. Farghānī, *Mashāriq*, 28.
128. *Iḥyā' 'ulūm al-dīn*, 4:480.
129. M. Muṣaffā, ed., *Dīwān-i Sa'dī* (Tehran: Kānūn-i Ma'rifat, 1339/1960), 780.
130. Tirmidhī, *Zuhd* 14; Ibn Māja, *Zuhd* 3.
131. *Iḥyā' 'ulūm al-dīn*, 4:481.
132. Annemarie Schimmel, *And Muhammad Is His Messenger: The Veneration of the Prophet in Islamic Piety* (Chapel Hill: University of North Carolina Press, 1985).
133. Giffen devotes a chapter to "The Marytrs of Love" and also describes a fourteenth-century "alphabetically arranged dictionary containing the accounts of those who died of pure but tragic love" (*Theory of Profane Love*, 33–34). Al-Daylamī provides a good selection of anecdotes on the topic in *Treatise*, chaps. 22–24.
134. Qur'an 41:31.
135. Ḥāmid Rabbānī, ed., *Munājāt* (Tehran: Kitābkhāna-yi 'Ilmī-yi Ḥāmidī, n.d.), 20.
136. Pourjavady, *Sawāniḥ*, 25. Persian has no gender (and no capital letters), so pronouns are ambiguous; this helps explain why Persian poetry has always spoken to every lover, whether the object of love was "true" or "metaphorical."
137. Abū Nu'aym al-Iṣfahānī, *Ḥilyat al-abdāl* (Cairo: Maṭba'at al-sa 'āda, 1971), 10:78.
138. Qur'an 29:2.
139. Bukhārī, *Marḍā* 3; Tirmidhī, *Zuhd* 57; Ibn Māja, *Fitan* 23.
140. Nicholson, *Mathnawī*, book 1, v. 629.
141. Rabbānī, *Munājāt*, 16.
142. Pourjavady, *Sawāniḥ*, 17.
143. *Futūḥāt*, 2:653, line 25.
144. Hirawī, *Rawḥ*, 51.
145. Qur'an 2:165.
146. Maybudī, *Kashf al-asrār*, 1:447.
147. 'Usayrān, *Tamhīdāt*, 97.
148. Farghānī, *Mashāriq*, 21.
149. Nicholson, *Mathnawī*, book 5, vv. 588–90.
150. Qur'an 2:256.
151. Furūzānfar, *Kulliyyāt-i Shams*, v. 15136.

7 The Humanity of Divine Love

The Divinity of Human Love

VIGEN GUROIAN

LOVE IS PERSONAL, and that which is personal is communal, Love draws others into its orbit. The model is God who is Trinity. St. Gregory of Nyssa observes that God "is a sort of continuous and indivisible community,"[1] a perfect communion of the Father, the Son, and the Holy Spirit in which love is given freely and completely to the others, and each receives love in the same measure that he gives it. Yet, this love communion is not mere diversity. This communion of love is a perfect unity such that the three are not several gods but one God (*Theos*), one Being (*Ousia*), three divine Persons *Hypostases*). The Persons do not divide the divine nature (or being) between themselves; rather, each is wholly God. Yet neither are the Persons reducible to an impersonal divine substance. The Father is the *arche*, the origination, of the triune Godhead. It is the Father, writes the twentieth-century Russian theologian Vladimir Lossky, "that distinguishes the hypostases" in an eternal movement of love."[2] Out of the ground of his absolute freedom and infinite love the Father eternally begets the Son and "breaths forth" (processes) the Holy Spirit. In and through his love, the Father communicates the divinity that is the common being of all three Persons. Within the economy of redemption, the Son, who is the very Image of the Father, offers himself back to the Father in an act of self-donative and self-sacrificial love that is for the salvation of the world. The Holy Spirit, who is sent by the Father through the Son into the world, breathes the newness of life into the world. He brings the gift of God's love and the knowledge of salvation in Christ to the world so that all who love and believe in Christ are sanctified and may become participants in the divine life.[3]

The Personal Nature of Love

Love is freely given or it is not love at all. Love issues from persons, whether these persons are uncreated, as are the divine Persons of the Holy Trinity, or created, as are the multitude of human beings. "Personhood," writes Lossky, "is freedom in relation to nature."[4] Persons enact their own nature. Nature may be *what* they are (e.g., human, angelic, or divine), but the nature does not determine *who* they are. "A personal being," Lossky continues, "is capable of loving someone more than his own nature, more than his own life."[5] Freedom and love are thus the cardinal attributes of personhood. This freedom to enter into loving relationships with others, this personhood, is the image of God in man. Personhood thrives and is perfected through reciprocity and intercourse, more still in and through communion. This deep reciprocity and intercourse of communion is not merely sociality. Human beings together with much of the rest of the animal kingdom exhibit sociality among their own kind. But sociality may be determinate, governed by the animal nature. Sociality need not entail freedom or love, whereas communion does.[6]

Among human beings, love appears to spring from feelings and emotions. Thus, some mistakenly characterize love as irrational. But love transcends feeling and reason. Love is not rationally justified, nor is it just a "natural" affection. At its source, love is a divine reality. Love, as I have stated, is rooted in freedom, in the absolute freedom of God and, next, in the relative freedom of the creature. Love is the subsistence of God, and it is the flowering of the divine image (*imago Dei*) in humankind.

"In perfect love persons do not merely engage in a reciprocal exchange of self," writes Romanian theologian Dumitru Staniloae. "They also affirm themselves reciprocally and personally and establish themselves in existence through giving and receiving."[7] Love that is at once wholly self-donative and perfectly reciprocal is divine. The love that is communicated between the Father, the Son, and the Holy Spirit, however, is not merely shared as between three individuals but binds an indissoluble triunity in which there is no "distance" between the three divine Persons, a perfect coinherence and interpenetration of personal life as one being. The *telos* of love is union minus extinction of relation, complete intimacy without compromise of integrity.

Love is perfectly efficacious within the Godhead. In other words, within the Godhead, freedom and love and love given and love reciprocated are commensurate. Nor in the mutuality that the Persons share is there pause, interlude of expectation, distance, or diminishment of personal integrity either for lack of reciprocation or reason of self-absorption. Father, Son, and Holy Spirit are One and yet "other" to one another. Within the Godhead, love that is virtue and love that is self-gift are one, so that, as I have said, love is the divine subsistence common to the Three. Love is their oneness: their oneness is love.

Communion and Human Existence

In summary, the divine communion of the Father, the Son, and the Holy Spirit is the establishment (the instantiation) of love among the divine Persons in perfect freedom. Love presupposes the other in his or her freedom and integrity while it also seeks intercourse and union with the other. Communion is the ideal milieu of personal existence. Rather than reducing multiplicity to uniformity, it is the blossoming of multiplicity within an unreservedly and uninterruptedly shared life.

Human existence is similar to divine existence in that it is personal. Yet, even if we discount the divisive and mortal effects of sin, we must take into account that human beings are individuated physically and psychologically. Within human existence, there is a certain order and sequence of freedom and love, love-gifted and love-reciprocated. Love's movement is modified by a certain expectation and waiting upon reciprocation, which may or may not be forthcoming. Even when communion is joined, it lacks the uninterrupted immediacy of the relation of the Father, the Son, and the Holy Spirit. Love and communion are attendant to finitude within a spatiotemporal world. Among human beings love always is threatened by death. Nonetheless, human beings are capable of giving love without expectation of return, even in the face of the mortality that threatens to shatter communion. Human love and communion approximate divinity, but they also await salvation.

Communion and Salvation

In a fallen and sinful world, love and communion are expectant upon salvation. More than this, the imperfect communion that love achieves in such a world is an intimation of salvation, for there is no such thing as solitary salvation. The salvation and *theosis* (deification) of the human person is the process by which God graciously narrows the "gap" between freedom's movement and love's substantiation as communion that sin and death have brought about. The Son brings the love of the Father into this world, and the Holy Spirit inspires this love and spreads it among all who believe in the Son. The gift of the Holy Spirit dissolves not only the gap that sin and death have brought about between God and humanity, but also remedies the division of humanity into selves who are existentially alienated from one another and die spiritually for want of love. The communion of the saints is the approximation of the triune life of God.

The gift of the Holy Spirit transfigures human persons through a holy communion. This is the meaning and aim of the prayer of *epiclesis*[8] in Orthodox liturgy. This prayer invokes and petitions the Holy Spirit not only to reveal the elements of the bread and wine as the body and blood of Christ but also to bring all who participate in the liturgy within a bond of love and togetherness. Thus, for example, the hymn of the Kiss of Peace in the Armenian Orthodox rite announces: "Christ in our midst is revealed; / . . . This Church has now become one soul, / The kiss is given for a full bond. / The enmity has been removed; / And love is spread over us all."[9]

Furthermore, absolute love, the love of the triune God, is ecstatic and effluent. It is an unceasing outgoing of "self" to meet and embrace the other and give life to the other, joyfully affirming and uniting with the other. The character of God is not a necessity of a divine nature—for if we must attribute a "nature" to God, this "nature" is the love itself of which we speak—but rather, as I have said, this character is grounded in God's absolute freedom. God the Father loves humankind no differently than he loves the Son and the Holy Spirit, as he draws us into the perfect communion of the divine life, all the while respectful of our creaturely freedom. "[Love] is the same and universal," writes St. Maximus the Confessor of the sixth and seventh centuries. By and through love, God and man come together in a single embrace. By and through his Incarnation, the Son has consummated this "embrace." In him, divinity and humanity are joined forever so that we need not assign "one form of love to God and another to human beings."[10] Christ reveals that the norm of humanity is quite simply love.

God Is Love

St. John writes that "God is love."[11] But in this instance, he is not speaking of the divinity in general. He has in mind God the Father "who sent his Son"[12]—the Father whom "no one has seen"[13] and who "has given us of His Spirit."[14] This aligns with the church's teaching that the Father is the *arche* or "source" of the Godhead. God, the Father, however, is never alone Godself. It also is perfectly appropriate to say that "God is Love (1 John 4:16) signifies that God subsists as Trinity,"[15] writes the Greek theologian John Zizioulas. There was never a time when this triune love that is Trinity was not.

Love that is not shared is not love at all. A god who is a simple monad is neither person nor love. "Love, as God's mode of existence, 'hypostacizes' God"—that is, makes God person—"constitutes His being," Zizioulas continues. Love is God's eternal mode of existence. His existence as love and person are not contingent upon Creation. Love is not a quality, property, or characteristic of a simple divine substance but is, rather, "that which makes God who God is, the one God,"[16] who is three Persons in perfect union and communion. Love is "*the supreme ontological predicate*." It transcends all other forms of predication. Love is the absolute. *God = Love. Love = God*. Insomuch as human beings love, they grow into the likeness of God; they enter into communion with others.

The Trinitarian Structure of Love

As we already have seen, the structure of love is trinitarian. Even the love that two share is incomplete and imperfect. Even the most self-giving and self-communicating relation between two is inherently egocentric, limited in its horizons, and subject always to the erotic fixation of each upon the other, an "absorption . . . [in] a mutual love that is indifferent towards the presence of any other."[17] "Communion between two does not open up an unlimited horizon" such as befits an infinite God, writes Staniloae. "A third enlarges the dimension of existence to in principle include all that can exist."[18]

Family as Image of Trinity

The Trinity exceeds our comprehension. The knowledge that divine revelation gives us of this mystery, however, opens to us a deeper understanding of God and love than might otherwise be possible. In his Letter to the Ephesians, St. Paul writes, "I bow down my knees to the Father of our Lord Jesus Christ, from whom the whole family in heaven and on earth is named, that He would grant you according to the riches of his glory . . . to know the love of Christ which passes knowledge; that you may be filled with the fullness of God."[19] According to St. Paul, God the Father is the head of a single family—another way of saying communion—of whom Jesus Christ, the only begotten Son of the Father, "is the firstborn of all creation."[20] Re- flecting on this scripture, Dionysius the Areopagite (Pseudo-Dionysius) of the sixth century observes that "all fatherhood and all sonship are gifts bestowed by that supreme source of [divine] Fatherhood and Sonship on us."[21] Staniloae adds, "Only a God who is Father and Son explains the whole reality of earthly paternity and sonship. . . . The warmth of differentiated human relationships derives from the existence of a God who is no stranger to the affection of such relationships."[22]

The "fullness of God" that St. Paul invokes is trinitarian. It includes not only the Father and the Son but also the Holy Spirit. The entirety of St. Paul's writings justifies our saying so, even though he does not refer explicitly to the Spirit in the Ephesians passage. God would not be full and God would not be love without the Spirit. The Spirit is the "third" that completes the love bond of the Trinity. This "third," however, is not reducible to a number within a sequence. The Trinity transcends enumeration. Three is a symbol of ontological fullness, personal existence, and communion.

Human love "finds its explanation in the fact that we are created in the image of the Holy Trinity, the origin of our love."[23] And within the Christian tradition this insight has directed theological eyes to marriage, and the family that marriage produces. God has inscribed the trinitarian structure of love within the marital bond and the family. Biblically speaking, the family is a community of the man (husband), the woman (wife), and the child (son or daughter) born of their love, attendant upon the sexual nature and generative powers of male and female. Here then is the primordial three that mysteriously comprises the *imago Dei*. As the book of Genesis states, God "made man; in the image of God he made them; male and female he made them. Then God blessed them; and God said to them be fruitful and multiply."[24]

Marital Love: A Model of Trinitarian Love

In the fourth century, St. John Chrysostom drew an important analogy between the marital bond and the unitive power of love in its trinitarian form. He described how love and being are the same in God, and that within humankind we find an approximation to this. God, observes Chrysostom, created humankind male and female and providentially made their "fleshly" love union (with its procreative power) a manifestation of the mystery of God's own triune being.

In his homily on Colossians 4:18, Chrysostom poses the rhetorical question, "How is marriage a mystery?" And he answers, "The two have become one." He adds, "This is not an empty symbol. They have not become the image of anything on earth, but of God Himself. . . . They come to be made into one body. See the mystery of love."[25] Chrysostom, however, immediately points out that the human nature that male and female share in common does not in and of itself secure the trinitarian character of their sexual and procreative union. Among all of the animal species, males and females share a common nature, yet God does not call them or their union his image.[26] Something more is needed, and that something is love that draws persons into communion.

In his homily on Ephesians 5:22–33, Chrysostom urges, "A man should love his spouse as much as he loves himself, not merely because they share the same nature; no, the obligation is far greater because there are no longer two bodies, but one. . . . I say that husband and wife are one body in the same way as Christ and the Father are one."[27] In turn, the child that the lovemaking of husband and wife engenders is not just a visible sign of their one flesh union but is their very flesh, the same substance as themselves. He likens the child to "a bridge connecting mother to father . . . [and] the bridge is formed from the substance of each." "That is why," he continues, "Scripture does not say, 'they shall be one flesh,' but that they shall be joined together 'into one flesh,' namely the child."[28] The three by virtue of not just the flesh but also their love for one another constitute an image, an icon, of the Trinity. For this reason as well, marriage is the preeminent sacrament of love.

Last, Chrysostom finds an image of the communion of the Trinity within marriage.[29] There is an ontological *prius* and *posterius* (or spiritual hierarchy) in the Trinity that would not be found in marriage, in as much as an originating act of the Father differentiates (and orders) the three Persons of the Godhead.[30] The communion of Father, Son, and Holy Spirit is, however, a love of equals; each is fully God, and in this sense there is not a fixed ranking of first, second, and third. Likewise, within the triad of father, mother, and child there may exist a fluid communion such that the child, who is third for husband and wife in their mutual love, may become a second for each in his or her relationship with the child. In this relationship, each spouse may experience the other as third whose love is born and reflected in the child. But the child also may experience father or mother as third in whom his (her) love for him or her is perfected by the love he or she has for the other spouse (parent). The *imago Dei* is love as love can only be in its perfection, love completely shared, love unselfishly given and unselfishly reciprocated. Such love given and received is not mere exchange, but rather gift of shared love without respect to station, self-forgetful and indivisible love that reaches to embrace yet another and another in communion.

Sin and Sacrifice

The Sinful Self

Human beings are individuated; God is not. This individuation, by reason of material and psychological existence, however, does not, in and of itself, frustrate the full blossoming of love. Rather, sin is the hindrance. Sin grows like a weed in the soil of personal existence, and the fruit of sin is the "detestable self." All of the great ascetics of the Christian faith argue that this weed must be pulled and the sinful self be put to "death" in order that the image of God may grow in its place. The sinful self is distinguished by a "self will" that sets the self up as a small "god" that asserts itself over and against other selves as it seeks to possess what it desires. Of course, sin also afflicts the family, so even this "icon" of divine communion has been tarnished. "In the creaturely, sinful world," writes Russian theologian Sergius Bulgakov, "love for one's own, that is, in essence love for oneself, acquires the character of self-love and prejudice in virtue of which this 'one's own' is prized not at its essential and true worth, but precisely as one's own."

"This," Bulgakov continues, "is the egotistical admiration of one's own image."[31] Such self-love is the ruination of marriage and family.

Adam's first act earned divine condemnation not because he behaved in a self-determining manner. Rather, Adam and Eve chose to make themselves (i.e., self-gratification) the sole end of their self-determination. This transmuted their natural individuality into an instrument and expressivity of a newly born self-will or autonomous self, the self that makes itself its own law and is moved by a love of self to the exclusion rather than inclusion of others, most especially God.

"Self love . . . separates[s] men from one another," writes Maximus the Confessor, "and splits the single nature (of those endowed with a single nature) into many parts."[32] Love corrupted into selfishness (or self-centeredness) shatters the unity of a single nature from which grows genuine communion. The biblical fall brings about the ruin of the original *imago Dei*. Henceforth, men and women are moved by an egocentric (self-possessive and self-assertive) principle that alienates the male from the female[33] and pits brother against brother.[34] This principle spreads so that the human environment is charged with a contention of wills, alienation, and conflict of every sort.

Vocation and Self-Sacrifice

"Sacrifice is the most natural act of man,"[35] argues Russian theologian Alexander Schmemann. The "religious" vocation to which God has called every human being is priestly in character. We are to receive creation from God as the "food" of communion with God and return it to God as our very "body" with love and thanksgiving.[36] In Adam, humankind has rejected this priestly vocation of sacrifice, or as the Orthodox Eucharistic liturgies proclaim, rendering up "Holy things to the Holy."

Instead, sacrifice in a fallen world has become of necessity self-sacrifice, or, in other words, "the rejection of all selfishness in the very form of sin."[37] In paraphrasing St. Cyril of Alexandria, Staniloae states, "Wherever sin exists there no pure sacrifice is found."[38] Christ is the sole human being in whom sin is not found. Only his sacrifice is pure and completely efficacious for restoring complete communion with God. Christ reclaims and fulfills in his person the vocation that God gave to humankind at Creation. The Incarnation is the revelation that love is sacrificial (is sacrifice) and comes from God. Christ obediently, lovingly, and selflessly gives himself over to the Father even as he is put to death. He was destined to do this from all eternity. He is "the Lamb slain from the foundation of the world."[39]

Thus, in Christ, the contradiction of love as self-sacrifice and love as mutuality is overcome. In baptism, the new Christian gives himself over to the Father and allows his sinful self to be put to death in order that Christ's pure self is born within him. In Orthodox worship, chrismation and first communion follow immediately upon baptism in one continuous sacramental action. The gift of the Spirit, symbolized by anointing with oil, is freedom from the hold of sin that imprisons the self within itself. "Now the Lord is the Spirit, and where the Spirit of the Lord is, there is liberty."[40] This liberty is the "law of Christ."[41] It is the image of God restored in the person. It is the person once again "rooted and grounded in love."[42] It is the liberty—as love and freedom are the same in God—that enables persons to enter into communion with one another. Baptism is not just a sacrament of repentance, as it has sometimes been imagined, but a sacrament of illumination, liberation, love, and communion. Love, writes St. Paul, "binds everything together in perfect harmony . . . in one body."[43]

Thus, through the Incarnation, God and humanity are reconciled and communion is restored, not according to a substitutionary formula or measure of infinite satisfaction for sin in God's mind, but by the power of divine love, first in Christ the God-man and second in the creature. The love of God in Christ moves the human being to turn toward God (*metanoia*, conversion) in a manner reflective of God's love and eternal turning toward his creature. And the Holy Spirit makes of he or she who "turns" a temple of God. For "the love of God . . . [is] poured into our hearts by the Holy Spirit who . . . [is] given to us."[44]

Incarnate Love

Jesus' parable of the Good Samaritan[45] has often served as a touchstone for reflection on the meanings of human and divine love. And to that end, I would like to turn to it briefly. I propose a reading, however, that differs from standard interpretations of Christian neighbor love and *agape* that modern Protestant theology, in particular, has espoused. According to this theology, Christian love is, preeminently, self-sacrificial love, so-called *agapic* love, that ideally is not motivated by the expectation of reciprocation. It is argued that the Good Samaritan story illustrates precisely such a pure benevolence that affirms the other person's humanity without prejudgment or precondition.

A Different Reading of the Parable

Let me begin by conceding for the sake of discussion that the Samaritan does respond to the plight of the wounded traveler from a profoundly disinterested regard for him as *qua human existent*. Nonetheless, it is a mistake to restrict the intention or the meaning of the Samaritan's act to this alone. St. Luke says that the Samaritan "had compassion" (*splanchnizomai*)[46] for the traveler. This compassion is a basic, viscerally human, response of pity or mercy toward another who suffers and is helpless. Empathy and compassion are necessary preconditions for community. They pave a "natural" path to *agape*, though even my use here of *agape* is broader than benevolence or even self-sacrificial love.

St. Luke introduces the story of the Good Samaritan with the question the young Pharisee asks: "Teacher what shall I do to inherit eternal life?"[47] "Love the Lord your God with all your heart, with all your soul, with all your strength, and with all your mind, and your neighbor as yourself,"[48] Jesus responds. In turn, the young man inquires, "And who is my neighbor?"[49]

In spite of the fact that it is often claimed that the neighbor in this story is the wounded traveler, this is not what St. Luke reports. Rather, he informs us that the Samaritan has made *himself* a neighbor to the wounded man.[50] This is no small difference. On the one hand, if the wounded traveler is the neighbor, he has become so by the Samaritan's unilateral action and remains a passive recipient of the Samaritan's kindness. But, on the other hand, if, by his gesture of kindness and compassion, the Samaritan has declared himself the neighbor of the wounded traveler, then a dynamic dimension is added to the equation. The Samaritan *acts* as a neighbor. He has made a clear gesture to establish a bond of friendship with a Jew, whose people are traditional enemies of the Samaritan people. The parable of the Good Samaritan should be seen as not merely concerned with disinterested love but indicative of the path that leads to friendship, neighborly relations, and even reconciliation between enemies.

Agape is not just sacrificial love or self-donative love; it also is love that opens onto reciprocity, intimacy, and communion with others. I am arguing that the parable of the Good Samaritan suggests this. *Agape* is more like a gerund than a noun proper. It is a dynamic process that moves toward communion. It is no accident that the early church also used *agape* to connote the Eucharistic fellowship itself, in particular the meal of fellowship shared at the liturgical gathering.

St. Luke does not tell us whether the traveler eventually befriends the Samaritan. There is no strong likelihood of this in the Palestine of Jesus' day. But this does not rule out the possibility. The parable certainly suggests that God desires this to be so, and beckons the listener to act in that spirit. We need only recall Jesus' own gesture of forgiveness and kindness in St. John's story of his encounter with another Samaritan, the woman at Jacob's well.[51] This story is a reminder that the one who told the parable of the Good Samaritan strove in his own encounters with strangers and enemies to establish a lasting bond of friendship. The Gospels as a whole invite us to imagine that the Samaritan's act of compassion is the initial movement of a love that establishes fellowship and communion.

The root error of the standard readings of the story of the Good Samaritan is that they view *agape* narrowly through the crucifixion severed from the Resurrection. The work of Incarnate Love does not end on the cross. It is finished only when all who are of goodwill toward God and man are gathered together in the resurrected life. Love's work is completed only when communion in the Body of Christ replaces the sinful divisions that afflict humanity, when the trinitarian image of love is fully restored to human nature and death is overcome by eternal life.

Agape and *Eros*

Thus far, we have been concerned almost entirely with *agape,* the preeminent form of love. *Agape* most properly expresses love from a divine point of view. *Agape* knows and treats the other as Thou, as neighbor, and not as merely an object for selfish use or pleasure. Nevertheless, in closing, I want to argue that *agape* does not stand alone, that the fullness of love includes the love that is called *eros*. Love of neighbor is not just a handshake; it is an embrace. If we see the face of God, the image of God, in the other, then we will *desire* communion with the other as we desire union with God. In the final analysis, *agape* and *eros* are one love; much as human and divine love are one. "Let us not fear this title of 'yearning' [*eros*] nor be upset by what anyone has to say about these two names [*agape* and *eros*], for, in my opinion, the sacred writers regard 'yearning' [*eros*] and 'love' [*agape*] as having the same meaning,"[52] writes Dionysius the Areopagite. And he sets the tone for the Orthodox Christian tradition until this day.

In a fallen world, *agape* and *eros* do indeed break apart, and they become distortions of their true character in God. *Eros*, severed from *agape*, degenerates into carnal desire and finally a God- and man-denying narcissism. *Agape* severed from *eros* narrows into mere benevolence, then altruism, and finally ethical egoism. Salvation entails the reintegration of *agape* and *eros,* much as it calls for the Incarnation itself.

In Christ, *agape* and *eros* obtain "the same exact meaning" with respect to his divinity and with respect to his humanity. In him, *eros* signifies not selfishness, as some have suggested, but "a capacity to effect a unity, an alliance, and a particular commingling in the Beautiful and the Good."[53] Without *eros*, God would not be Trinity nor would the Word have united with human nature. Without *eros,* God would not have brought the creation into existence, nor would God have redeemed it. "The divine yearning [*eros*] is Good seeking good for the sake of the Good"[54] and "Beauty seeking beauty for Beauty's sake," the Areopagite continues. For as God yearns for Godself, Father, Son, and Holy Spirit, so also God yearns for the world in all of its original goodness and beauty, and especially for humankind whom God created in his very own image and likeness.

Likewise, love of neighbor, the beginning of divine love in this world, is inexplicable without the presence and pull of *eros.* Christ's dual love commandment draws no distinction between divine Persons and human beings, or between *eros* and *agape*. When we love properly, we love in God; and through God's love for us, we are inspired to act the same toward others. We recognize the face of God in human beings and are drawn to them because God has loved them even before we were moved to do the same.

Rayber's Terrifying Love

In her novel *The Violent Bear It Away*, Flannery O'Connor, that gifted twentieth-century Roman Catholic writer of American fiction, makes the case for *eros* as I have been describing it. The lesson is in the personal tragedy of the character Rayber. Rayber is a single father with two sons. His great uncle, Mason Tarwater, a backcountry religious fanatic who regards himself as a prophet and aims to pass the mantle of prophecy on to the boy, has raised the oldest son, Francis Mason Tarwater. The youngest son is in Rayber's care. His name is Bishop, and Rayber regards him as his "idiot child." Bishop apparently is a Down syndrome child, though O'Connor does not name his condition.

Rayber wants Francis back. But he is outraged at the training that the old man has given the boy and repulsed by the boy's beliefs and behavior. Meanwhile, his own love for Bishop frightens Rayber because it seems irrational and uncontrollable. "He was not afraid of love in general," O'Connor writes. Rayber knew the value of it and how it could be used. But this particular love for Bishop "could not be used for the child's improvement or his own . . . . It was completely irrational and abnormal." Rayber believes that so long as this love for Bishop remains focused on the child alone, he can control it and is safe, but if anything should happen to Bishop, "he would have to face it in itself. Then the whole world would become his idiot child."[55]

Rayber is comfortable with benevolence as a principle of life—he is an educator—but he steers clear of deep and intimate relationships, even with his two sons. His love for Bishop is a crack in Rayber's rational egoism and utilitarian ethos. This love, this *eros*, that moves Rayber to embrace Bishop with his whole heart, not just his mind or intellect, is the remedy for his egocentrism and loneliness. Nonetheless, he fights it back because it threatens to broaden and expand so that he might even embrace God, whose existence Rayber vehemently denies. Nor is Rayber able to disentangle his love for Bishop from the attraction he still feels, in spite of his resistance and denial, for the life he once lived as a child with Mason Tarwater, especially the old man's longing for the Bread of Life and his vision of a transfigured world. O'Connor vividly likens this longing to "an undertow in his blood dragging him backwards to what he knew to be madness."[56]

In self-defense, Rayber transfers to Bishop his self-hatred and denial of God. In contradiction to his love for the boy, he thinks of him "as an *x* signifying the general hideousness of fate." This hideous fate is the severe and wrathful God of Mason Tarwater's extreme religious imagination. And that twisted image blinds Rayber to the authentic image of God within himself and his son. "He did not believe that he himself was formed in the image and likeness of God," O'Connor writes, "but that Bishop was he had no doubt. The little boy was part of a simple equation that required no further solution, except at the moments when with little warning he would feel himself overwhelmed by the horrifying love."[57]

Here O'Connor has brought us face-to-face with *eros* in ourselves through his characterization of Rayber, just as the lesson of Rayber's resistance to it betrays how necessary *eros* is in our lives in order for love to blossom into communion. Within this milieu of love sparked by *eros*, we see beauty where before we might have seen ugliness, and we are attracted to it. We see goodness where before we might have seen evil, and we are drawn to it. We see integrity where before we might have seen corruption, and we desire it. We see a neighbor where before we might have seen a stranger or an enemy, and we love that person.

Were Rayber able to surrender to his love for Bishop, the legitimate status of his son's humanity might come into view, the image, not of some hideous fate, but of the God who is love and whose love for humankind (God's *philanthropia*) abides in every human being. Ironically, love is more alive in the "idiot child" than in the educated father. The hope and possibility for Rayber's salvation from the deadening entropy of his own egocentrism and isolation lies mysteriously in his afflicted son. Bishop is a sacramental sign of Christ's presence, Christ who draws us nearer and nearer to himself through our neighbor, or an "idiot child," like the magnet's pull or gravity itself.

As regards Rayber, *eros*'s immediate object may be the "idiot child," but its final resting place is God. *Eros* beholds beauty even in the "beast" and opens the human heart to the joy that is beyond all earthly suffering. Rayber is afraid of this and withdraws into himself. At the moment that he could rescue Bishop from drowning he is unable to act to save the boy and, by extension, also himself.

Conclusion: *Eros* and *Agape* United: Love That Is Both Human and Divine

Eros and *agape* united belong to the original image of God in man. As O'Connor demonstrates through her storytelling, benevolence alone cannot restore that image. Rather, a love communion is necessary. It may start with love of neighbor, love of spouse, or a parent's love for her child. It reaches out to embrace others. *Eros* enjoins *agape*. The love that is the Trinity is the exact same love that unites God and man in Christ. The love that restores the image of God in humanity is also this love that is both *eros* and *agape*. In St. Augustine's words, "The very same person is at once God and man, God our end, man our way,"[58] Jesus Christ.

"God," writes Byzantine theologian Nicholas Cabasilas, "has emplanted the desire [*eros*] into our souls by which every need should lead to the attainment of that which is good, every thought to the attainment of truth. . . . For those who have tasted of the Savior, the Object of desire is present. From the beginning human desire was made to be gauged and measured by the desire for Him, and is a treasury so great, so ample, that it is able to encompass God." In other words, *eros*'s repose is Christ, in whom it is translated into universal love. "Those, therefore, who attain to Him," Cabasilas adds, "are hindered by nothing from loving to the extent that love was implanted in our souls from the beginning."[59]

In Christ, man's "natural" "inner" movement toward the Godhead is consummated, and man's capacity to reciprocate God's love is perfected in communion. In Christ, human love and divine love are commensurate: they are one in his Person. The heart of the christic human being has a "burning love [*eros*] of its charity [*agape*] for God,"[60] says Maximus the Confessor. *Agape* is the fullness of love, while in the creature *eros* is the way to that fullness. When grace has purified it, *eros* in the creature is stripped of the selfishness that sin has introduced and is elevated to *agape*. The human being is once more an unblemished reflection of the express Image [*karakteer*, stamp] of God,[61] Jesus Christ himself.

Notes

1. Gregory of Nyssa, "On the Difference between *Ousia* and Hypostasis 1–4," in *Documents in Early Christian Thought*, ed. Maurice Wiles and Mark Santor (Cambridge: Cambridge University Press, 1975), 34. Although traditionally included among the letters of St. Basil, this work is now generally attributed to Gregory of Nyssa.
2. Vladimir Lossky, *The Mystical Theology of the Eastern Church* (Cambridge: James Clark, 1975), 60.
3. John 1:14; John 15:26; John 14:26; 2 Peter 1:3–4.
4. Vladimir Lossky, *Orthodox Theology: An Introduction* (Crestwood, NY: St. Vladimir's Seminary Press, 1978), 42.
5. Ibid., 72.
6. I am a beekeeper, and I marvel at the complicated social organization of the beehive. It is accurate to say that bees have a society. Nonetheless, it is false to attribute communion to a beehive.
7. Dumitru Staniloae, *The Experience of God*, trans. Ioan Ionita and Robert Barringer (Brookline, MA: Holy Cross Orthodox Press, 1994), 257.
8. The *epiclesis* in Orthodox rites is the invocation of the Holy Spirit over the elements of the bread and the wine not merely so that they are revealed as the body and blood of Christ but to bring about communion. The Armenian prayer of *epiclesis* states, "We bow down and beseech and ask thee, beneficent God, send upon us and upon these

gifts set forth, thy co-eternal Holy Spirit"; *The Divine Liturgy of the Armenian Apostolic Orthodox Church*, trans. Tiran Nersoyan (London: Saint Sarkis Church, 1984), 79.

9. Ibid., 71.
10. Maximus the Confessor, "Letter 2: On Love," in *Maximus the Confessor*, ed. Andrew Louth, Early Church Fathers Series (London: Routledge, 1996), 90.
11. 1 John 4:8 (NKJV).
12. 1 John 4:10 (NKJV).
13. 1 John 4:12 (NKJV).
14. 1 John 4:13 (NKJV).
15. John Zizioulas, *Being as Communion* (Crestwood, NY: St. Vladimir's Seminary Press, 1985), 46. Much of this discussion is drawn from Zizioulas.
16. Ibid.
17. Dumitru Staniloae, *Theology and the Church*, trans. Robert Barringer (Crestwood, NY: St. Vladimir's Seminary Press, 1980), 93. This belongs to an original (or first) version of a chapter titled, "Holy Trinity: Structure of Supreme Love," revised in *The Experience of God*, such that this passage has been expurgated.
18. Staniloae, *Theology and the Church*, 93.
19. Ephesians 3:14–15, 19 (NKJV).
20. Colossians 1:15 (RSV).
21. *The Divine Names in Pseudo-Dionysius: The Complete Works*, trans. Colm Luibheid, Classics of Western Spirituality Series (New York: Paulist Press, 1987), 62 (chap. 2:8).
22. Staniloae, *The Experience of God*, 246.
23. Ibid., 245.
24. Genesis 1:27–28 (NKJV).
25. *St. John Chrysostom on Marriage and Family Life*, trans. Catherine P. Roth and David Anderson (Crestwood, NY: St. Vladimir's Seminary Press, 1986), 75 (Homily 12: On Colossians 4:18).
26. I want to add here that my statement, which for rhetorical reasons may lack nuance, does not discount that traces of the image of God and personality are present in other animal species.
27. *St. John Chrysostom on Marriage and Family Life*, 52 (Homily 20: On Ephesians 5:22–33).
28. Ibid., 76 (Homily 12: On Colossians 4:18).
29. Chrysostom does not advance the argument so often found in Western theology since Augustine that the Holy Spirit is the love shared between the Father and the Son. Orthodox theology distinguishes this attribute of relation within the Trinity from hypostatic subjectivity and identity. The child in the parent and child nexus is not strictly associated with the Holy Spirit either as the love shared between the parents or in the strong sense of hypostatic subject. Nonetheless, it may be said that, like the Holy Spirit, the child is the one in whom the communion is completed.
30. Sergius Bulgakov, *The Comforter* (Grand Rapids: Wm. B. Eerdmans, 2004), 70.
31. Sergius Bulgakov, *The Lamb of God*, trans. Boris Jakim (Grand Rapids: Wm. B. Eerdmans, 2008), 105.
32. Maximus the Confessor, "Contemplative and Active Texts," in *Early Fathers of the Philokalia*, ed. R. Kadloubovsky and G. E. Palmer (London: Faber & Faber, 1954), 365.
33. Genesis 3.
34. Genesis 4.

35. Alexander Schmemann, *For the Life of the World* (Crestwood, NY: St. Vladimir's Seminary Press, 1973), 35.
36. Romans 12:1–2.
37. Staniloae, *Theology and the Church*, 195.
38. Ibid.
39. Revelation 13:8 (NKJV).
40. 2 Corinthians 3:17 (NKJV).
41. Galatians 6:2 (NKJV).
42. Ephesians 3:17 (NKJV).
43. Colossians 3:14–15 (RSV).
44. Romans 5:5 (NKJV).
45. Luke 10:25–37.
46. Luke 10:33.
47. Luke 10:25 (NKJV).
48. Luke 10:27 (NKJV).
49. Luke 10:29 (NKJV).
50. Luke 10:36–37.
51. John 4:5–26.
52. *Divine Names in Pseudo-Dionysius*, 81 (chap. 4:12).
53. Ibid., 82 (chap. 4:12).
54. Ibid., 79 (chap. 4:10).
55. Flannery O'Connor, *Three by Flannery O'Connor* (New York: New American Library, 1983), 192.
56. Ibid., 193.
57. Ibid., 192.
58. Augustine, *City of God* (New York: Modern Library/Random House, 1950), 347 (book 11, chap. 2).
59. Nicholas Cabasilas, *The Life in Christ* (Crestwood, NY: St. Vladimir's Seminary Press, 1974), 96–97 (book 2).
60. Maximus the Confessor, "The Four Centuries on Charity," in *St. Maximus the Confessor*, trans. Polycarp Sherwood, Ancient Christian Writers Series 21 (New York: Newman Press, 1955), 138 (century 1:10).
61. Hebrews 1:3.

8 I Love, Therefore I Am

A Relational and Charismatic Model of Love

Clark H. Pinnock

Compared to love, as we say, there is nothing greater and nothing better. Therefore, it needs to be studied. What does it mean to love? For starters, to love someone requires us to affirm the basic dignity of the other person and to promote the other person's humanity. Love presupposes a concern for the other and wants the other person to flourish. More than sentimentality and mere feelings, love acts intentionally and sympathetically in response to the other. Love promotes well-being. Love is an act of self giving for the empowerment of others. Love is the ideal of the Christian life and character. It is what it means to be "perfect," as God is perfect. Love summarizes the moral law of God. It bonds the human community, and (one could add) it bonds the triune communion, too. Because of God's love for us, Christ died and rose again. It is safe to say that, if a person lacks love, he or she does not know God. The converse is also true. If a person radiates love, we know where it came from.[1]

No Life without Love

The philosopher Descartes once said, "I think, therefore I am." *If I find myself thinking,* he reasoned, *I must exist!* A minimalist argument to be sure, but true, I suppose. However, I would much prefer to say, "I love, therefore I am." I say that because (surely) not thought but love stands at the heart of human existence. There is nothing more important in the whole world. This is why countless books and poems, songs, and letters exist that exalt love on every level imaginable. Contrary to the Beatles, love is not "all you need" and certainly not in the way that they likely understood it. Julian of Norwich got it right: "Our life is founded and rooted in love and without love one cannot live."[2] The love of God for us and in us and flowing out from us is a very great treasure and is life most abundant.[3] Paul asks why become drunk and stupid when there is divine love to intoxicate and elevate the senses?[4] To know the love of God in the power of the Holy Spirit is a central feature of the gospel and a continuing source of strength in trying circumstances.

The happiness that God makes possible for his higher creatures is the happiness of loving and being loved by God and our fellow creatures. Life does not get much better than that.

It can be an ecstasy of delight comparable only to a romantic love between a man and a woman. Our God-given freedom is something precious, but it is not an end in itself. It exists for the sake of love and makes it possible.[5] Charismatic believers (I find) are more comfortable perhaps than most with such categories. For them, the love of God poured out is much more than a concept. Through the baptism in the Spirit, one can experience the Spirit directly and have a joy that no one can take away. Ideally, it is not exhilaration for its own sake but God's own refreshing breath blowing through them. *Agape* does not have to be emotional. Certainly not! It can be calm and deliberate. But love can also stir us profoundly and, when it does, do not downplay experience. The hotter the fire, the deeper the love. Let us seek a lively faith in the Spirit, one characterized by intensity. God is not a distant figure, but can be an overwhelming presence.

Through the Spirit, we can know God's love, and through God's love we can know God's very self, who is love. By love God is chiefly known. Paul writes, "We all have knowledge; but knowledge puffs up, while love builds up. Anyone who claims to know something does not yet have the necessary knowledge. But anyone who loves God is known by him."[6]

Love Supreme and Unsurpassed

Love is God's gift to the world and holds a central place in the gospel of Jesus Christ, our Lord. It is made wonderfully clear in the parable of the Prodigal Son.[7] It is a familiar story. A certain father (we read) had a young son who demanded his inheritance before his father's death and promptly squandered it. Having been reduced to poverty and homelessness, the boy reckoned that, if he went home in a suitably penitent spirit, he might secure work as a slave on his father's estate. Mind you, even this was far from certain, given the fact that grabbing the inheritance ahead of time was like wishing his father dead. But it was worth a try, and the boy set out for home.

But while he was still far off, his father saw him and was filled with compassion for him. He ran and put his arms around him and kissed him. Then the son said to him, "Father, I have sinned against heaven and before you; I am no longer worthy to be your son." But the father said to his slaves, "Quickly, bring out a robe—the best one—and put it on him; put a ring on his finger and sandals on his feet. And get the fatted calf and kill it and let us eat and celebrate. For this son of mine was dead and is alive again! He was lost and is found!" And they began to celebrate. Because of the love and mercy of God, the ungodly and sinners are free to come home and claim their belovedness. This parable is most eloquent in defining the nature of God's love for humankind.[8]

Paul the Apostle expresses the same kind of thought in spatial terms when he says that God's love is *broad* enough to encompass all mankind, *long* enough to last for eternity, *deep* enough to reach the most degraded person, and *high* enough to raise humankind to glory. In this text,[9] Paul echoes what he had written to the Romans that, whether one goes forward or backward or whether one goes up to the heights or down into the depths, nothing will separate us from the love of God in Christ Jesus.[10] Paul also spoke of faith, hope, and love (each of them priceless), but singles out love as particularly special—special because, unlike the others, it is not just for "now" but for "eternity." One day faith will become sight and will not be needed, and one day hope will become fulfilment and not be so important as now. But, as for love, it will remain just what love is through the transition to new creation. Prophecies will pass away (Paul says) and tongues will cease and words of knowledge will become superfluous, but love is everlasting. It will always be supremely relevant: "Love never ends."[11]

God's Love in the Old Testament

According to the Old Testament, the love of God was the basis of Israel's election as his people, and she experienced his faithfulness and leading in good times and in bad. In many scriptures, we overhear the Israelites thanking God: "I will sing of your steadfast love, O Lord, forever; with my mouth I will proclaim your faithfulness to all generations."[12] God's covenant love (*chesed*) was the foundation of their existence, and they could love because God loved them first. They sang, "Your steadfast love, O Lord, extends to the heavens and your faithfulness to the clouds,"[13] and, "How precious is your steadfastness, O Lord. All peoples take refuge in the shadow of your wings. O give thanks to the Lord for he is good and his steadfast love endures forever."[14] God's desire was and is to have a loving relationship with his people. Even though Israel often betrayed the relationship, God would not give them up or hand them over to their enemies. God says, through the prophet Hosea, "My heart recoils within me. My compassion grows warm and tender." Yet God says that he will not bring judgment on those who have been made his bride.[15] The relationship matters to him and his love extends even to suffering, as when his people are unfaithful and the relationship is broken. In such situations, God laments and even weeps. Love is a great theme of the Hebrew scriptures. The loving father of Jesus the Christ is (it would seem) the God of the Old Testament scriptures, too.[16]

One must be honest here. Not every biblical author keeps to this standard. I suppose that God employs the talent that was available to him so that sometimes we gain a very different impression. We come across texts that make us wonder just how loving God is, places where God seems to be an instigator of suffering and violence. To be fair, we cannot pretend that there is a single and unambiguous concept of God's love in the Bible. The diversity of the texts does not support such a notion. One has to wrestle with the biblical material in order to distill the deep teaching of the divine love. Often when we do so the difficulties are lessened.

In Genesis 22, God instructs Abram to sacrifice his only son Isaac. How barbaric of God to command such a murder! But things appear a little differently when you look at the ancient context. The point for Abram is that offering his firstborn to God would not be thought of as "murder." Neither would his neighbors have viewed it in that way. The firstborn was offered to God as a sacrifice in those days so that the land would be fertile. The scandal lay elsewhere. The command forced Abram to ask himself where his heir would come from now that Isaac was dead. It was a challenge to Abram's faith, not to his ethics. If Isaac died, everything would be back at square one. It was a huge testing of Abram's faith. It forced him to trust

God radically. The "problem" in the text then dissolves in the presence of a more culturally sensitive interpretation.

A similar issue arises when it comes to holy war. Reading some of these texts, too, can make the modern reader cringe. But here, too, it is not about killing as much as it is about faith. The issue was about this: will God take care of Israel or not? (Remember that they had no Pentagon to do strategic planning or a large army in reserve.) It was plain and simple: Israel could not win this battle over armed Canaanites apart from miracles. God would have to help them or they would be done for. In this sort of war you cannot trust in kings or in armaments. You need men of faith, men who would stand still and see the salvation of God.[17] Faith was the scandal. Did Israel have a faith strong enough to survive this test? Paradoxically, when you start thinking about it, warfare in such terms led the great prophets later on to propose nonresistance as the way of obedience. No more holy wars! What may seem like a contradiction to us may not actually be one.[18]

What about divine wrath, then? We are all aware that the Lord threatens wrath in certain circumstances and sometimes carries it out. What are we to make of that? Is God loving in these circumstances? This, too, requires a culturally sensitive reading. God's wrath should not be taken in isolation. Listen to the subtlety in God's words: "For a brief moment I forsook you, but with great compassion I will gather you. In the overflowing wrath for a moment I hid my face from you but with everlasting love I will have compassion on you, says the Lord, your redeemer."[19]

Let us be honest now. Sometimes, in the context of evildoing, wrath is the appropriate response. In that case, not to show anger would be wrong. Sometimes showing righteous indignation is the right thing to do. Sometimes God must show that he is not indifferent to iniquity. Wrath can be then a tragic necessity. But, in such cases, wrath is the secondary emotion and not the ruling passion. The fact is that God is slow to anger. Wrath, when it occurs, is always a tragic necessity. It is not an "attribute" of God's but a disposition that may be unavoidable. Cheap love that ignores justice is morally repugnant. Justice and love go together. The city of Nineveh deserved judgment but escaped it when the people repented and God relented. Let a people repent and God's anger disappears because God delights in doing us good, not ill.[20] What I am trying to say here is that some seemingly difficult texts like these must not prevent us from celebrating the tender mercies of our God.[21]

Divine Love in the New Testament

God's love was manifested most clearly, according to the New Testament, in Jesus Christ. It was communicated to us, not as an intellectual concept but through a historical event—the event of the Incarnation. John writes, "God so loved the world that he gave his only Son so that everyone who believes in him may not perish but may have eternal life"[22]—not that we loved God but that God loved us and sent his son to be the atoning sacrifice for our sins. God's love was revealed among us in this way: "God sent his only Son into the world so that we might live through him."[23] In Romans we read that, while we were still weak, at the right time Christ died for the ungodly. Rarely will anyone die for a righteous man—though perhaps for a good man someone might even dare to die. But God proves his love for us in that, while we were sinners, Christ died for us.[24] John the Apostle states, "God is love. It is God's very essence. It is what God is about. That love is not just an attribute among others. Love is of his very essence. Such that, if one abides in love, one abides in God."[25] God's love should be the structuring principle that brings unity to all the other doctrines. Love is the center of Christianity and its fundamental motif.[26]

"Beloved, let us love one another, because love is from God and everyone who loves is born of God and knows God. Whoever does not love does not know God, for God is love."[27] Since God loves us so much, we ought to love one another. Jesus said, "You shall love the Lord your God with all your heart. and with all your soul, and with all your mind." This is the greatest and first commandment. And the second is like it: "You shall love your neighbor as yourself."[28] Eight times in the New Testament we are summoned to love our neighbor as we love ourselves (the neighbor being the person in need whom you meet). In his teaching, Jesus expected a new kind of human being—one who loves God with all his heart and pursues the dignity and well-being of humanity, even of the enemy, as well as having a readiness to forgive without limit and a willingness to serve others in menial ways.

Despite the strong evidence of God's unlimited love in the gospel, some still manage to find interpretations there to limit the scope of divine love.[29] In the tradition of Augustine, for example, some endorse double predestination—which has God playing favorites, giving grace to one while denying it to another, seemingly unaware of the negative impact of believing that sort of thing on our confession of God's good character. Another distortion of interpretation that also reflects badly on the character of God is the widely held theory of atonement in traditional thinking named the theory of penal substitution. It is made to sound as if God cannot pardon sin without receiving satisfaction first, as if, when the now penitent prodigal returns, the father says to him, "My son, I am sorry but I cannot forgive you. There is a penalty to be paid first."

The real situation, however, is very different. From the cross, God reaches out in grace and mercy to welcome sinners home. The cross was an act of the self-sacrificing love of God. Christ's suffering expresses God's suffering forgiveness, and God's justice is restorative not retributive justice. What we discover in the atonement is the justice-making activity of God—his liberating, forgiving, and transforming justice—his costly identification with us in our plight. The death of Christ is a work of justice—not because it entails retribution, but because it demonstrates God's unfailing faithfulness to his people and because it liberates and restores them. In Jesus, we discover who God really is, and this enables us to repent. The love of Christ constrains us and gives us the motivation to believe.

There has been a change in the hierarchy of truths in Christian faith in our time. The primary importance of the universal salvific will of God has become a truth of primary importance, with baptism and church membership becoming lessened in prominence.[30]

Flame of Love

Thus far we have considered God as a loving subject but not yet as triune communion. Trinity expresses our belief in one God who does not live a solitary life but is a loving communion of love marked by overflowing life. No one can claim to know very much about the inner life of God, and I have no secret information about that to share. But I can point the reader to a thrilling mystery of a totally shared life at the heart of the universe. The triune God is not a static being but a dynamic, pulsating energy—maybe even a kind of dance. God may or may not need us. Except that he wants more partners in the dance.

Father, Son, and Spirit are three modes of consciousness in the divine communion. The members constitute a community of persons in reciprocity as subjects of one divine conscious life. Each is an "I" in self-awareness of its own self, knowing and loving the others. By virtue of the interplay, each person disposes himself toward the others in knowing and loving that each person gains his own unique identity. The one divine consciousness is a shared consciousness, shared by the three persons. We seem to be dealing with three subjects who are reciprocally conscious of each other by reason of one and the same consciousness that the three subjects possess each in his own proper way. As to the consciousness of the three persons, (1) each person is conscious of himself in the fullness of the deity; (2) each person is conscious of himself as distinct from the other persons; and (3) at the same time, each person is conscious of himself as a total and reciprocal communication. The Trinity is a circle of shared love which is large enough to take us all in.

To me the Trinity is something of real beauty. It pictures God as fundamentally personal and relational through all eternity. One can imagine the joy of interaction and the communication that is always going on at the very center of the being of God. The shared life is not one of sorrow, loneliness, or emptiness. God is never lonely, sad, or depressed. Living in fellowship, God is essentially and eternally happy. The triune God participates in a dance of shared life that is full and rich and passionate, creative and good and beautiful. God loves to share what he has with others and draw people into the circle of this life. The perfection of love and community is the antithesis of aloofness, isolation, and domination. Relationality is an essential aspect of God's being and the ultimate ontological category.

God is pure love. Loving activity, not power, is his primary perfection. Father, Son, and Spirit enjoy everlasting relationships of love toward one another. They are involved in a tri-personal community in which each gives and receives love. Loving relationships are an essential aspect of God. God is not a solitary potentate, forcing God's will on others. The members of the Trinity mutually share with and relate to each other. Personhood is the ultimate ontological category. Personhood, relationality, and community—not power and independence—become the center for understanding the nature of God. Whereas the main motif of the Neoplatonic concept of God is that of distance and unrelatedness, the Christian doctrine of the Trinity asserts that to be God is to be related in love. God did not need to create in order to love. But if creating is what God is normally doing (maybe always doing—who knows?), God's loving activities are more extensive than we can imagine.[31]

The Trinity experiences and manifests a fullness of love. In loving freedom, the triune God decided to bring into being creatures with whom to share this love. God in love shows himself open to others who could experience love and enter loving relationships. Ours is a God who is antecedently relational and self-sufficiently free to create significant others and enter into genuine reciprocal relations with them. The triune God, as both lover and beloved, is free to take the initiative of opening the love of God to others. It was love that brought creation into being in order to have relationality. God wanted significant others who could experience the divine love and reciprocate that love both to God and to creatures. God's aim was and is to create a human community that would reflect the divine life. The very creation of the world comes (I think) as the outflowing of the eternal love relationship within the triune God. The Trinity provides a symbolic picture of shared life at the heart of the universe.[32]

A Cosmology of Love

Metaphysically speaking, God is not an absolute being, unaffected by the world. Rather, God is One who enjoys real relations with creation. By "real relations," I mean that both parties (God and people) enter into and are affected by the relationship, not only the people.[33] God is "open" to the world and open to receiving creaturely input. God not only acts but reacts. The world has significance for the life of God. We impact God's experience. God is love and as such is sensitive and compassionate. Wanting loving relations, God does not exercise complete control over the world. As a relational and personalist theologian, I believe that restraints on God's power are voluntary, not necessary. God's nonintervention in history is therefore God's choice and not because it lies beyond God's capacity. God's inner life itself is social and relational, and the Trinity allows us to attribute to God sociality and relativity, while preserving the central insight that God is creator of everything. In a cosmology of love, God is open to the world and empties himself. The freely chosen self-limitation of God is central to the model.[34]

"Open theism," which could be called "relational theism" or "voluntary panentheism" (what one calls it is not the issue), is an understanding of God in which the deity chooses to be involved with the world and takes us up into his own life. In this model, God and the world are ontologically distinct and God transcends the world, even while the world is "in" God ontologically. As the poet put it, "In him we live and breathe and have our being."[35] We reject classical theism, which places God outside of the created order and does not explain how God acts inside the world. Open theology accounts for God being engaged in the world and having an ontological relation such that the world is conceived as "within" the being of God but "distinct" ontologically from God.[36]

According to open theism, God is antecedently actual, relational, and self-sufficient in relation to the world and free to perform what God chooses. God, who is eternally social in Godself, can perform the more than necessary feat of opening up the divine sociality to what is other than God-self. And, because God deals with a nonnecessary world, grace enters into the picture. God responds freely to the world and not out of necessity. One should not say that the world is a necessary coexistent alongside God, as if God required the world to be what God is.[37] Divine love makes "room" for the world, I suppose. God accepts some limitations voluntarily so that creatures may exist and flourish. I call it a kenotic act of self-constraint—a joyous, kind, and loving attitude that is willing to give up selfish desires and make sacrifices on behalf of others for the common good and for the glory of God. The "place" of creation is in God's life. There is no place for it to be "outside" of the Trinity.

Love brought creation into being (I believe) for the purpose of interpersonal relationships, which means that God created the world "out of love." It gave God the opportunity to share what God has with us. It is not that God gives up any divine properties to make room for the creature. Self-giving love has a way of adding value to the divine experience. God does not suffer loss, but has a way of realizing possibilities that had not yet been realized. God created the world "out of love." God could also have created the world *ex nihilo*. Maybe God did. It is an old tradition. Of this I am a little less sure, partly because Genesis 1, a major creation text, does not teach it, but rather depicts the Creator confronting resistance to his efforts.[38] This is not the picture of a God in complete control. The cosmology here does not suggest that the creatures are "nothing." They are "something" that is posing a real threat. Why does this matter? It tells us that the God-and-creation relationship is a serious one. God did not give us just a little bit of power that could be snatched away at a whim. No, the relationship is much more serious than that.[39]

God's Love and Human Love

Often we make the distinction between God's love, which is gift-love, and human love, which is need-love. God's love is unlike any other. It is free and total and unconditional self-giving. More than anything else, God's love is an indescribable gift.[40] It is gift-love to the core. It is unlike our love, which is so full with need, such as the need to be accepted or the need to be healed. God's love is mostly gift-love, while man's love is mostly need-love. "For you know the gracious act of our Lord Jesus Christ that though he was rich, yet for your sakes he became poor so that by his poverty you might become rich."[41] God's love at its heart is an act of self-sacrifice.[42] "See what love the Father has given us that we should be called the children of God!"[43]

God's love is so special because of its association with sacrifice. "We know love by this that he laid down his life for us—and we ought to lay down our lives for one another."[44] God took the initiative and loved us first because God is love and all love comes from him. God's love stoops down and embraces sinners and the ungodly. Without expecting anything in return, God's love gives itself away. It is generous and willing to forgive. God's love is moved with pity.[45] God's love takes up the towel and washes the disciples' feet.[46] Foot washing is associated with servanthood.[47]

The fruit of love is very sweet. It has great vitality, rich beauty, and strong fidelity. Love enhances both the lover and the beloved. The world for the lover is endlessly giving and constantly surprising. Love has eyes that can see what is unique and special about the beloved. It affirms the goodness of what it is and what it can become. Her hands reach out to help and to resist any errant tendencies. Human love's prayer joins with God's own love in redeeming the world.

Love celebrates God's participation in the world. It has the power and the dynamism for fulfilling God's goals for the world. God's love is overwhelmingly gift-love, but it does not follow that it is solely gift-love. There is something else—something related to God's interacting with creatures and God's commitment to a relational world. Humans need to be loved. Does God need that? It may be.

Does God not desire to hear the creature say "yes" to his call? In a relational world, God wants love to be reciprocated. It is not as if God receives nothing from relationships. God is not indifferent to us. He does not say to himself, "I don't need those creatures!" Quite the reverse! God loves us so much that he is willing to suffer in relationship. The world matters to God. I grant you that God's love is mostly gift-love. But God also gets something in return. By making the world, God added to his experiences dimensions of true value—dimensions that, though always possible, were not yet actualized. Even self-sacrifice brings with it some benefits. Where did we ever get the idea that God is so complete in himself that our existence is neither here nor there—as if God could take it or leave it, so little does it matter to him? Do you really want to say that God would be perfectly happy with or without us? Remember the sparrow then—how God cares for every one of them. Love is a two-way street. Love gets given and returned. If God does not need us at all, there is no relationship.

Human Love

On the human side, Jesus embodied a remarkable orientation in his own person. As the beloved of the Father, he knew what God wanted for humans. He wills nothing for himself. His cause is the human cause, man's well-being, man's true greatness and dignity. Jesus, who is ordinarily faithful to the law, does not hesitate to act contrary to it, for man's sake. Love of the neighbor is the central issue and was a matter of action, not talk. The neighbor is the one who needs me now. Love does not consist primarily in words, sentiments, or feelings. Love for God is validated or falsified by the love of neighbor. Love is not a love of "man in general" or love of one with whom we are not personally involved. To love God is to care for and forgive the neighbor. This is the yardstick.

One has love for God to the extent that we love the other. It is not enough to teach grace unless we exercise it concretely—a simple rule that embraces the whole of life and yet applies to particular cases, too. For Jesus, love is understood, not as feelings, but as goodwill to others, even enemies. Put in a nutshell, love is good in any situation.[48]

Human love begins with need-love but must not stay there. It must move in the direction of divine gift-love, which is not an impossibility. Paul commands us, "Be imitators of God, dear children, *as I am of Christ*."[49] Our goal is to become "like him." In Wesleyan terms, our Lord commands perfect love: "Be ye perfect as God is perfect."[50] Paul urges us, "Let the same mind be in you that was in Christ Jesus."[51] Over time, God willing, we will experience a deepening of our love for God as we live the life of loving attention and a growing union with God. It is possible to grow in grace. Reinhold Niebuhr aside, love is not an impossible ideal for the community, unless (of course) the community is unwilling to suffer. (Then all bets are off.) Paul issues a strong call for love: "Let love be genuine."[52] "Owe no one anything except to love one another; for the one who loves another has fulfilled the law."[53] "Love does no wrong to a neighbor: therefore, love is the fulfilling of the law."[54] "We who are strong ought to put with the failings of the weak and not to please ourselves."[55] "Christ did not please himself."[56]

The importance of love, according to Paul, cannot be exaggerated:

> If I speak in the tongues of mortals and of angels and do not have love, I am a noisy gong and a clanging cymbal. And if I have prophetic powers and understand all mysteries and knowledge and if I have all faith so as to remove all mountains but do not have love, I am nothing. If I give away all my possessions and hand over my body so that I may boast but do not have love, I am nothing.[57]

The qualities of love are beautifully conceived:

> Love is patient, love is kind. Love is not envious or boastful or arrogant or rude. It does not insist on its own way. It is not irritable or resentful. It does not rejoice in wrong doing but rejoices in the truth. It bears all things, believes all things, hopes all things, endures all things.[58]

The spirit of it all is captured in the prayer of St. Francis:

> Make me an instrument of your peace. Where there is hatred, let me sow love. Where there is injury, pardon. Where there is doubt, faith. Where there is despair, hope. Where there is darkness, light. Where there is sadness, joy. O divine master, grant that I may not so much seek to be consoled as to console. To be understood as to understand. To be loved as to love. For it is in giving that we receive. It is in pardoning that we are pardoned. And it is in dying that we are born to eternal life.[59]

Love then is the criterion for our Christian life and behavior. It is the test of Christian realities. Love (however) itself is not a charism. It is the virtue of character which the gifts are meant to foster. "The fruit of the Spirit is love."[60] Love is not an obligation. It is a spontaneous drive of the heart. People who do not love do not know God. God lives in all who do love. If we love one another, God lives in us and God's love is perfected in us.[61] "Beloved, let us love one another, because love is from God and everyone who loves is born of God and knows God. Whoever does not love does not know God, for God is love."[62] Since God loves us so much, let us love one another for love is of God. Service (however) is a charism—not a display of power, but a manifestation of grace. Paul mentions a variety of such "services," all of which "serve" the community.[63] I think that the gift itself is the act of serving and sharing. The gift is not a latent power that one controls. The actual deed and word is the charism. It is not a person's private possession.

What does it mean to love? To love a person means that you affirm a person's basic human dignity. I love you because you are you. I love you because you are here. I want to participate in the promotion of the other person's full humanity. I want the other person to flourish. "Let us love, not in word or speech, but in truth and action."[64] With love, there is a readiness to subordinate my own agenda so as to be able to help the other person to be able to fulfil their needs.[65] God does not call us to love humanity. He calls us to love the neighbor. The neighbor is the person who needs your help now. Who is my neighbor? The Good Samaritan.[66] Such acts are precisely what God wills. Not some theoretical or poetic or universal love but a practical and concrete deed that builds up.

Vacek writes as follows:

> Love is an actively receptive movement of the heart that creatively enhances the value of both the lover and the beloved through a union that affirms their respective dynamisms. Where there is love, there is greater value, richer beauty, deeper ideas, and stronger fidelity and more profound religion. The world for the lover is endlessly over flowing, constantly surprising. Love's eyes see the unique and the special in the beloved. Love's heart beats with the dynamism of the beloved and affirms the beloved for what it is and what it can become. Love's hands reach out to help the beloved in need and to resist its errant tendencies. Love's prayers join God's own love and redeem the world by enfleshing God's own participation in the world. The perfection will be reached when God is in all and all is in God. Love is the dynamism for fulfilling this ultimate goal.[67]

The love that Jesus commanded—be it directed toward the neighbor or the enemy—is understood in just this way: as active goodwill toward the other and the affirmation of him or her: "Beloved, let us love one another, because love is from God. Everyone who loves is born of God and knows God. Whoever does not love does not know God, for God is love."[68]

When you see the fruit of the kingdom, "the cup of cold water," you know where it came from. If a person does justice, loves kindness, and walks humbly with God—this is the ethical criterion. God's love embraces all people. However, many have not been reached by the message. In this case, I think that the message of Jesus will be the norm by which God judges us all: have they done the works of love that are in accord with that message?

Love is central to who we are as God's beloved children. Our identity is not what we do. It is not our power. Our identity is not what people say. It is not our popularity. Our identity is not what we possess. It is not our success. How fragile is the life that depends on such things. We have so little control over them. What if we lose our job or our fame or our wealth because of events completely beyond our control? Jesus came to give us a new identity. He says we are the beloved children of God. Therefore, let us claim our belovedness. That will enable us to live free from the traps and snares of this world. Listen to the voice that says, "You are my beloved."

The Victory of Love

Will God's love win out over the powers of hatred? I hope and believe that it will. Has God not reconciled the world in Christ? Has God not decided not to count our trespasses against us? Does it not sound as if God wants hell empty of occupants? But hoping is not knowing. If it were a matter of coercion, then God would surely "win." But what kind of "victory" would that be? Not a relational victory, for sure. Not if human freedom counts in the equation. Consider the elder brother in Jesus' parable of the Prodigal Son. Did he relent? Did he repent? Jesus does not say that he did. The father issued the invitation to him also. One hopes that he came to the celebration. But it would be as a person that he comes (if he comes), not as a robot. God offers us God's love and inspires us to respond. But the invitation is not causal. There is still the possibility that one may exclude oneself from the community of salvation. Such is the condition surrounding our God-given freedom. It gives to our lives great weight. There is a power to say "no," even to God.

In closing, I invite you, my readers, to open yourself to a baptism of the Spirit that will give you a foretaste of divine glory and a renewal of the realities of Pentecost. Do not seek chiefly impulses of power over much, but seek rather the power of love. More than anything else, we need not a high-voltage baptism but an immersion in the sanctifying grace of love.

Notes

1. 1 John 4:21.
2. George M. Newlands, *Theology of the Love of God* (Atlanta: John Knox Press, 1980); and Edward Collins Vacek, *Love, Human and Divine: The Heart of Christian Ethics* (Washington, DC: Georgetown University Press, 1974).
3. Vincent Brummer, *The Model of Love: A Study in Philosophical Theology* (Cambridge: Cambridge University Press, 1993); and Daniel D. Williams, *The Spirit and the Forms of Love* (New York: Harper & Row, 1968).
4. Ephesians 5:18.
5. C. S. Lewis, *Mere Christianity* (London: Collins/Fontana Books, 1952), 49.
6. 1 Corinthians 8:1–3; Thomas J. Oord, ed., *The Many Facets of Love* (Newcastle, UK: Cambridge/Scholars, 2007).
7. Luke 15:11–24.
8. Thomas J. Oord, *Science of Love: The Wisdom of Well-Being* (Philadelphia: Templeton Foundation Press, 2004).
9. Ephesians 3:18.
10. Romans 8:38–39.
11. 1 Corinthians 13:8.
12. Psalms 89:1.
13. Psalms 36:5–10.
14. Psalms 136:1.
15. Hosea 11:9.
16. Barnard V. Brady, *Christian Love* (Washington, DC: Georgetown University Press, 2003); and Terrence E. Fretheim, *The Suffering of God: An Old Testament Perspective* (Philadelphia: Fortress Press, 1989).
17. Exodus 14:14.
18. John Howard Yoder is particularly good at picking up on such cultural issues. See John Howard Yoder, *The Original Revolution* (Scottsdale, AZ: Herald Press, 1971), chap. 5, and Yoder, *The Politics of Jesus* (Grand Rapids: Eerdmans, 1972), chap. 4.
19. Isaiah 54:5–8.
20. Jeremiah 32:41.
21. Abraham J. Heschel helpfully clarifies the meaning of wrath in the Hebrew Bible. See Abraham J. Heschel, *The Prophets* (New York: Harper and Row, 1962), chap. 16. See also George H. Tavard, "God's Love and God's Wrath," in *A Way of Love* (Maryknoll, NY: Orbis Books, 1977), chap. 6. The wrath of God amounts to *agape* experienced in the situation of sin.
22. John 3:16.
23. 1 John 4:9.
24. Romans 5:6–8.
25. 1 John 4:16.

26. Benedict XVI, *God Is Love: Deus Caritas Est*, Encyclical Letter (San Francisco: Libreria Editrice Vaticana/Ignatius Press, 2006).
27. 1 John 4:7–8
28. Matthew 22: 37–39.
29. R. H. Gundry sees God's love being limited to a believing elect and not a universal principle. So also D. A. Carson, *The Difficult Doctrine of the Love of God* (Wheaton, IL: Crossway, 2000)..
30. Mildred B. Wynkoop, *A Theology of Love: The Dynamic of Wesleyanism* (Kansas City, MO: Beacon Hill, 1972).
31. C. Baxter Kruger, *The Great Dance: The Christian Vision Re-visited* (Jackson, MS: Perichoresis Press, 2000).
32. Stephen G. Post, *A Theory of Agape: On the Meaning of Christian Love* (Lewisburg, PA: Bucknell University Press, 1990).
33. Aquinas used the analogy of a person in relation to a column. We move in relation to the column but the column does move. In my view, both God and people move in relation to the other. There is real reciprocity.
34. Nancey Murphy and George F. R. Ellis, *On the Moral Nature of the Universe: Theology, Cosmology, and Ethics* (Minneapolis: Fortress, 1996).
35. Acts 17:28.
36. John W. Cooper, *Panentheism: The Other God of the Philosophers, from Plato to the Present* (Grand Rapids: Baker Academic, 2006), 190–92.
37. Samuel M. Powell, "A Trinitarian Alternative to Process Theism," in *Thy Nature and Thy Name Is Love: Wesleyan and Process Theologies in Dialogue*, ed. Brian P. Stone (Nashville: Kingswood Books, 2001), 143–67.
38. Genesis 1:2.
39. See Michael Lodahl, *God of Nature and of Grace* (Nashville: Kingswood Books, 2003), chap. 3, for the *ex nihilo* option.
40. 2 Corinthians 9:15.
41. 2 Corinthians 8:9.
42. Thomas J. Oord, *The Many Facets of Love: Philosophical Explorations* (Newcastle, UK: Cambridge Scholars, 2007); and Kevin J. Vanhoozer, "The Love of God: Its Place, Meaning, and Function in Systematic Theology," in *First Theology: God, Scripture, and Hermeneutics* (Downers Grove, IL: InterVarsity Press, 2002), chap. 3.
43. 1 John 3:1.
44. 1 John 3:16; Post, *Theory of Agape*; and Irving Singer, *The Pursuit of Love* (Baltimore: Johns Hopkins University Press, 1994).
45. Anders Nygren, *Agape and Eros* (Philadelphia: Westminster Press, 1953).
46. John 13.
47. John C. Thomas, *Footwashing in John 13 and the Johannine Community* (Sheffield, UK: Sheffield Academic Press, 1991).
48. I need to say something here about the insufficiency of a purely selfless *agape*. But in love there is always giving and receiving. There must be some regard for the self in a complete Christian life. A life solely of selfless, self-forgetting, self-sacrificial *agape* would not be a well-balanced life. Self-love is not necessarily selfish. Self-denial is not always a good thing. Consider Vacek, *Love, Human and Divine*, chap. 7.
49. Ephesians 5:1 (emphasis added).
50. R. Newton Flew, *The Idea of Perfection in Christian Theology: An Historical Study of the Christian Ideal for the Christian Life* (Oxford, UK: Clarendon Press, 1968).

51. Philippians 2:5.
52. Romans 12:9.
53. Romans 13:8.
54. Romans 13:10.
55. Romans 15:1.
56. Romans 15:3.
57. 1 Corinthians 13:1–3.
58. 1 Corinthians 13:4–7.
59. Francis of Assisi, *The Prayers of St. Francis*, trans. Ignatius Brady (Ann Arbor, MI: Servant, 1987), 119.
60. Galatians 5:22.
61. Flew, *Idea of Perfection.*
62. 1 John 4:7.
63. Romans 12:7; 1 Peter 4:12.
64. 1 John 3:18.
65. Brady, *Christian Love*, 265–73.
66. Luke 10:30–37.
67. Vacek, *Love, Human and Divine*, 66.
68. 1 John 4:7–8.

Conclusion

Divine Love and Human Dignity

STEPHEN G. POST

DIVINE LOVE is variously conceptualized in the preceding chapters, all of which point to some source of love in this universe that is higher and more reliable than our own. Flawed creatures that we surely are, arrogance and group insularity often distort the power of divine love when we do experience it. We remain earthen vessels, so those who report such experiences can and do go amiss. Very often, however, such experiences and beliefs give rise to consistent and inspiring lives of profound humility and a love of all humanity without exception.[1]

Still, consistent with perennial wisdom, the authors emphasize that in our connectedness with this divine love lies our greatest dignity as human creatures.[2] Such discussion may sound quaint and a tad irrelevant in our busy techno-world, but this is far from true. These days, we are bombarded by offers to "enhance" ourselves as human beings through BOTOX, anabolic steroids, growth hormone to make our children a little taller, and the dubious promises of a fountain of youth—all are for sale but none add to dignity or a deeper happiness.[3] Let us focus our attention not on the external vessel of our bodies, but instead on the capacity for a generous love that already lies within us waiting to be more fully unveiled and actively engaged through the enhancing power of divine love. Without this divine love, we are poor even if we do not know it, for in it rests ultimate hope for a better world, and without it despair is always close at hand.

What kind of love are we talking about? Elizabeth Alexander of Yale

University wrote a poem titled "Praise Song for the Day," which she read at Barack Obama's presidential inauguration. One stanza reads:

> Some live by *love thy neighbor as thyself,*
> others by *first do no harm or take no more*
> *than you need.* What if the mightiest word is love?[4]

Love is the fundamental emotional dynamic that moves us to "do unto others" in kindness and generosity. It is what makes our lives meaningful. In love, we affirm the value of others as well as of self, and we act creatively; in hatred, we diminish value and act destructively. I do not have in mind "love" in the modern sense that limits it to the nearest and dearest; rather, I am talking about a love of humanity that is typically at the core of our great spiritual and moral-political traditions. It is believed that such love, in infinitely vibrant creativity, underlies the universe.

A bold statement on the power of love in hard times was that of Franklin Delano Roosevelt in his Christmas Eve address of 1941. He wondered how men and women could rejoice in the spirit of love in a time of such concerted war against radical evil, with "sons and brothers" endangered. He asked, "How can we light our trees? How can we give our gifts? How can we wake and worship with love and with uplifted spirit and heart in a world at war, a world of fighting and suffering and death?" He answered, "Against enemies who preach the principles of hate and practice them, we set our faith in human love and in God's care for us and all men everywhere."[5] And it was with this affirmation of universal love, he said, that the sacrifices of sons and brothers could be properly solemnized and honored. FDR learned this from his Episcopal religious upbringing and extended the concept to the throes of conflict with a Nazi regime that preached the brutal elimination of so-called inferiors.

It is easy to lose hope in the power of love but for faith that in the sweeping drama of history God set the universe in motion and wrote the play so that love would be victorious in the final act, despite startling scenes of immense cruelty and hideous violence in which evil fills the stage. Thus, St. Paul linked together faith, hope, and love in 1 Corinthians 13:13. Without faith and hope, love does not hold our hearts in the darkness. Faith declares that despite all the cruel tyrants and wanton abusers of life, godly love has already won the day. Hope sets its sights on a real future in accordance with God's promises.[6]

I write as an Episcopalian Christian who is appreciative of the human capacity for other-regarding love, but who wishes to assert that this capacity is limited to greater or lesser degree, even when we have the benefits of caring parents, functional environments where love is modeled and celebrated, a culture that affirms generous living, and a faith community that exhorts us to serve others. I also write as one who appreciates the experience of divine *agape* love as quickening and enlivening our naturally evolved capacities for love, expanding them in profound and mysterious ways.[7] In this mystery, we are surprised by a joy that far transcends other forms of happiness, for it includes tears for the neediest. I am not the heavily Calvinist Protestant who is so pessimistic about the evolved human substrate as to assert that any expression of natural human love must be inauthentic, manipulative, and constricted by an iron law of reciprocity. The human substrate, however imperfect, is somewhat better than that, elevated by divine love rather than abolished by it.[8]

In this epilogue, several themes are taken up not because they follow one from the other, but rather because they are areas of some confusion that have been on this author's mind over the years as a Christian thinker.

A Protestant Love Eudaemonism

Divine love should not be confused with dry principle. It is buoyant and effervescent in the lives it touches, and it does not destroy the human desire for a deeper happiness, but rather fulfills it.[9] As St. Paul wrote, "God loves a cheerful giver."[10] The "fruit of the Spirit" includes "love, joy, peace, patience, kindness, generosity, faithfulness, gentleness, and self-control."[11] These are not arid things, dry as the dust. There has been a Protestant tendency to inject too much *nomos* into *agape*.[12]

Our lives are all a mixture of light and shadow, and we are all somewhat broken by loss, disappointment, illness, bitterness, and hurts imposed by others or by our own foolishness. Thus, glib happiness is never very honest. I am a Christian *eudaemonist* in asserting that all deeper and more honest happiness comes through discovering and acting upon the power of love within us, especially when elevated at some "point of contact" with divine love[13]—a "point" that is either a neurological pathway or some nonmaterial soul, or both.[14] The eudaemonistic thesis can be captured with a phrase: *In the giving of self lies the discovery of a deeper and happier self.* Here lies the perennial truth that unites all the great religions of which I am aware.

And here lies the inner core of human enhancement and dignity, which has nothing to do with posthumanist goals of remaking human nature by technological gadgetry.

A natural love lies within, but alongside it are competing hurtful tendencies. The dignity and joy of a life depend upon bringing forth this innate inner love, rather than its opposites. Jesus said, "The kingdom of heaven is within you."[15] We all encounter people who have a radiant and joyful love, and their smile seems to light up a room. Even when life circumstances take a downturn, they seem able to muster an inner strength that serves as a beacon of hope to others. These sorts of people become especially interesting to us when they report an animating and sustaining experience of divine love.

Phenomenologically considered, there is an inner freedom connected with divine love. We all treasure our physical liberty to go and come as we please. Spiritual freedom is even more significant, for it involves an unlimited potential to dream about a better world, to inspire others, to set visionary goals, and to accomplish them. People of great love are the ones who speak out for change and can sometimes be quite irreverent because the power of love overwhelms the power of fear. When I think of the personalities of people who engage the world with love, I conclude that love rarely, if ever, stands alone. In addition to this internal freedom, it coincides with gratitude, hopefulness, and peace. Love leads into a family of positive emotions that are closely connected and blend together into a unity of virtue. It is impossible to imagine love not giving rise to a spontaneity and liberation from all those emotions that weigh us down, to a joy and delight in the beloved, to inner peace and gratification that by its nature denies violence in emotion, word, intention, or deed. So love leads right into a whole set of positive emotions that shape a virtuous life, and make each of us passionaries who shape the world around us for good.

Joy is also part of this family of spiritual emotions. No one who is feeling anger or fear, for example, can simultaneously feel happy. But when we love others, we move into a state of internal harmony that is also a state of deep happiness. Washington Irving understood this inner joy when he wrote, "Love is never lost. If not reciprocated, it will flow back and soften and purify the heart."[16] Simply to abide in a spirit of love is to abide in a joyful warmth and harmony with oneself. Love is its own emotional and spiritual reward, and no one can take this away—even in the absence of reciprocation. Of course, love often does beget love, just as hate usually begets hate.

We often find joy in the deeper relationships and connections that love brings into our social lives. But we cannot count on reciprocity and should not depend on it or even seek it. We have only to love people and hope, as Jesus taught, that they will be inspired to "go and do likewise."[17]

Certain people claim to be called by divine love to acts that are risky. But they are not seeking the cross, anymore than did Dietrich Bonhoeffer.[18] However, sometimes the cross finds them, and they must accept it with courage, however reluctantly. Anything else would be a form of masochism and self-immolation, which are only pseudo-expressions of love. Let us say a few more things about the calling.

Love's Calling

Divine love can never be fully implemented by a human creature because we are finite and it is infinite. Thus, many who report on the experience of divine love refer to the notion of vocation, to some special task that they have been called on to pursue in love. They have received a "call" to love some particular constituency of the neediest, and they try to live out their lives accordingly.

In October 1999 the Institute for Research on Unlimited Love (www.unlimitedloveinstitute.com) was beginning to take shape through a conference convened in Cambridge, Massachusetts. Among the leading lights of godly love whom I invited to speak about their lives was the remarkable Templeton Laureate Dame Cicely Saunders, then eighty-three years of age, and known all over the world as the creator and founder of the hospice movement. Indeed, she took the name "hospice" from the medieval notion of a place where wayfarers might spend the night, and, as she viewed dying as a journey, Dame Cicely first applied the word in the modern sense of a safe haven where people can die in love and grace, and without a tube in every orifice natural and unnatural. Dame Cicely, who flew in from St. Christopher's Hospice in London, began her dinner plenary address by stating that her entire life's work was guided by God and by her experience of divine love, however much the standard professional textbooks manage to leave this out. Indeed, Christian bookstores in England sometimes have entire sections on Dame Cicely, who gained nursing and medical degrees in the process of building up her credibility for a single task—that of enabling people who are dying to experience a sense of significance. No, they are not beyond "care" simply because they are dying, nor need they be warehoused in dehumanizing and depersonalizing highly technological settings as though a few machines could afford them a sense of self-worth. Dame Cicely changed the world and did so because she felt so deeply that God loves people who are dying and wants their final months to be opportunities to sense the significance of their lives. At the end of her talk, Dame Cicely said that God has never allowed her to retire, and that she still goes into St. Christopher's to change bedpans, to listen attentively and express love, and to do all the small chores of hospice life with great love. She did die several years later, and across the globe virtually every news organization printed voluminous obituaries to a modern saint who gave significance even to those who could no longer be rescued from death.

There are many people who, like Dame Cicely, act upon the call of divine love. Millard Fuller felt called to build houses for the homeless,[19] Heidi Baker feels called to care for orphans in Mozambique,[20] and the list goes on. Not everyone is likely to describe the elaborate mystical experience of divine love, but they will quickly speak of what they feel God has called them to do.

Some are called to an engaged spirituality that explicitly confronts social, political, and economic structures deemed unjust and contributory to the suffering of some needful group. Mahatma Gandhi, Dr. Martin Luther King Jr., Rabbi Abraham Heschel, and Bishop Desmond Tutu are obvious examples. Their moral appeal is to human dignity and human rights, and their endeavor is to effect structural change. The psychological dynamic involved in these efforts requires the persistent confrontation of entrenched powers that are recalcitrant to change. This is a calling that is left to the most courageous.[21] When we read about such lives we sense that the love manifested hinted at divine love, something about which all these exemplars taught.

Divine Love Is Not Human Love

Divine love is not to be confused with human love.[22] It far exceeds any human emotion, even at our impressive best, because it is at a different level of magnitude and stability than anything human. This does not mean that human love lacks authenticity and immense importance within the natural order, or that it is not the substrate upon which divine love acts. Human love nevertheless pales in comparison to the overwhelming experience of pure divine love.[23]

As Sorokin suggested in his classic work, *The Ways and Power of Love*, a first dimension of love is *intensity*. Low-intensity love makes possible minor actions, such as giving a few pennies to the destitute or relinquishing a bus seat for another's comfort; at high intensity, much that is of value to the agent is freely given. Human love can be intense or weak at any given moment, for we are subject to the ups and downs of the heart. Divine love is *perfectly intense*, meaning that its energies are infinite and constant. Human love falls short.

Sorokin's second dimension of love is *extensivity*: "The extensivity of love ranges from the zero point of love of oneself only, up to the love of all mankind, all living creatures, and the whole universe. Between the minimal and maximal degrees lies a vast scale of extensivities: love of one's own family, or a few friends, or love of the groups one belongs to—one's own clan, tribe, nationality, nation, religious, occupational, political, and other groups and associations."[24] Our human love tends toward insularity and has a strongly myopic tendency unless it is enlarged by the power of divine love.

Whom should we love? Everyone, though obviously we finite creatures must establish functional priorities in ordering love.[25] Even in doing so, we can still be leaning out toward all humanity. The Greeks felt that love should be confined to those who are worthy of it. We should only love someone as a friend, argued Aristotle, if they are virtuous. Thus did the seventeenth-century Anglican Divine Jeremy Taylor write, "When friendships were the noblest things in the world, charity was little."[26] It is fair to state that in the West, with the impact of divine love as Christianity has understood it, love in its most profound form is not something that another person merits. No one has to earn divine love.

Sorokin next added the dimension of *duration*, which "may range from the shortest possible moment to years or throughout the whole life of an individual or of a group."[27] For example, the soldier who saves a comrade in a moment of heroism may then revert to selfishness, in contrast to the mother who cares for a sick child over many years. Romantic love, he indicates, is generally of short duration as well. Human love is notoriously fickle. It gives up on people when they have been wounded by life, or when they fail to measure up to some standard of achievement. Divine love is perfectly reliable and enduring; human love is not.

The fourth dimension of love is *purity*. Here Sorokin wrote that pure love is characterized as affection for another that is free of egoistic motivation. By contrast, pleasure, advantage, or profit underlie inferior forms of love, and will be of short duration. Pure love—love that is truly disinterested and asks for no return—represents the highest form of emotion. Human love is at best a mix of other-regarding and self-regarding motives, whereas divine love is pure.

Finally, Sorokin included the *adequacy* of love. Inadequate love is subjectively genuine but has adverse objective consequences. It is possible to pamper and spoil a child with love, or to love without practical wisdom. Adequate love achieves ennobling purposes, and is, therefore, anything but blind or unwise. Certainly love is concerned with the building of character and virtue, and love will shun overindulgence. Successful love is effective. Human love is sometimes very destructive in its application. We destroy our children by loving them in ways that breed bad habits and irresponsibility. Divine love is perfectly creative because it is perfectly wise.

Sorokin argued that the greatest lives of love and altruism approximate or achieve "the highest possible place, denoted by 100 in all five dimensions," while persons "neither loving nor hating would occupy a position near zero."[28] Gandhi's love, for example, was intensive, extensive, enduring, pure, and adequate (effective). Of special interest to Sorokin was the love of figures such as Jesus, Al Hallaj, and Damien the Leper. Despite being persecuted and hated, and therefore without any apparent social source of love energy, they were nevertheless able to maintain a love at high levels in all five dimensions. Such love seems to transcend ordinary human limits, which suggested to Sorokin that some human beings do, through spiritual and religious practices, participate in a love energy that defines God.

Sorokin was convinced that such perfect love can best be explained by *hypothesizing an inflow of love from a higher source that far exceeds that of human beings*. Those who were despised and had no psychosocial inflow of love to sustain them must receive love from above.

> The most probable hypothesis for them (and in a much slighter degree for a much larger group of smaller altruists and good neighbors) is that an inflow of love comes from an intangible, little-studied, possibly supraempirical source called "God," "the Godhead," "the Soul of the Universe," the "Heavenly Father," "Truth," and so on. Our growing knowledge of intra-atomic and cosmic ray energies has shown that the physico-chemical systems of energies are able to maintain themselves and replenish their systems for an indefinitely long time. If this is true of

> these "coarsest" energies, then the highest energy of love is likely to have this "self-replenishing" property to a still higher degree. We know next to nothing about the properties of love energy.[29]

Sorokin believed that those people of great love who, when surrounded by adversity, sustained love were graced. Those who are high in all five aspects of love reflect, he conjectured, a divine love energy.

On a scale of one to ten on each aspect of love, most of us would rate ourselves relatively low. If divine love is a perfect ten on duration, I would rank Dame Cicely Saunders, who founded the hospice movement, a clear eight for her loyalty to the dying. I would rate Millard Fuller, who founded Habitat for Humanity, a clear eight for his loyalty to the homeless. But I would rank myself low, perhaps at about five, even though I consider loyalty a personal strength. Divine love never fades away.

So when we think of divine love, we feel the gap between its perfection and our imperfection. Sometimes we can only forgive ourselves because we know that God loves us so perfectly, and that we are therefore already forgiven by a power far beyond ourselves. Divine love inspires, but it also judges, drives us to repentance, and lures us in the direction of greater holiness. It is always a direction we take, rather than a place at which we fully arrive. And yet, in deference to the perfectionists, I do think that some people come very close to it, but they are rare and we call them saintly.

Divine love breaks through to us from above. It need not be the dramatic conversion experience, or involve a loud shout. Anglican poet W. H. Auden described his quiet experience of Godly love as follows:

> One fine summer night in June 1933 I was sitting on a lawn after dinner with three colleagues, two women and one man. We liked each other well enough but we were certainly not intimate friends, nor had anyone of us a sexual interest in another. Incidentally, we had not drunk any alcohol. We were talking casually about everyday matters when, quite suddenly and unexpectedly, something happened. I felt myself invaded by a power which, though I consented to it, was irresistible and certainly not mine. For the first time in my life I knew exactly—because, thanks to the power, I was doing it—what it means to love one's neighbor as oneself. I was also certain, though the conversation continued to be perfectly ordinary, that my three colleagues

> were having the same experience. (In the case of one of them, I was able later to confirm this.) My personal feelings towards them were unchanged—they were still colleagues, not intimate friends—but I felt their existence as themselves to be of infinite value and rejoiced in it.[30]

Auden captures an experience that is subtle and deeply emotional, a Godly love animating and enlivening his sense of awe for the gift of others. His description begins to capture the "feel" of divine love. Auden expressed his sense of divine love through creativity as the great Christian poet that he was, but there are other modulations or expressions of love allowing us to draw on our strengths and gifts accordingly.

The Modulations of Divine Love

Divine love cannot be reduced to any single modulation or expression. It is too responsive to particular needs for such expressive monism. Love is always a deeply emotional and intellectual affirmation of the significance of others, but there are various spokes that fan out from this hub in more specific forms.

Human beings are broken creatures who cannot heal themselves, and none of whom can be called consistently good. Sickness, depression, loneliness, fear, rejection, losses, failures, selfishness, bitterness, hurtful pasts—we are none of us whole, we all carry wounds and regrets, some of which are of our own making and some are received from others. Divine love is thus a *compassionate* love bestowed on creatures who struggle with life's innumerable challenges.

Yet human beings are also creatures who have their dignity in small actions of concern for others, in creativity, in perseverance, in the capacity to sacrifice for others, in hope, gratitude, courage, and forgiveness. Divine love is thus a *celebratory* love that recognizes human achievements and virtue. Indeed, some theologians and mystics describe this love as even *mirthful*.[31]

Divine love is *loyal*. It is not an extinguishable project. Its sincerity and honesty in intention are demonstrated in fidelity and permanence over time. Constancy provides security and safety for human creatures. Here is the greatest emotional safe haven, and it is readily at hand. Our greatest drive for attachment is with the Source of our being.

Forgiving is more complex than giving. It does not displace the need for contrition and justice, though just as forgiveness without justice is sheer chaos, justice without forgiveness is brutality. Divine love is a *forgiving* love because human creatures all fall short.

Divine love, as variously described, is a *respectful* love, for it includes a quiet reverence for the mystery of other lives, and a freedom from the desire to manipulate.[32] It is a *listening* love, attentive to human prayers of supplication. It is a love of *confrontation*, holding creatures accountable for destructive and self-destructive actions. Perhaps above all, it is a *creative* love, inspiring us to use our gifts for noble purposes.[33]

Whatever modulations of love are our own, they all add dignity to our lives, and they confer upon others the sense that their lives are worthy of love, and significant in God's eyes.

The Human Need for Significance

Why does the experience of divine love transform lives so powerfully? More specifically, what fundamental human need does divine love respond to in us that makes it so compelling? Godly love responds to the deepest of human needs—the need for *significance*. It reflects back to the beloved their significance, dignity, and even sacredness. In the stress and struggle of life, as William James concluded, "The deepest principle of Human Nature is the craving to be appreciated."[34] The need for significance is sometimes distorted into a human quest for fame or renown that will usually be ruinous because it lacks a grounding in God, who alone provides the significance that we seek.

It is divine love alone that can be trusted to see equal significance in every human being. We are loved by God, all of us, and therefore our significance is firm in the universe. Our lives do not rest on some cosmic error, but on the hand of a loving God who cherishes all. Our highest human dignity comes from the love that is within us by nature, and enhanced by God. There is no higher significance than this. We become, as it were, co-Creators in divine love. In all the experiences people have of this love, they seem to radiate with a sense of just how amazingly precious and significant they feel in the deeply personal love of God.

In the Christian perspective, a compassionate divine love brings Christ into the world to liberate and heal the broken, affirming a human significance that is worth suffering over. In other words, to cite the most succinct and powerful summary of divine love, "For God so loved the world that he gave his only Son, so that everyone who believes in him may not perish but have eternal life."[35] Each and every one of us, no matter how much we have been tossed around by life, is worthy of infinite divine love. Jacques Maritain, the French Christian philosopher, once remarked that all human rights are based on the idea that Christ came to the world in the form of a human being, rather than in the form of some other creature. Each of us is equally significant and equally worthy of being adopted in the family of God.

Divine Love as Adoptive

The idea of adoption as central to divine love was contributed to Christian tradition by St. Paul. Four of Paul's texts mention adoption as a means of obtaining permanent enjoyment of an improved status as legal heir and having old debts canceled.[36] The Pauline appropriation of a theology of adoption is exceedingly technical and too complex for this discussion, except to note that adoption in some broad sense is a part of his vision of Christian membership and salvation. Somewhat simplistically stated, human beings are *not* by nature the *fully* adopted children of God, although they are otherwise still within the range of divine love. Jesus, as the Christ, however, is the Son of God, and God is prepared to fully adopt as children those who accept Christ. Adoption is thus at the very core of the Christian narrative of salvation by faith.

Adoption is also central to Christianity because Jesus of Nazareth was himself raised by a de facto adoptive father. According to orthodox theology, Jesus was conceived by the Holy Spirit—a prospect made more plausible against the background of our increasing scientific capacities to engage in nonprocreative reproduction. He was the Son of God in a way that did not involve Joseph as a biological father. Indeed, Joseph might easily have rejected Jesus as illegitimate. But instead, Joseph became the social father of Jesus, protecting him from fatherlessness and from public scorn, and Mary from a desperate fate. So it is that in the Christian narrative, we are saved by the birth of a child who was also an adoptee.

Early Christianity endorsed adoption theologically as metaphor for salvation; although more historical study is needed, it was also endorsed in practice as a necessary response to human contingencies. In ancient Rome, relinquishment occurred under a mythological canopy: a statue of a she-wolf suckling the foundlings Romulus and Remus stood over the forum in Rome from the third century BC, conveying the potentially happy outcomes for abandoned children. The benefits of relinquishment were thus creatively ensconced in cultural symbol and ethos. With the development from Roman antiquity to Christianized Europe in the fourth and fifth centuries, a new sacred canopy captured the happy prospects of the relinquished infant and the acceptability of the birth mother's gift, which at that time took on deeper religious meaning. The Christian self-perception was that they had been adopted by God to substitute spiritually for the biological lineage of Abraham. Given the centrality of this theology to the post-Constantinian formation of Western culture, Christian literature includes numerous examples of idealized images of adoption. Converts all believed that they were adopted into the faith, sometimes setting aside hostile biological families. They were provided with a "birth" through baptism—a kind of rescue from abandonment. The convert had "spiritual parents" who took special care in nurturing his or her faith; these parents "took up" a child, much like adoption.

Among the Protestant theologians, Karl Barth offers an elevation of adoption that is both influential and intriguing. While he rightly emphasizes that while the idea that birth parents should rear their child is central to Christian thought, he goes further than other Protestant thinkers of whom I am aware in stressing that it should not be absolutized. There will be practical circumstances ("ought implies can") that make rearing impossible to fulfill for biological parents. And "under divine command parenthood will necessarily involve readiness for exceptional circumstances" when it may be disturbed by God's "extraordinary claims and constraints" through providential necessity. More importantly, Barth holds that parents must realize "*it is not their relationship to their children which is divine but the will of God in which this relationship is rooted.*"[37] The authority of parents ensconced in the command to honor father and mother is based on a "spiritual mission." While "biological fatherhood has a weight and honor," the mission of parenting can be fulfilled "even apart from physical parenthood."[38] In the last analysis, "No human father, but God alone, is properly, truly, and primarily Father."[39] Thus the biological parents are relativized under divine freedom.

Divine love adopts us into the family of Christ, making us true sons and daughters, and heirs to the kingdom. Even when we are loved by our parents, that love is penultimate beneath divine adoptive love.

Taking Divine Love More Seriously

Believers in all faiths need to take the idea of God as love seriously. We think of the power of God and wage wars in God's name. We think up definitions of God that, even if inspired, are still products of the human mind and fail to make love central. When religions have put doctrine and force above love, they have created a history of massive evil from torture to terror, from coercion to conflict. Religious wars have been manifestations of a human tribalism and arrogance that bring out the worst in us. We forget that God is love.[40]

Hatred, hostility, and revenge are strong enough emotions to overwhelm our deeper sense of Godly love. The pseudo-spirituality of hatred is contrary to all genuine spirituality, which is always an adventure in love. The love of power can sometimes overwhelm the power of love, so we must be humble and on guard to prevent this. How little we know about God, but we can still experience divine love. Most of religion and spirituality lies in rightly inspired healing emotions. The world will never know sustained peace in the twenty-first century without all religions living up to their inherent ideals of a Godly love that applies to all humankind without exception.

Only by taking divine love much more seriously than we do—even to the point of a profound love of ancient enemies—can we expect to avoid increasing destruction.[41] The world shows no signs of becoming greatly less religious; we as humans will always have a passion for an ultimate truth that provides a safe haven of emotional security. To the extent that truly divine love can be captured in the ritual worlds that religions create, and expressed in spiritual emotions such as forgiveness and compassion, we will have a human future. To the degree that religions fall short of universal divine love, violence will overcome us all. Godly love alone can rightly align the world in harmony and peace, although it must do so through human agents who are so imperfect.[42] Too many kill in God's name under the assumption that they alone know the unfolding purposes of God. Our human knowledge of such purposes should be regarded as profoundly limited.

Envoi

When it comes to divine love, we would concur that words are never enough. There is a passion and compassion underlying divine love, and those who experience it deeply sometimes report an overwhelming divine desire for reconciliation with a lost humanity. Abraham Heschel, for example, captured this in his classic book *God in Search of Man*.[43] In the end, a test of the depth of our experience of divine love lies in the degree to which we transcend self and actively lift up those for whom God cares so profoundly. Divine love is at some level directed at activity in the world.

The human future will depend primarily on the prospects for *allophilia*, for real love and appreciation between the three great Abrahamic faiths. Mere tolerance will not suffice, for this evaporates quickly under the right conditions. We must move to respect and to love, and study the ways in which such a universal love can have its roots in the particular teachings and practices of an individual religious tradition in all its enthusiasm.

Our whole being can be reordered and rightly organized by divine love, and thus countless people have done good in the world with renewed and even unbounded energy despite adversity. Their hearts are not disheartened. Hate and fear are abandoned, and spiritual emotions are harmonized in their proper dominance. Separation from Godly love is to live without fullness.

Notes

1. Richard Maurice Bucke, *Cosmic Consciousness: A Study in the Evolution of the Human Mind* (1900; repr. New York: Penguin Compass, 1991).
2. Hans Urs von Balthasar, *Love Alone Is Credible*, trans. D. C. Schindler (1963; repr. San Francisco: Ignatius Press, 2004).
3. C. S. Lewis, *The Abolition of Man* (1944; repr. New York: Simon & Schuster, 1996); see also Jürgen Moltmann, *Science & Wisdom*, trans. Margaret Kohl (Minneapolis: Fortress Press, 2003).
4. Elizabeth Alexander, *Praise for the Day* (Minneapolis: Graywolf Press, 2009).
5. Franklin Delano Roosevelt "Christmas Eve Message to the Nation, December 24, 1941," *The American Presidency Project*, Document Archive, http://www.presidency.ucsb.edu/ws/index.php?pid=16073.
6. Jürgen Moltmann, *Theology of Hope: On the Ground and the Implications of a Christian Eschatology*, trans. James W. Leitch (1967; repr. Minneapolis: Fortress Press, 1993).
7. C. S. Lewis, *The Four Loves* (San Diego, CA: Harcourt Brace & Company, 1960).
8. See Philip Clayton and Jeffrey Schloss, eds., *Evolution and Ethics: Human Morality in Biological and Religious Perspective* (Grand Rapids: Wm. B. Eerdmans, 2004).
9. Servais Pinckaers, O.P., *The Sources of Christian Ethics*, trans. Sr. Mary Thomas Noble, O.P. (1985; repr. Washington, DC: Catholic University of America Press, 1995).
10. 2 Corinthians 9:7.
11. Galatians 5:22.

12. Anders Nygren, *Agape and Eros*, trans. Philip S. Watson (1932; repr. Chicago: University of Chicago Press, 1982).
13. Emil Brunner and Karl Barth, *Natural Theology*, trans. Peter Fraenkel (1946; repr. Eugene, OR: Wipf and Stock Publishers, 2002).
14. Warren S. Brown, Nancey Murphy, and H. Newton Maloney, eds., *Whatever Happened to the Soul? Scientific and Theological Portraits of Human Nature* (Minneapolis: Fortress Press, 1998).
15. Luke 17:20; see Leo Tolstoy, *The Kingdom of God Is within You: Christianity Not as a Mystic Religion but as a New Theory of Life*, trans. Constance Garnett (1894; repr. Lincoln: University of Nebraska Press, 1984).
16. Washington Irving, available online, http://www.famousquotesandauthors.com/authors/washington_irving_quotes.html (accessed June 12, 2009).
17. Luke 10:37.
18. Dietrich Bonhoeffer, *The Cost of Discipleship*, trans. R. H. Fuller (1937; repr. New York: Simon & Schuster, 1995).
19. Bettie B. Youngs, *The House That Love Built: The Story of Millard and Linda Fuller—Founders of Habitat for Humanity and the Fuller Center for Housing* (Charlottesville, VA: Hampton Road Publishing, 2007).
20. Heidi Baker, *Compelled by Love* (Lake Mary, FL: Charisma House, 2008).
21. Paul Tillich, *Love, Power and Justice: Ontological Analysis and Ethical Applications* (London: Oxford University Press, 1954).
22. Henri Bergson, *The Two Sources of Morality and Religion*, trans. R. Ashley Audra and Cloudesley Brereton (1932; repr. Garden City, NY: Doubleday, 1935).
23. Kenneth E. Kirk, *The Vision of God: The Christian Doctrine of the Summum Bonum*, abridged ed. (1931; repr. Harrisburg, PA: Morehouse Publishing, 1991).
24. Pitirim Sorokin, *The Ways and Power of Love* (1954; repr. Philadelphia: Templeton Foundation Press, 2004), 16.
25. Garth L. Hallett, *Priorities and Christian Ethics* (Cambridge: Cambridge University Press, 1998).
26. Quoted in Gilbert C. Meilaender, *Friendship: A Study in Theological Ethics* (Notre Dame, IN: University of Notre Dame Press, 1981), 1.
27. Sorokin, *Ways and Power of Love*, 16.
28. Ibid., 19.
29. Ibid., 26.
30. W. H. Auden, from his "Introduction," in *The Protestant Mystics: An Anthology of Spiritual Experience from Martin Luther to T. S. Eliot*, ed. Anne Fremantle (New York: Mentor Books/New American Library, 1964), 30–31.
31. See G. K. Chesterton, *Orthodoxy* (1908; New York: Image/Doubleday, 1959).
32. Margaret A. Farley, *Compassionate Respect: A Feminist Approach to Medical Ethics and Other Questions* (New York: Paulist Press, 2002).
33. Dorothy L. Sayers, *The Mind of the Maker* (San Francisco: HarperCollins, 1979).
34. William James, "To His Class at Radcliffe College Which Had Sent a Potted Azalea to Him at Easter" [1896], in *The Letters of William James*, vol. 2, ed. Henry James (Boston: Atlantic Monthly Press, 1920), 33.
35. John 3:16.
36. Romans 8:15; Romans 8:23; Galatians 4:5; Ephesians 1:5.
37. Karl Barth, *The Doctrine of Creation, Part 4*, vol. 3 of *Church Dogmatics* (Edinburgh, UK: T & T Clark, 1961), 285 (emphasis added).

38. Ibid., 244.
39. Ibid., 245.
40. Allen Dwight Callahan, *A Love Supreme: A History of the Johannine Tradition* (Minneapolis: Fortress Press, 2005).
41. Nancey Murphy and George F. R. Ellis, *On the Moral Nature of the Universe: Theology, Cosmology, and Ethics* (Minneapolis: Fortress Press, 1996).
42. See Margaret M. Poloma and Ralph W. Hood Jr., *Blood and Fire: Godly Love in a Pentecostal Emerging Church* (New York: New York University Press, 2008).
43. Abraham J. Heschel, *God in Search of Man: A Philosophy of Judaism* (New York: Farrar, Strauss, and Cudahy, 1955).

Contributors

Jeff Levin, PhD, an epidemiologist and religious scholar, holds a distinguished chair at Baylor University, where he is University Professor of Epidemiology and Population Health, Professor of medical humanities, and director of the Program on Religion and Population Health. He has authored over 150 scholarly publications, mostly on the instrumental functions of religion for human well-being, including seven books, notably *God, Faith, and Health*. According to the Institute for Scientific Information, since 1981 Dr. Levin has been one of the most highly cited social scientists in the world. His most recent work focuses on the influence of religion on population health and aging, biblical and rabbinic perspectives on the role of divine love in Jewish moral theology, theories of healing and the work of healers, and the history and future of discourse on Judaism and health. He is also adjunct professor of psychiatry and behavioral sciences at Duke University Medical Center and currently serves as scientific chair of the Kalsman Roundtable on Judaism and Health Research, based at Hebrew Union College-Jewish Institute of Religion. Dr. Levin lives in Texas with his wife, Dr. Lea Steele, research professor of biomedical studies at Baylor.

Stephen G. Post, PhD, is professor of preventive medicine, head of the Division of Medicine in Society, and director of the Center for Medical Humanities, Compassionate Care, and Bioethics at Stony Brook University. He is currently a senior fellow in the Center for the Study of Law and Religion at Emory University, and an elected Hastings Center Fellow. He served as editor-in-chief of the third edition of the five-volume *Encyclopedia of Bioethics*, is an elected member of the Medical and Scientific Advisory

Panel of Alzheimer's Disease International, and in 2003 was elected a Member of the College of Physicians of Philadelphia for "distinguished contributions to medicine." Dr. Post is also president of the Institute for Research on Unlimited Love, established in July 2001 with support from the John Templeton Foundation. He completed his PhD at the University of Chicago, where he was an elected University Fellow, a preceptor in the Pritzker School of Medicine, and a fellow in the Martin E. Marty Center for the Advanced Study of Religion. He has published over 150 articles in peer-reviewed journals such as *Science*, *Annals of Internal Medicine*, *The Journal of Religion*, *American Journal of Psychiatry*, *JAMA*, and *The Lancet*, and has authored or edited over twenty books. His research has been supported by the National Institutes of Health and the National Endowment for the Humanities. Dr. Post is a lifelong member of the Episcopal Church and is currently a Trustee of the John Templeton Foundation (2008–11).

William C. Chittick, PhD, is professor of religious studies in the Department of Asian and Asian American Studies at Stony Brook University. Born and raised in Connecticut, he finished his BA at the College of Wooster and then went to Iran, where he completed a PhD in Persian literature at Tehran University in 1974. He taught comparative religion for five years in the humanities department at Aryamehr Technical University in Tehran, and left Iran right before the revolution. He has lectured around the world and published thirty books and numerous articles on Islamic intellectual history, concentrating on the interface between Sufism (Islam's mystical dimension) and philosophy. His books include *Imaginal Worlds: Ibn al-'Arabī and the Problem of Religious Diversity*, *The Heart of Islamic Philosophy*, and *Science of the Cosmos, Science of the Soul.*

Vigen Guroian, PhD, resides with his wife, June Vranian, in Culpeper, Virginia, where he tends to his large perennial and vegetable gardens. He received his BA from the University of Virginia (1970) and his PhD in Theology from Drew University (1978). He is presently professor of Religious Studies at the University of Virginia. He is senior fellow of the Center on Law and Religion of Emory University; senior fellow of the Trinity Forum; Permanent senior fellow of the Russell Kirk Center for Cultural Renewal in Mecosta, Michigan; and an ongoing fellow of the Wilberforce Forum under the Prison Fellowship Ministries founded by the honorable Chuck Colson. Dr. Guroian has published more than 150 articles in books, journals, and encyclopedias on a range of subjects including Orthodox theology, marriage and family, children's literature, education, politics, ecology, genocide, liturgy, and medical ethics. Dr. Guroian is the author of nine books, including *The Fragrance of God*, *Incarnate Love: Essays in Orthodox Ethics*, and *Ethics after Christendom: Toward an Ecclesial Christian Ethic*.

Ruben L. F. Habito, DLittC (Tokyo), is professor of World Religions and Spirituality at Perkins School of Theology, Southern Methodist University. He is the author of *Healing Breath: Zen for Christians and Buddhists in a Wounded World*, *Experiencing Buddhism: Ways of Wisdom and Compassion*, *Living Zen, Loving God*, and a dozen other works in English as well as in Japanese. He is a Zen Master (Rōshi) in the Sanbō Kyōdan lineage, and guides the Maria Kannon Zen Center in Dallas, Texas. Married to Maria Dorothea Reis Habito, they have two sons, Florian and Benjamin.

William K. Mahony, PhD, is Charles A. Dana Professor of Religion and chair of the Department of Religion at Davidson College. Educated at Williams College (BA, 1973), Yale University (MDiv, 1976), and the University of Chicago (PhD, 1982), his teaching, research, and writing interests center on the religions of South Asia and particularly of India. A recipient of a National Endowment for the Humanities Fellowship, Professor Mahony's publications include *The Artful Universe: An Introduction to the Vedic Religious Imagination* and, as coauthor, *Meditation Revolution: A History and Theology of the Siddha Yoga Lineage*, as well as numerous journal articles and reviews. Dr. Mahony served as an editor and major contributor to the sixteen-volume *Encyclopedia of Religion*, first edition, which received the Hawkins Prize and the Dartmouth Medal from the American Library Association for the best work in any category of publishing. He is a former member of the board of directors of the American Academy of Religion and of its executive committee and is a past president of the American Academy of Religion Southeast Region and Past Chairman of the Southeast Commission for the Study of Religion. He is the founding president, head of the Academic Council, and member of the board of directors of the Muktabodha Indological Research Institute.

John S. Mbiti, PhD, born in Kenya between the two world wars, was educated in Uganda, the United States, and England, where at Cambridge in 1963 he obtained his doctorate in New Testament. He has been awarded several honorary doctorates by universities and theological seminaries in Switzerland and the United States. He has taught theology and religion at universities in Uganda, England, the United States, Germany, and Switzerland, and has done pastoral work in England, Uganda, and Switzerland. Now retired, he embarked on the exciting and challenging task of translating the New Testament from Greek into his mother tongue of Kiikamba, which he finished in 2008. Married to Verena, a teacher of languages (English, French, and German), they have four children and five grandchildren, live in Switzerland, and keep strong ties to his home in Kenya.

Jacob Neusner, PhD, is Distinguished Service Professor of the History and Theology of Judaism, and senior fellow, Institute of Advanced Theology, Bard College. He also is a member of the Institute for Advanced Study, Princeton, New Jersey, and life member of Clare Hall, Cambridge University, in England. He has published more than one thousand books and unnumbered articles—scholarly and academic, popular and journalistic—and is the most published humanities scholar in the world. He has been awarded nine honorary degrees, including seven U.S. and European honorary doctorates, and holds fourteen academic medals and prizes, as well as numerous other academic awards. He received his AB from Harvard College in 1953, his PhD from Columbia University and Union Theological Seminary in 1961, and Rabbinical Ordination and MHL from the Jewish Theological Seminary of America, in 1960. During his graduate studies he also was Henry Fellow at Lincoln College, Oxford University, 1953–54, and Fulbright Scholar at the Hebrew University of Jerusalem, 1957–58. He has held two fellowships from the American Council of Learned Societies and two fellowships from the Guggenheim Foundation as well as an NEH Fellowship at the Institute for Advanced Study and many other research awards. He was president of the American Academy of Religion (1968–69), the only scholar of Judaism to hold that position, and a member of the founding committee of the Association for Jewish Studies (1967–70). He founded the European Association of Jewish Studies (1980–81), and also served, by appointment of President Carter, as member of the National Council on the Humanities (1978–84) and, by appointment of President Reagan, as member of the National Council on the Arts (1984–90). He is editor of the *Encyclopaedia of Judaism* and its Supplements, chairman of the Editorial Board of *The Review of Rabbinic Judaism*, and editor-in-chief of *The Brill Reference Library of Judaism*. He is editor of *Studies in Judaism* for University Press of America, was editor for Judaism of both the Harper/AAR's *Dictionary of Religion* and the Britannica/Merriam Webster's *Encyclopaedia of Religion*. Dr. Neusner resides with his wife in Rhinebeck, New York. They have a daughter, three sons and three daughters-in-law, and seven granddaughters and two grandsons.

Clark H. Pinnock, PhD, is professor emeritus of systematic theology at McMaster Divinity College, member of the Faculty of Theology at McMaster University, and author of over a dozen theological monographs. He is a Baptist and free church Protestant and he approaches the subject of divine and human love from a Pentecostal and charismatic perspective. Author of *Flame of Love: A Theology of the Holy Spirit*, his theology has moved over the years to a greater concentration on the love of God, as seen in *A Wideness in God's Mercy: The Finality of Jesus Christ in a World of Religions* and *The Openness of God: A Biblical Challenge to the Traditional Understanding of God*. To be baptized in the Holy Spirit, he claims, is to be immersed in God's outpoured love.

David Tracy, STD, is the Andrew Thomas Greeley and Grace McNichols Greeley Distinguished Service Professor Emeritus of Catholic Studies and Professor of Theology and the Philosophy of Religion in the University of Chicago Divinity School, and also a member of the Committee on Social Thought. Dr. Tracy had taught a wide variety of courses in contemporary theology: philosophical, systematic, and constructive theology and hermeneutics, and courses dealing with issues and persons in religion and modern thought. His publications include *The Analogical Imagination: Christian Theology and the Culture of Pluralism* and *On Naming the Present: Reflections on God, Hermeneutics, and Church*. Dr. Tracy is currently writing a book on God.

Index